Localized Bargaining

Localized Bargaining

The Political Economy of
China's High-Speed Railway Program

XIAO MA

OXFORD
UNIVERSITY PRESS

OXFORD
UNIVERSITY PRESS

Oxford University Press is a department of the University of Oxford. It furthers
the University's objective of excellence in research, scholarship, and education
by publishing worldwide. Oxford is a registered trade mark of Oxford University
Press in the UK and certain other countries.

Published in the United States of America by Oxford University Press
198 Madison Avenue, New York, NY 10016, United States of America.

Library of Congress Control Number: 2022903686
ISBN 978–0–19–764822–3 (pbk.)
ISBN 978–0–19–763891–0 (hbk.)

DOI: 10.1093/oso/9780197638910.001.0001

3 5 7 9 8 6 4 2

Paperback printed by Marquis, Canada
Hardback printed by Bridgeport National Bindery, Inc., United States of America

献给我的父母
For My Parents

Contents

List of Figures

List of Tables

Acknowledgments

This book is about how local governments in China extract policy benefits (railway investments in particular) from their superiors. In the long journey leading to the completion of the book, I have "extracted" help, guidance, inspiration, and companionship from countless family, friends, colleagues, and mentors. This book would not be possible without them. While I tried my best to list every name of the people and institutions that have helped me along the way, there will inevitably be omissions. My apology in advance for those whose names I forget to include.

First and foremost, I owe a significant debt to my advisors at the University of Washington, Seattle: Chris Adolph, Victor Menaldo, Joel Migdal, and Susan Whiting. They not only guided me through the completion of my dissertation, which this book is based on, but also trained me as a scholar. I hope the book will live up to their expectations.

Chris is always sharp in pointing out pitfalls in my research design and methods application, while being extremely helpful in suggesting ways to improve them. He was also instrumental in guiding my first few publications on the central committee members of the Chinese Communist Party.

Victor is an inspirational teacher both in and outside the classroom. We had countless discussions and debates on a wide range of political economy topics during his office hours and at meals after the comparative politics workshops. These discussions and his style of engaging students greatly shaped my research interests and my own pedagogy when I started to teach my own classes.

Joel joined my dissertation committee in my second year at UW. He pressed me to think beyond the world constructed by rational choice models and more about the nuances of the interactions between state and society. He is always generous in sharing his time with his students. He not only read through the original dissertation but also the revised book manuscript, and provided extensive written comments. Joel is also a role model for mentoring students. I have benefited tremendously from his wisdom about how to survive in academia.

I could not ask for a better dissertation committee chair than Susan. She invited me to join her research projects and generously shared her data during our very first meeting after I arrived in Seattle. These opportunities provided me with firsthand experience in conducting serious empirical research, and some of these later turned into coauthored publications. Susan was both a stern critic and an ardent defender of my dissertation project. I spent hours in her office as she grilled me about details in my dissertation proposal. Thinking back, I feel very fortunate that someone other than me could care so much about the success of this project.

I am also very fortunate to have encountered numerous teachers who provided valuable intellectual guidance during different stages of my time as a student. I want to thank David Bachman, Matt Barreto, Lance Bennett, Madeleine Yue Dong, Darryl Holman, Tony Gill, Margaret Levi, John Mercer, Aseem Prakash, Scott Radnitz, Emma Spiro, and Judy Thornton at the University of Washington; Daniel Botsman, Deborah Davis, Koichi Hamada, Bill Kelly, and Jun Saito at Yale University; Masaru Mabuchi, Tetsuji Murase, and Naofumi Sakamoto at Kyoto University; and Alita, Andong Ma, Weidan Sheng, Chuchu Wang, Xiaofan Wang, and Kahori Yumoto at Zhejiang University.

This project would also not have been possible without the help of Qi Gao, Youxing Lang, Jigang Li, Warren Wenzhi Lu, Xiaoshun Zeng, Zheng Zhang, Shukai Zhao, and Xinxin Zhou, who introduced me to key informants or helped me gain access to policy documents or archives. Many of my informants in China chose to remain anonymous for obvious reasons. I am grateful to them for sharing their time and insights.

Since I left graduate school, I have revised and extended the original draft significantly. Yuen Yuen Ang, Yue Hou, Sunia Kale, and Scott Radnitz attended my book conference in March 2020 (which, like many things that spring, was moved online at the last minute) and offered detailed, constructive suggestions for improvement. Kyle Jaros also read through the manuscript and provided extensive written comments. For insights and comments on the initial ideas, draft papers that later became chapters in this book, or the completed manuscript, I want to thank Yongshun Cai, Kyle Chan, Jidong Chen, Ling Chen, Shuo Chen, Yanhua Deng, Iza Ding, Mary Gallagher, Xiang Gao, Stephan Haggard, Enze Han, Jean Hong, Haifeng Huang, Chengyuan Ji, Ruixue Jia, Junyan Jiang, Pierre Landry, Youxing Lang, Zhenhuai Lei, Margaret Levi, Lianjiang Li, Tao Li, Chuyu Liu, Hanzhang Liu, Lizhi Liu, Mingxing Liu, Peter Lorentzen, Fengming Lu, Warren Wenzhi Lu, Xiaobo

Lü, Liang Ma, Dan Mattingly, Ciqi Mei, Tianguang Meng, Emerson Niou, Julia Payson, Victor Shih, Yu Sasaki, Susan Shirk, Dan Slater, Shiping Tang, Ran Tao, Tuong Vu, Erik H. Wang, Zhengxu Wang, Barry Weingast, Jeffrey Weng, Saul Wilson, Guoguang Wu, Yiqing Xu, Feng Yang, Xuedong Yang, Zhenjie Yang, Qingjie Zeng, Jing Zhao, Changdong Zhang, Luke Qi Zhang, Yong Zhang, Shukai Zhao, Tan Zhao, Xueguang Zhou, and Xufeng Zhu.

Colleagues at Peking University, and those in the School of Government in particular, have provided a collegial and intellectually stimulating environment that has been indispensable for the completion of this project. I want to thank Muyang Chen, Hao Dong, Haiting Fei, Kaidong Feng, Zengke He, Anping Jin, Xingkun Liang, Mingxing Liu, Yanjun Liu, Yinan Luo, Mingming Shen, Ming Sun, Kai Tian, Xianglin Xu, Tianyang Xi, Jie Yan, Jirong Yan, Feng Yang, Wenhui Yang, Yi Yang, Ruijun Yuan, Keping Yu, Yu Zeng, Changdong Zhang, Pengfei Zhang, and Nuo Zhao, for their support, encouragement, and occasionally, constructive critiques.

A key privilege of teaching at Peking University is the opportunity to get to know some of the most talented students in the world, many of whom also contributed to this project. For able research assistance or useful input, I want to thank Zhishuo Fu, Jialei Ma, Liu Peng, Xuanning Shi, Yihang Sun, Yongkang Tai, Zezhong Wang, Zhihao Wang, Tingwei Weng, Zemin Wu, Dian Yu, Xinyu Yun, Lingyun Zhang, Yifan Zhang, and Yinsheng Zhou.

The process of writing a dissertation and later turning it into a book is grueling and lonely, and the support and companionship of friends make it a lot easier. I want to thank Aaron Erlich, Dan Berliner, Anne Greenleaf, Vanessa Quince, Zhaowen Guo, Shihao Han, Meredith Loken, Dave Lopez, Walid Salem, Yu Sasaki, Hanjie Wang, Yunkang Yang, Daniel Yoo, and Tan Zhao for their comradeship in graduate school, and Muyang Chen, Qian He, Minli Lai, Xialu Li, Ying Liang, Lin Lin, Yiyu Tian, Xiaoshun Zeng, Can Zhao, Lijuan Zhang, Keran Zheng, and the late Richard Wesley for filling my life in Seattle with joy. Jason Qiang Guo, Benmo Jiang, Chuyu Liu, Dongshu Liu, Yuchen Liu, Li Shao, Yujing Tan, Erik H. Wang, and Can Zhao attended graduate school at roughly the same time I did, and we exchanged intellectual and emotional support. Since I moved to Beijing, Kunrui Li, Xingkun Liang, Yizhi Mao, Ruobing Xie, and Haozhe Xu have made my life as a *beipiao* a lot easier. Muyang Chen and Yitian Xia played crucial roles in making sure that I stuck to my writing plans. I also want to thank my old friends Frank Qiji Chen, Chengrong Chu, Yulong Ma, Xiaomeng Ren, and Kaichen Weng for being an enthusiastic audience when I talked about my research and life developments. Liyang Xu offered valuable suggestions on the cover design.

Fengming Lu deserves special thanks. Very few people have the privilege of having a classmate from kindergarten who later becomes a colleague and a coauthor. Fengming first cultivated my interests in politics through our numerous discussions in middle school, and pointed me to the field of political science during my time in college. We entered graduate programs in the same year, and our shared interests turned into coauthored research projects. Now, we both have begun to teach political science at different universities, and we have continued our discussions on all things politics that we have been enjoying since middle school. These discussions are always important sources of inspiration to me.

The research in this book was made possible by generous financial support from the following institutions: the China Studies Program, the Department of Political Science, the Henry M. Jackson School of International Studies, and the Center for Statistics and the Social Sciences at the University of Washington; the Social Science Research Council, the China Times Cultural Foundation; the Institute for Public Governance, and the School of Government at Peking University; the National Natural Science Foundation of China (project ID: 72004004), Beijing Social Science Fund Project (project ID: 21DTR018), the Ministry of Education Project of Key Research Institute of Humanities and Social Sciences at Universities (project ID: 16JJD810001), and the Fundamental Research Funds for the Central Universities by the Ministry of Education, People's Republic of China. A special thanks to the China Studies Program at the University of Washington and the School of Government at Peking University for providing additional funding to support the publication of this book.

Chapter 6 of the book is based on a previously published article, "Consent to Contend: The Power of the Masses in China's Local Elite Bargain" in The China Review (Vol. 19, No. 1, February 2019). I want to thank The China Review and the Chinese University Press for granting me the permission to reprint.

I am grateful to my editor David McBride at Oxford University Press for his faith in my project, and to Emily Benitez for guiding me through the publication process. Two anonymous reviewers provided valuable comments and suggestions for revisions. I also want to thank Kate Epstein for her expert editing of the manuscript.

Finally, I am exceptionally lucky in my family. I was very close to my grandparents and two aunts when I was growing up. They taught me how to be a good person and have always been proud of my achievements. My paternal grandmother passed away shortly after I submitted the manuscript for external review, and I know she would have been so proud to see this book coming out. And, as the only child in my family—a typical situation for people in my age in China—I have the good fortune to share fun memories of growing up with two little cousins I love dearly.

I find words are inadequate to express my gratitude to my parents, Jianbo Ma and Ying Wang, for their unconditional love, support, and faith in me my whole life. I dedicate this book to them.

Abbreviations

CCP	Chinese Communist Party
CRC	China Railway Corporation
CREPRI	China Railway Economic and Planning Research Institute
EMU	Electric Multiple Unit
GDP	Gross Domestic Product
KM	Kilometer
NDRC	National Development and Reform Commission
NRA	National Railway Administration
PLA	People's Liberation Army
PPP	Public Private Partnership
RMB	Renminbi

1
Introduction

On November 5, 2019, five weeks before the newly built Xuzhou–Huai'an–Yancheng high-speed railway began operation, the official newspaper of Yancheng published a front-page article describing the locality's decade-long quest for high-speed railway service.[1] A communist base during the Chinese communist revolution, Yancheng is a coastal, industrial city of Jiangsu province with over eight million residents. The article recounted how the province's high-speed railway construction plan released in 2008 originally did not include service to Yancheng. It is a major regional center in the northern part of the province, and the neighboring city of Huai'an, which has fewer than six million residents and plays a less prominent role in the region's economy, was to have service. According to the article, the city's leaders had been advocating for service to Yancheng since the plan's release, tirelessly traveling to the relevant departments in Beijing and the provincial capital to make the case for the city's inclusion in the plan. It described countless meetings by the city's then party secretary and the city's mayor, and that reports about the need for an extension that would connect Yancheng by way of Huai'an were "pil[ing] up like a mountain."

Yancheng officials' efforts paid off in 2011 when the Jiangsù provincial government agreed in principle to extend the planned rail network to Yancheng. But before Yanchengers could celebrate, things took an unexpected turn. The construction plan the Ministry of Railways released listed the design speed of the extension segment to Yancheng as only 160 kilometers per hour, significantly slower than the above 200 kilometers per hour speed of the state-of-the-art high-speed trains. According to the report, Yancheng officials again mobilized a response. They visited the National Development and Reform Commission, a powerful regulatory agency that oversees infrastructure investments, and the China Railway Corporation, the successor to

---

[1] See *Yanfu People's Daily*. (2019, November 5, front page). 逐梦通衢，理想照进现实 ——来自盐徐高铁建设一线的报告之一 *(The dream of building thoroughfares has finally come true: A report from the construction frontline of the Yancheng-Xuzhou high-speed railway)*. ycnews.cn, retrieved from http://www.ycnews.cn/p/437671.html.

Localized Bargaining. Xiao Ma, Oxford University Press. © Oxford University Press 2022.
DOI: 10.1093/oso/9780197638910.003.0001

the Ministry of Railways after 2012, numerous times, seeking an upgrade of the key parameters of the railway. The National Development and Reform Commission revised the designated speed of that segment of the railway twice, first from 160 kilometers per hour to 200 kilometers per hour in 2013, and then to 250 kilometers per hour in 2015, when the railway finally received approval for construction.

The Xuzhou–Huai'an–Yancheng intercity high-speed railway began operation on December 16, 2019. As the newspaper headline exulted, "A Long Dream Eventually Comes True." While a decade might not be a long time in which to build a railway by international standards, China's high-speed railway has developed much more quickly in some other places. For example, it only took 19 months from finalizing the construction design to operation for the Shanghai–Hangzhou intercity high-speed railway, which is located roughly 300 kilometers south of Yancheng.

Yancheng's case is the tip of the iceberg: many local governments have had similar battles since the Chinese central government released the Medium- to Long-term Railway Network Plan, proposing the construction of 12,000 kilometers of high-speed railways in 2004. As the addition of the Huai'an–Yancheng extensions suggests, the construction has exceeded the original plans. Fifteen years after the release of the initial plan, in 2019, China had over 35,000 kilometers of railway track running trains at or above the speed of 250 kilometers per hour. That is twice the length of high-speed track in every other country in the world combined.[2]

Yet, coverage has not been even. In 2017, the Chinese government announced that the high-speed rail network would cover 80% of cities with at least one million population by 2020.[3] My calculations indicated that 74.3% of 334 Chinese municipalities had at least one high-speed rail station by the end of 2019.[4] The Chinese government states that it will build another 25,000 kilometers by 2030, but in the meantime cities are experiencing significant inequality of service. The disparate experience of Yancheng and Huai'an is typical, as proximate localities with, at best, similar needs for rail service have received approval for rail construction many years apart. Variations in the

---

[2] See Fan, X. (2019, November 22). 我国高铁营业里程年底将达3.5万公里 (*The lengths of high-speed rails in operation reach 35,000 kilometers by the end of this year*), Xinhua News Agency, retrieved from http://www.xhby.net/tuijian/201911/t20191123_6416057.shtml.

[3] See the Xinhua News Agency. (2017, March 1). 2020年，高铁覆盖80%以上超100万人口城市 (*High-speed rails to cover 80% of municipalities with more than one million population by 2020*), ifeng. com, retrieved February 10, 2020, from http://inews.ifeng.com/50742525/news.shtml?&back.

[4] The standard for high-speed rail is that the trains run at least 250 kilometers per hour.

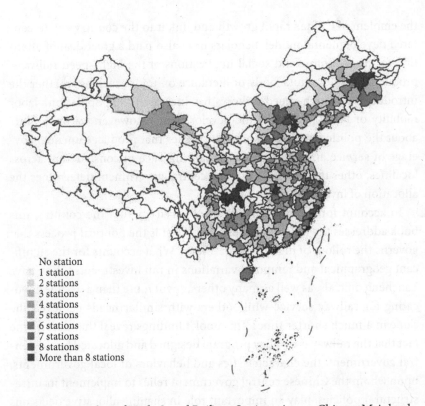

Figure 1.1 Number of High-Speed Railway Stations Across Chinese Mainland Cities (By the End of 2019)

$129 BLN/year RR

number of stations also exist among those places that already have service, as shown in Figure 1.1.

Uneven coverage does not reflect a lack of investment. China's annual investment in railways has skyrocketed from 51.6 billion RMB (6.3 billion US dollars) in 2004 to over 800 billion RMB (129.2 billion US dollars) *every year* since 2013.[5] To put that number in context, the US interstate highway system cost in total, *over four decades* of projects, $259.61 billion in 2021 dollars.[6] By any measure, China's high-speed railway program is the largest state-directed infrastructure program in human history. It has received wide media attention both at home and abroad. Many consider it

[5] Author's data.
[6] See US Department of Transportation, Federal Highway Administration. *Highway History*, fhwa. dot.gov, retrieved from https://www.fhwa.dot.gov/interstate/faq.cfm#question6. About 89% of this amount was federal money. The estimate of $128.9 billion was made in 1991.

Largest state-dir. infrastructure in history

the emblem of China's rapid growth and link it to the country's state-centered developmental model. Scholars have also paid a great deal of attention to the economic and social implications of the high-speed railways, producing a voluminous body of literature on topics such as whether the introduction of high-speed railways has increased the population's labor mobility or facilitated economic development.[7] However, we know little about the political process behind the scenes that produces unequal coverage of service and determines the varying pace of construction across localities, other than the fact that the central government determines the allocation of investment.

To account for the uneven rollout of service across the country, this book addresses the following questions. What is the political process that governs the rollout of high-speed railways? What accounts for the significant geographical and temporal variations in rail investments? Why have Yancheng officials, as well as many others, spent more than a decade advocating for railway service while others with similar needs achieved the same in a much shorter time? This book's findings reveal that despite the fact that the railway is a policy program designed and allocated by the central government, the characteristics and behaviors of local governments, upon whom the Chinese central government relies to implement its infrastructural policies, play an important role in shaping allocative decisions on high-speed rail. I call the bottom-up solicitation of policy benefits by local authorities *localized bargaining*. Localities with greater bargaining power, derived either through institutional or extra-institutional sources, are better positioned to procure investments and other policy benefits from higher levels of government authorities. Through the lens of high-speed railway construction, this book helps readers gain a deeper understanding of how policy resources are allocated among different actors across China's party-state hierarchies, and also provides a novel perspective on the factors contributing to the resilience of China's one-party system.

---

[7] Yao Yang, the dean of National School of Development at Peking University and an editor of the *China Economic Quarterly*, once complained in public that he got tired of reading endless submissions on the economic consequences of high-speed railways to the extent that he began to wonder whether Chinese economists have any other questions they might ask. See Yao, Y. (2019, March 29). 姚洋：当下中国经济学的出路 (*Yao Yang: The path for the economics discipline in China*), finance.sina.com.cn, retrieved from https://finance.sina.com.cn/china/2019-03-29/doc-ihsxncvh6662618.shtml.

1.1 The Politics of Distribution under Authoritarianism

Railway construction has long been an issue with political valence. Many late-developing countries have taken on railroad construction as a state project in order to modernize the economy and tighten the state's control over its territory (Kale, 2014, pp. 9–10). The state's central role in railroads financing and construction is manifested through the creation of specialized bureaucracies dedicated to railway management in many parts of the world. Since the national rail system took shape in the 1910s, China has developed a robust railway administration that involves central, local, and occasionally military authorities (Köll, 2019). Besides China, countries such as India, Pakistan, Bangladesh, Japan, North Korea, and the former Soviet Union also have (or once had) a Ministry of Railways.

Beyond the benefits to the central government, railways confer tangible benefits on those localities that receive service. Localities gain fixed-asset investments and contracting opportunities in the short term during railway construction and accessibility in the longer term, with the central government largely footing the bill. The decision about where to invest in railways therefore becomes a political one. Lasswell (1936) once said that "politics is about who gets what, when, and how." There is no question more political than how, where, and when governments spend trillions of dollars that have lasting social and economic impacts, as they do with railways.

In China, politics take on a particular cast. While China's high-speed railway is the world's most advanced long-distance public transportation system, it has erected it through the efforts of a government that drastically differs from those in the West. China does not have competitive elections at any level except in some village communities. The ruling Chinese Communist Party (CCP) keeps tight control over all forms of media, and typically silences dissent with force. Certainly, electoral incentives or other conventional mechanisms of accountability are not shaping decisions, nor is electoral feedback or representative institutions. This raises questions. How does the Chinese government allocate investments across a country of vast population and territories in the absence of many institutions that political scientists deem crucial in shaping distributive decisions? Just how does the Chinese government pick winners and losers in allocating railway investments? In an authoritarian system that lacks clearly defined rules or impartial third-party enforcers to settle intra-regime conflicts, a mechanism that steadily allocates policy benefits among regime insiders while minimizing potential elite conflicts over allocation is also crucial to the survival of the regime.

1.1.1 The Limits of Existing Explanations

The conventional wisdom posits that in a polity like China, one that lacks robust institutions of open contestations and accountability, the ways government allocates resources often follow the logic of patronage (e.g., Eisenstadt & Roniger, 1980; Hicken, 2011; Scott, 1969). That is, the rulers tend to divert resources to an exclusive group of recipients—often based on some predetermined associations with the rulers—in exchange for their support and services (Bueno de Mesquita et al., 2005; Haber, 2007). I label this dynamic "loyalty purchasing." Existing research on electoral authoritarian regimes, and nascent democracies such as Mexico or India, has found that levels of support (or lack thereof) toward the incumbent politicians drive the distribution of government resources (e.g., Blaydes, 2010; Magaloni, 2006; Min, 2015; Rigger, 1999; Stokes et al., 2013; Treisman, 1999; Tremewan, 1994). Even in well-established democracies such as Japan, Spain, or Italy, scholars have found that electoral incentives are important drivers of variations in the allocation of government investments in infrastructure (e.g., Castells & Solé-Ollé, 2005; Golden & Picci, 2008; Saito, 2006).

The intuition that the incumbents use distribution to purchase loyalty has also withstood empirical examinations in the Chinese context, where institutions like semi-competitive elections that provide good information on incumbent support are absent. Leaders instead rely on personal ties to identify targets of distribution. These ties are often formed along the lines of shared lineages, hometowns, work and education experiences, and so forth. Numerous studies on China have found that the allocations of government-controlled resources such as bank loans, fiscal transfers, and government appointments tend to favor people who have personal ties to the decision-makers (e.g., Jiang & Zhang, 2020; Shih, 2004, 2008; Shih et al., 2012; Tsai, 2007). Research in other developing countries has also found that the patterns of distributions often reflect shared ethnic identities or local ties with the leaders (e.g., Habyarimana et al., 2007; Hodler & Raschky, 2014).

Another set of arguments, which I call the "technocratic solution," focuses on the role of bureaucracy. Students of this school contend that elite technocrats in bureaucracies play a decisive role in formulating policies with distributive consequences. These bureaucrats enjoy relative autonomy in policymaking. They have the ability to resist pressures from politicians and from members of society (Evans, 1995) and are able to make decisions based on what they believe will serve the country's welfare, on issues ranging from where to build roads to which industries to subsidize (e.g., Johnson, 1982). This framework suggests that distributive patterns reflect technocratic solutions that states adopt to solve development issues. Scholars of many late-industrialized countries embrace this logic in explaining how the engagement of the state in the economy has contributed to economic growth (e.g., Chen, 2018; Evans, 1995; Gerschenkron, 1962; Haggard, 1990; Johnson, 1982; Kohli, 2004; Woo-Cumings, 1999). In contrast to the "loyalty purchasing" explanation, this model suggests policy considerations rather than power plays determine state actions. The variations in the assignment of government benefits, therefore, reflect bureaucrats' technocratic calculations to optimize the effectiveness of policy instruments.

Both the loyalty purchasing and the technocratic solution models have a far-reaching impact on our understanding of distributive politics. Yet they still fall short in offering satisfactory answers to the questions we raised earlier, for two reasons. First, both theories assume that those who control resources and those who have the power to make decisions purposefully plan the observed distributive patterns. The story suggests a straight line from what the decision-makers have in mind—either to enrich their friends or to strengthen the development—to what ordinary citizens eventually receive. This view is often an oversimplification of the world we live in (e.g., Evans, 1995; Migdal, 2001). For a large, complicated project like the high-speed railway program, between the moment the ruler conjures the idea and the moment a train hits the track for its maiden journey, numerous other actors get involved, and some become middlemen. The ruler has to rely on the expertise of the technocrats to turn his ideas into executable blueprints; the technocrats in the central bureaucracies also need the help of grassroots authorities to gather information on local conditions and to implement the blueprints; these local authorities might have different opinions on their superiors' decisions and want to increase their own shares in the project; citizens whose livelihood the project would affect might also get mobilized to influence the delivery of the policies.

Some of these middlemen, such as local leaders, are agents of their superiors. But they also experience the impact of policies those superiors have made. They might have as much influence as their superiors in shaping

Railroads ⟷ Spatial conflict

the formulation and implementation of distributive decisions. The classical model of "fragmented authoritarianism" in the Chinese politics literature recognizes that the Chinese state is far from monolithic, and that tension, conflicts, and competition among government departments and territorial administrations have played important roles in shaping policy outcomes (e.g., Lieberthal, 1992; Lieberthal & Oksenberg, 1988; Mertha, 2009). Indeed, Jaros (2019) makes the point that investments like railway projects, which "affect where in space resources go" are "particularly likely to awaken and bring into conflict the territorial interests of central, provincial, and local governments" (p. 17). The loyalty purchasing and the technocratic solution arguments suggest that localities are passive takers of decisions made by their superiors, as recipients of policy benefits without influence. Neither explains the experience of Yancheng's local leaders or those of many other localities in China.

Second, distributive politics does not take place in a vacuum. Institutions that shape the incentives of policy actors in distributive politics might be byproducts of macro-level institutional arrangements. They are embedded in a broader institutional context. It is by no means clear that the logic of loyalty purchasing or technocratic solutions are compatible with the incentive structures that perpetuate authoritarian rule in China. A satisfactory explanation for distributive politics in China, therefore, should also withstand testing by theories of authoritarian politics. For example, how does the ruler make sure that elites whose loyalty the ruler purchases through policy benefits will return the favor? What additional mechanisms allow the ruler to punish disloyal recipients? What scholars have identified as a "commitment problem" (e.g., North & Weingast, 1989; Williamson, 1983) is especially acute when the types of goods being distributed include infrastructure. The ruler can hardly withdraw the benefits of an infrastructure program (e.g., roads, airports, rails) *ex post* to punish disloyal recipients. Similarly, how do recipients make sure that the ruler with whom they entrust power and support will not harm their interests in the future? In electoral authoritarian regimes, periodic elections provide mechanisms that mitigate the commitment problem between the ruler and his supporters (Magaloni, 2006, 2008). China's lack of semi-competitive elections at the national level closes this option. This raises the question, what institutions tie the hands of the autocrats and ensure that various interests of the regime insiders are protected? The technocratic solution model also begs similar questions. If the ruler delegates the power of making decisions to a group of bureaucratic elites, then what prevents these bureaucrats from attempting to challenge the ruler? Operational dependence generates moral hazard problems under authoritarianism (Debs, 2007; Svolik, 2012). Bureaucrats who make all the important decisions are generally not eager to be subordinates forever. Rulers must grant them some autonomy while reducing possible threats associated with power delegation, raising the question as to what institutional arrangements make this possible. Conversely, what prevents the authoritarian ruler from interfering in bureaucratic policymaking or even reversing bureaucratic delegation at will? Unless we pay attention to these theoretical inconsistencies, the existing explanations for distributive politics are at best partial equilibria.

1.2 Localized Bargaining

This book proposes a theory that focuses on how proactive actions on the part of those who receive policy benefits could make a difference in policy outcomes. I argue that bottom-up bargaining by territorial administrations, or what I call *localized bargaining*, importantly shapes the allocation of policy benefits like infrastructure investments. While ordinary citizens are the eventual recipients of government policies, they do not directly negotiate policy details with the decision-makers. Thus I focus on the actions of intermediary recipients. The intermediary recipients of China's high-speed railway program are territorial authorities such as the provinces, the municipalities, the counties, and their functional departments. Their nominal job is to implement the policies of higher authorities. However, they benefit personally if their superiors' allocative decisions give their jurisdictions greater shares of policy resources. A multitude of factors, including a mismatch of resources and responsibilities, constantly present career incentives, pressures from local constituents, and sometimes even a sense of localism, motivate Chinese local authorities and their administrators to solicit policy resources from their superiors. In a parsimonious diagram in which the process of distribution flows from the decision-makers on the left end to the eventual recipients of policy benefits (i.e., the citizens) on the right end, these "intermediary recipients" are slightly right of center. To ordinary citizens, these actors appear as a part of the government authority, whereas within the government, their superiors see them as recipients of policies.

The term *localized bargaining* is a play on the more commonly used term "collective bargaining." In collective bargaining, employees with shared interests form a group to negotiate work conditions with their employers. In localized bargaining, localities share the same goal of gaining access to more resources from their superiors. There are also important distinctions. Unlike unionized workers, localities seldom coordinate their actions. In negotiating for resources they often compete with one another, as policy resources at any given time are limited. Inter-jurisdictional competition can be fierce. Consequently, the actions of bargaining remain localized and, unlike a unionized workforce, localities differ in their paths in gaining access to resources. This book reveals which factors give particular localities greater bargaining power than others. The word *localized* also describes the scope of the bargaining. Localities are seeking to bring policy resources to their jurisdictions in these processes. They are not trying to change or overthrow the broader institutional framework that defines and regulates central–local relationships in China.

1.2.1 Differential Bargaining Power

Bargaining power sets territorial administrations apart in localized bargaining. Margaret Levi (1988) defines the bargaining power of state actors as the "degree of control over coercive, economic, and political resources" (p. 2). The research on the allocation of high-speed railway investments in this book points to two important sources that give subnational actors in China bargaining power in bottom-up policy solicitations. The first is political: localities' positions in the party-state hierarchy. Leaders of territorial administrations at various levels may be selectively represented in the leadership group immediately above their levels. Such concurrent appointments create what I call, borrowing from congressional politics literature, "cardinal" localities and "cleric" localities.[8] The administrations of cardinal localities, like individual members of the US Congress who hold leadership positions in congressional committees, enjoy a range of advantages that give them leverage in negotiation. They have privileged access to the ears of decision-makers at higher levels. They also hold additional power to influence the drafting of crucial policy documents that affect resource allocation at lower levels.

---

[8] See, for example, Berry and Fowler (2016). Members with leadership positions differ significantly from cleric legislators without such leadership roles in their ability to get earmarks for their constituents.

The second source of bargaining power comes from localities' abilities in bringing extra-institutional forces into their bargains with higher-level authorities. Zhang and Liu (2019) show that local officials who were marginalized by their superiors formed alliances with grassroots elites to survive during the tumultuous political movements of the Mao era. In bargaining for policy resources, localities without much institutionalized influence within the party-state rely on what I call the "power of the masses" (Ma, 2019) to strengthen their bargaining positions. They strategically tolerate or mobilize spontaneous expressions of demand for policy benefits by grass-roots constituents (e.g., protests) to put pressure on their superiors and extract policy concessions. Unlike their placement in the party's hierarchy, this source of bargaining power does not vary systematically across localities. It instead emerges sporadically, contingent upon idiosyncratic factors such as whether local citizens and officials have similar preferences and whether local officials can invoke the assistance of local societal elites to mobilize the citizens. Officials embrace this bargaining strategy even though it is risky because of some inherent contradictions in the party-state's incentive structure, including the ineffectiveness of promotion incentives among grassroots officials.

1.2.2 What Allows Localized Bargaining to Take Place?

Two conditions are necessary for localized bargaining to take place. The first is a mismatch between resources and responsibilities across government hierarchies. The superiors at higher levels control a significant amount of policy resources waiting to be spent locally, whereas local authorities are responsible for a wide range of government functions but are starved for revenue. While local authorities have other incentives (such as doing well in performance evaluations), this gap alone gives local authorities a strong impulse to try to influence higher levels' allocative decisions. Since 1994 the tax-sharing system has directed a large portion of local revenue to China's central government while keeping local expenditure responsibilities largely intact, leaving local governments highly reliant on central transfers (Lam, 2009; Wong & Bird, 2008). The tax sharing system also does not specify division of revenue below the provincial level, intensifying bargaining among lower tiers of authorities to gain access to more resources (Shih & Zhang, 2007; Wong, 1997). Revenue is not the only resource upper tiers of government

Taxation

control. The legacies of the planned economy leave a significant amount of regulatory power over social and economic issues within the purview of central government (Yeo, 2009). Numerous specialized central agencies, along with state-owned enterprises, decide whether localities will receive permission to pursue their development ambitions. The interests associated with such regulatory power also become targets for local lobbying activities.

A second, more important condition for localities to take initiative in influencing their superiors' policies is the fact that political leaders in the tiers above their immediate superiors do not interfere in the allocation of policy resources like infrastructure investments. If central leaders micromanaged every policy decision, localities would have no reason to bargain with their immediate superior, and China's authoritarian system gives them no sway over the central leaders. But central leaders delegate allocations to a rather independent bureaucracy. While central leaders could intervene in policymaking by giving direct orders to the bureaucrats, these leaders rely on bureaucracies to keep them in power while sparing them the quotidian exercises of governance. Such delegation creates spaces for localities to influence policy decisions.

The bureaucracy with which localities bargain for railway resources does not function as a logically coherent, unitary actor. Policy conflicts routinely take place among different domains of functional agencies and territorial administrations (e.g., Lampton, 1992; Lieberthal, 1992; Lieberthal & Oksenberg, 1988; Mertha, 2006, 2009). Decision-making power is decentralized across a wide range of specialized agencies; as I found, the making and implementation of decisions regarding high-speed railways involve close to a dozen of ministries in the central government, including the National Development and Reform Commission, the Ministry of Transport, the Ministry of Natural Resources, and the Ministry of Ecology and Environment.[9] Receiving railway access requires the consensus and cooperation of these different agencies, which often have divergent, even competing interests and preferences. This means that each one of these agencies may be able to "veto" the allocation the locality desires (Tsebelis, 1995).

The fragmentation of bureaucratic authorities makes top-down interference in railway policies difficult. In the case of large-scale infrastructure such

[9] A major ministerial reorganization took place in 2018. The Ministry of Natural Resources replaced the now-defunct Ministry of Land and Resources, and the Ministry of Ecology and Environment succeeded the Ministry of Environmental Protection. In the book, I use the current and the previous names of these ministries interchangeably.

Bureaucratic Specialization

as the high-speed railway, such fragmentation is largely the natural consequence of bureaucratic specialization. The technical and logistical sophistication of the programs necessitates the institutional differentiation. A central leader who intends to interfere must force a variety of powerful bureaucracies to follow orders and coordinate policy actions. But in the meantime, central leaders also depend on these bureaucracies to govern over a much wider range of issues. If the goal of interference were to tilt the policies to favor certain associates of a central leader, it is far easier for the leader to offer his associates direct promotions than through intervention in the allocation of railway resources or other policy minutiae. As a result, as Nathan (2003) describes, since the beginning of the reform era, bureaucratic agencies have enjoyed a considerable degree of autonomy over the decisions in their purview, and the "sense that interference would be illegitimate" has also grown over time (p. 11).

While bureaucracies are shielded from top-down interference, they may respond to bottom-up solicitations because they need the cooperation of local authorities to accomplish policy goals. As Evans (1995) points out, bureaucracies rely on ties with the people in their society as a "source of intelligence" (p. 12) for successful policy implementation. While Evans was referring to the relationship between bureaucracies and firms in the making of industrial policies, the same logic applies to the relationship between central bureaucracies and local authorities in making and implementing infrastructure policies. To decide where to invest railway resources, the central bureaucrats need to know, for example, where transportation capacity is lower and which places are financially and logistically capable of handling the construction. Local authorities provide land, labor, and in some cases a significant portion of the funding for laying track and building stations. Central bureaucrats are more likely to accept localities' demand for investments if localities are willing to take on more responsibilities. The bottom-up policy solicitation therefore can be conceptualized either as a process in which localities bargain with their superiors over division of responsibility and benefits, or a process of localities supplying their superiors with information necessary for effective policymaking and implementation.

The outline of the argument can be recapitulated as follows. The ruler delegates the policymaking power to a bureaucracy with fragmented authorities, which creates space for territorial administrations, the intermediary agents, to influence the bureaucracies' allocative decisions. The outcomes of such policy solicitations vary in localities' bargaining power, which is derived from both institutional and extra-institutional sources.

1.3 Data and Methods

Probing bureaucratic processes is not easy in any political context. Executing research design becomes difficult in the field, as the government is often non-cooperative and nonresponsive. Requests to interview officials often receive no response. Access to data is another problem. Government withholding information is the norm in authoritarian states (Hollyer et al., 2018). Publicly available data are often of unreliable quality (e.g., Wallace, 2016). Some of the most insightful findings are often acquired through casual dialogues with officials, rather than from readings of coefficients of regression results (e.g., Solinger, 2006). The biggest challenge lies in the complicated processes of bureaucratic politics per se. While social scientists have placed increasing emphasis on causal identification, the intertwined nature of bureaucratic processes makes it hard to parse out clear directions of causal arrows.

To overcome these challenges and create a comprehensive picture of bureaucratic bargaining in China's high-speed rail project, this book draws on an array of evidence. This includes 60 interviews with government officials and experts between 2015 and 2020, archives of government documents at different levels, and an original, comprehensive data set on the construction of high-speed railways across different parts of China. I also collaborated with several cadre training institutions within Chinese universities and implemented a survey with 893 local Chinese officials. Using both direct questions and survey experiment techniques, I probed officials' perception of bottom-up bureaucratic bargaining and its role in influencing allocative decisions in the survey. The wide array of sources allows me to triangulate and ascertain the complex dynamics of intragovernmental bargaining within the Chinese state.

The interviews with local government officials and central bureaucrats provide insights to develop an understanding of the cumbersome bureaucratic steps leading to the approval of a high-speed railway project, and a labyrinth of central authorities that localities need to work with in this process. These interviews also illuminate various strategies localities have adopted to solicit preferential policy treatments in railway and other policy areas, and identify factors that contribute to successful outcomes in such pursuits. The survey results further corroborate the interview results. To circumvent social desirability bias in answering sensitive questions regarding the Chinese government, I embedded several list experiments in the survey to elicit more genuine opinions on bottom-up policy bargaining from the officials. The results suggest that frontline local officials recognize efforts in bottom-up policy bargains as a crucial determinant of preferential policy treatments from higher levels of authorities (see Chapter 3 for more details).

I then try to identify sources of varying degrees of bargaining power among different localities. Chinese provinces follow the example of the central government, and every five years they issue planning documents that determine the direction of resource allocation, including railway investments, at the provincial level for the next five years. Analyzing the text of two waves of these documents from 2011 and 2016, I found that municipalities whose leaders hold dual appointments at the provincial level are prominent in these policy documents to an extent out of proportion to the size of the economies or population of the municipalities they oversee. Additional analyses suggest that representations at higher levels (through dual appointment) enable these localities to exclude proposals by their competitors while inserting their own preferences into the provincial policy agenda. These analyses, provided in Chapter 4, suggest that representation at higher levels gives localities institutionalized bargaining power (what I call "cardinal" localities). To test how this power of cardinal localities affects the actual rollout of high-speed railway programs, I compiled a detailed data set of the construction of all high-speed railways and stations between 2005 and 2014. The results appear in Chapter 5. After accounting for a wide range of socioeconomic variables, I confirmed the theory, finding that cardinal localities receive quicker approval for construction from the central government, are connected to more lines, and have been assigned more stations. Finally, I used an in-depth case study to elaborate how localities without institutionalized bargaining power (the "clerics") use the power of the masses to gain leverage. The case study shows that officials in an eastern county tolerated local citizens' organization of a protest against their superior's decision to turn the county into a district, which normally their superiors would expect them to quell. While the redistricting case is not directly related to high-speed rail, such a strategic alliance between citizens and local officials also appeared in several "high-speed railway movements" in which protestors demanded the assignment of local stations. I call this phenomenon of officials tolerating protests and translating instabilities into bargaining power "consent instability." In addition, Chapter 6 explains a survey experiment I ran with local officials that corroborates my findings from interviews and case studies on consent instability.

While the majority of the book's empirical evidence is situated in the context of China's high-speed railway program, the argument and findings of the book could and should be extended to explain dynamics in other policy areas. For example, provincial five-year plans reveal that the "cardinals" and the "clerics," and their respective institutionalized bargaining power, would apply to policy domains other than rail. When examining officials' strategy of invoking the power of citizens in policy bargaining, I mainly focus on a case of resistance against a superior's redistricting decision among local officials in an eastern county. These cases share similarities with the high-speed railway program in the sense that they both involve simultaneous bargaining between localities and their superiors and the competition between localities. These cases are also indirectly related to the high-speed railway case. For example, the provincial five-year plans determine in general the allocation of resources at the provincial level across different issues in the next five years, and transportation investments are among the most contested by the localities when formulating these documents. Thus this book offers a broad understanding of Chinese policy processes as well as a detailed study of the policy dynamics behind China's high-speed railway program.

1.4 The Book's Contributions

To my knowledge, *Localized Bargaining* is the first book that offers a systematic examination of the politics and policy processes shaping China's high-speed rail program. The main text of the book provides rich empirical evidence on the workings of bureaucratic processes and logic that surround China's rail development. The book also seeks to advance our understanding of two important theoretical literature in comparative politics.

1.4.1 Contribution to Research on Distributive Politics

The question of who benefits from distributive policies motivates this book. The conventional wisdom posits that the patterns of distribution reflect strategic calculations by decision-makers. Whoever has the most power uses resources either to enrich associates and followers in exchange for their support, or to prioritize the development of certain sectors, industries, or regions. This book cuts against this wisdom and argues that the patterns of distribution could also reflect the actions and strategies of the potential recipients who each seek to increase their own share of the policy benefits. The recipients are not just passive takers of decisions from higher levels. Intermediary recipients who are tasked with implementing higher-level decisions also actively work to influence their superiors' decision-making. As Max Weber (2013) famously noted, politics is not just about the leadership, but also about the "influencing of the leadership" (p. 77). Differences in local agents' abilities to influence their superiors, derived from institutional or extra-institutional sources, are key drivers of the variations in the outcomes of localized bargaining.

In looking at the influences on leadership, this book does not seek to overturn existing conclusions in distributive politics, a field with extraordinary breadth and depth. Instead, the findings of this book call for greater attention to the contexts in which distributions take place and the types of benefits being distributed, rather than focusing on the decision-makers alone. In a review essay examining the distributive politics literature, Kramon and Posner (2013) point out that the outcomes (i.e., types of goods) scholars study often affect their findings. There are good reasons to believe that under authoritarianism, the allocations of benefits in areas such as national-scale infrastructure programs might follow a different logic than "loyalty purchasing" or "technocratic solutions." First, compared with other types of goods, the benefits associated with infrastructural investments are difficult to reverse. Yet the reversibility of policy benefits is at the core of a patron–client argument—the idea that the patron could punish disloyal clients *ex post* by withdrawing the benefits previously given to them (e.g., Hicken, 2011; Kitschelt & Wilkinson, 2007; Robinson & Verdier, 2013). The quid pro quo logic of patronage politics therefore is less persuasive in explaining the distribution of large-scale infrastructure investments. Second, the execution of these large-scale programs relies on the expertise and cooperation of numerous specialized bureaucracies at various levels. These actors are not just impersonal tools of their superiors (e.g., Jensen & Meckling, 1976; Ross, 1973). Leaders of these local institutions often identify more closely with their positions or departments than with their superiors (Falleti, 2005; Kornai, 1980). They use the power delegated to them to influence their superiors in order to advance their interests. Such localistic or departmental behaviors pervade the policymaking and implementation processes, and the eventual distributive outcomes can hardly be considered to reflect coherent, strategic calculations on the part of top decision makers.

There is a long tradition in studies of Chinese politics of looking at how local politics shape higher-level policies. Solinger (1986), for example, notes that China's economic reform has resulted in "decentralization in power and purse on a vertical dimension and redistribution of investment among sectors and regions on a horizontal one" (p. 379). This has given rise to "local advocacy." Local leaders become the "spokespersons for the areas under their jurisdiction" (p. 382), and appeal to upper-level allocators for expanded resources. The redistribution produces "a process of pluralization, involving bargains, battles, negotiations, and lobbying" (p. 379) among state entities across hierarchies. More recently Jaros (2019) finds that multilevel bargains between the central, provincial, and municipal governments produce variations in development policies across China. In places where provincial authorities have greater influence relative to central or local counties and municipalities, the provinces are able to make policies that prioritize the development of a few provincial centers. In places where the provinces are relatively weak, developmental policies tend to be more egalitarian across sub-provincial units. Jaros explains, "Power at the provincial level is thus associated with more metropolitan-oriented development" (p. 19). Relatedly, Wang (2014) finds that the bargaining power of asset holders at local levels determines the regional variations in the provisions of more robust legal institutions. Asset holders who are mobile (e.g., foreign investors) can make a credible threat that they will withdraw their resources from a particular locality, which gives them greater bargaining power vis-à-vis local officials. Places where such asset holders dominate local economies are more likely to build cleaner courts and experience the rise of "a partial form of the rule of law" that is more hospitable to investment. This book joins this growing body of research by arguing that bottom-up bargains by local authorities play important roles in pressing for favorable social and economic policies, and extracting policy concessions when upper-level decisions contradict local interests. In addition to institutional sources of influence, this book adds that localities can draw from extra-institutional sources, such as the pressure of local citizens, to strengthen their bargaining power. This finding echoes a recent line of work which suggests that authoritarian elites seek grassroots support to overcome the lack of superior backing in political competition (e.g., Radnitz, 2010; Zhang et al., 2013; Zhang & Liu, 2019).

The patterns and logic of distribution presented in this book are not unique to China. Scholars of other developing and developed countries have also found that the calculations of those who have the decision-making power do not always determine allocations of public resources. Rather, the actions of those who would bear the consequences of distributive policies could play a decisive role. In studying the regional variations in electrification in India, Kale (2014) finds that differences in political and social structures at the provincial level account for variations in patterns of infrastructural development. Places where rural constituents were successfully mobilized and became politically influential were more likely to make gains in electrification. Relatedly, Singh (2015) argues that the levels of welfare provision (e.g., education, health) in subnational India vary in the strength of the solidarity of local communities. Localities where local elites share a strong common identification place a higher value on collective interests, and thus are more likely to push for progressive social policies and further the welfare of local communities. In a recent book titled *Demanding Development*, Auerbach (2019) finds that the internal political organization of India's urban slum settlements and their leaders vary in ways that determine their ability to demand and secure development from the state. Informal slum leaders who are embedded in larger party networks are able to better mobilize residents to demand resources from the state, and consequently improve their access to public goods and services. In post-Soviet Russia, while Moscow tends to divert more subsidies, grants, transfers, and other resources to protests-prone regions for "selective fiscal appeasement" (Treisman, 1999), Robertson (2010) shows that regional elites with relatively weak influence actually encourage protests in order to gain access to more resources from Moscow. In a more general comparative study of developing countries, Wibbels (2005) finds that "a constant process of bargaining between national and regional leaders struggling for political survival" determines the degree to which federal states embrace transitions to market-based economies (p. 5). Factors that are similar to what we examine in this book, such as the bargaining power of national leaders vis-à-vis regional leaders, or whether regional interests are institutionally represented at the national level, affect the bargaining outcomes on policy coordination to achieve market transitions.

In studying the planned economies in East Europe during the transition period, a context that bears more resemblance to today's China, Kornai (1980, 1992) identifies a phenomenon of "plan bargaining" in which "[t]he central authority wishes more output from the firm for fewer inputs, while the firm asks for more input and promises less output" (Kornai, 1980, p. 564). While central planning seemed rigid and hierarchical, the planners and the firms routinely negotiated the planned output levels, the materials the state would supply, and how much surplus firms could retain for reproduction. These led to what Kornai (1980) famously conceptualizes as "the soft budget constraint." Planned production targets no longer bind most firms in today's China, and firms have various formal and informal channels to influence politics and policies (e.g., Hou, 2019; Kennedy, 2009). The bargaining similar to what Kornai (1980) identifies, as this book shows, still exists between different levels of government authorities in China, on policy issues such as infrastructure investments.

Finally, readers might even draw parallels in patterns of distributions between bargains under China's Leninist party-state hierarchies and lobbying by interests groups in electoral democracies (e.g., Hansen, 1991; Truman, 1951; Wright, 1996), two otherwise drastically different systems. Recent empirical studies in American politics have highlighted the existence of lobbying by local governments and the distributive implications of such actions (e.g., Goldstein & You, 2017; Payson, 2020a). This book shows that in China, governments also lobby governments, but their strategies in influencing their superiors might differ from those of their counterparts in the United States.

1.4.2 Contribution to Our Understanding of Authoritarian Political Institutions

Through the lens of distributive politics, this book also seeks to advance our understanding of authoritarian politics in general. While classical theories of political development predict that economic modernization will lead to either democratization (Lipset, 1959) or political instabilities (Huntington, 1968), China has emerged as a theoretical exception in the past four decades. In China, authoritarian rule has appeared "resilient" in adapting to shocks from unprecedented economic growth in the reform era (Dickson, 2016; Nathan, 2003). Elite conflicts have followed such shocks in many countries worldwide (e.g., Geddes, 2004; Smith, 2007) and serve as the single most important cause of authoritarian breakdowns (Svolik, 2012). Yet the CCP has maintained a cohesive elite coalition while gaining control over a significant amount of resources in the process of development, which raises the question as to how. What institutional arrangements credibly commit the ruling communist party to share power among influential actors in the regime? How does the regime allocate government resources in a way that minimizes elite tensions? The politics of distribution are a second-order puzzle under authoritarianism. The particular institutional configurations that sustain authoritarian rule also shape the ways in which wealth and resources are distributed among autocratic elites.

The virtue of authoritarianism—unchecked power in the hands of the few—often sows the seed of its own demise. In an authoritarian regime, one that lacks an impartial enforcer who has authority over the wielder of state power, if the ruler promises to share power and resources with other elites, he or she can hardly be considered credible. Fearing the ruler will expropriate them, elite members of the regime tend to invest their loyalty in the subversion—rather than the continued rule—of the incumbent ruler (Boix & Svolik, 2013; Magaloni, 2008; Svolik, 2012). A typical intra-elite conflict begins with a ruler consolidating his power with the support of a subset of elites (Geddes et al., 2018; Haber, 2007). Yet the consolidation of the ruler's power cultivates opportunism. Without effective challenges or punishment, the ruler could have attempted to exploit the very elites that launched him to power to enrich himself, or disproportionally favor a narrow group of protégés at the expense of the remaining elites, with whom the ruler once promised to share prestige and wealth (e.g., North & Weingast, 1989). When the costs of retaining such an opportunistic and exploitive ruler surpass a certain point, elites will take options to remove him or her despite the risk.

The key to a stable authoritarian rule therefore lies in mechanisms that give elites leverage to enforce agreements rulers make to share prestige and wealth (Myerson, 2008; Svolik, 2012). Even seemingly meaningless institutions can provide elites with venues or focal points for collective actions, thereby curbing opportunism on the part of autocrats and making elites more confident that power sharing will endure. Scholars have found that institutions such as political parties (Gehlbach & Keefer, 2011; Magaloni, 2008; Shirk, 1993), legislature (Gandhi, 2008; Malesky & Schuler, 2010), constitution (Albertus & Menaldo, 2012; Myerson, 2008), judiciary (Moustafa, 2007; Wang, 2014), hereditary succession (Brownlee, 2007; Kokkonen & Sundell, 2014; Menaldo, 2012), and term limits (Ma, 2016; Meng, 2020) promote durable authoritarian rule by tying the autocrat's hands such that elites have a relatively stable expectation of power sharing. Likewise the presence of electoral competitions, even largely manipulated ones, empower the elites by giving them an exit option—leaving the incumbent faction or party and running as opposition—that can impose credible threats against the ruler (Magaloni, 2008). Rulers allocate resources based on the need to secure electoral support, and the credibility of the ruler's redistribution promises is in turn safeguarded by the institution of elections per se (e.g., Acemoglu & Robinson, 2000)—rulers who failed to keep their promises would face punishment in future elections.

Research has generally not explained how institutions actually mediate the distribution of resources among the ruling elites. Indeed, the nominal functions of most of these institutions do not directly pertain to resource allocation, and China has no elections that are even semi-competitive at the national level. This fact leaves open the question as to what other institutions play the twin functions of curbing the opportunism of the ruler and ensuring a credible arrangement of sharing resources among powerful regime insiders.

This book focuses on the role of bureaucracy in power sharing in China. The fragmentation of bureaucratic authorities limits the ruler's ability to arbitrarily influence policymaking to favor his own associates, as the ruler would have to expend considerable political capital among a diversified group of bureaucratic elites on whom he relies to govern. Fragmentation also makes it harder for bureaucrats to act collectively, making bureaucratic delegation a safer option for the ruler. The fragmentation nevertheless creates opportunities for local authorities who are responsible for implementing central decisions to advance their interests. Their ability to move the gridlocked bureaucracy becomes a critical determinant of their receipt of resources. In this regard, the bureaucracy fulfills the twin functions of mediating resource allocation among regime insiders and making the resource-sharing arrangement more credible by limiting the extent to which the ruler can interfere in the daily policymaking and implementation processes.

While bureaucracies are often perceived as politicians' impersonal policy tools, the findings in this book point out that bureaucracy can also limit the power of authoritarian rulers. Social scientists have long been interested in theorizing how particular characteristics associated with bureaucracy, such as expertise, professionalism, and "organizational coherence" (Evans, 1995), create autonomous power among bureaucrats and curb the dictatorial tendencies of their political masters (e.g., Rosenberg, 1968; Weber, 2013). Scholars have indeed found empirical evidence that bureaucracy constrains executive power and preserves policy independence in various contexts, including imperial China (e.g., Qian, 1982), developmental autocracies (e.g., Campos & Root, 2001; Cheng et al., 1998; Haggard, 1990), and developed democracies (e.g., Knight & Miller, 2007; Miller, 2000; Miller & Whitford, 2016). Campos and Root (2001), for example, argue that autocrats in Taiwan and South Korea made their commitments to protecting property rights more credible by delegating parts of their decision-making powers to a technocratic bureaucracy. The intuition of this argument also helps to explain why, historically, certain despotic rulers sought to weaken or destroy bureaucratic institutions when they attempted to tighten their grip on power (e.g., Huang, 2000; Lewis, 2002; MacFarquhar & Schoenhals, 2009). This book thus joins a growing list of research that attributes authoritarian durability to the roles of various institutions in committing authoritarian rulers to share power (e.g., Boix & Svolik, 2013; Gehlbach & Keefer, 2011; Kokkonen & Sundell, 2014; Ma, 2016; Magaloni, 2006, 2008; Menaldo, 2012; Moustafa, 2007; Myerson, 2008; Svolik, 2012). Most extant studies associate the credibility of bureaucratic institutions with the costs of reversing bureaucratic delegation—in other words, the ruler cannot govern without the help of professional bureaucrats. This book argues that bureaucratic constraints also stem from the fragmentation of authorities within the bureaucracy, and such arrangements generate a distinctive pattern of distribution that cuts against predictions by conventional understandings of authoritarianism.

Relatedly, my argument also indirectly contributes to our understanding of political accountability under authoritarianism. Why do authoritarian officials embrace policies that benefit the economy and the population without elections holding them accountable? A highly influential strand of literature argues that certain institutions, such as merit-based promotions, help align the interests of local officials with the developmental goals of the regime (e.g., Bell, 2015; Li & Zhou, 2005; Whiting, 2001, 2004). An unanswered question is why rulers want to pursue growth- or welfare-enhancing policies in the first place. Authoritarian rulers are not by default benevolent. The same institution that disciplines local officials to pursue economic growth could also incentivize them to take atrocious actions, if the central leaders want to pursue bad policies (e.g., Arendt, 1963; Kung & Chen, 2011). The argument advanced in this book supplements existing theories by highlighting the role of bureaucratic institutions in tying rulers' hands. Bureaucratic constraints limit the abilities of authoritarian rulers to unilaterally impose decisions, and leave policies to be shaped by bottom-up bargains that incorporate different interests within the regime. While elections and legislative institutions in competitive democracies aggregate constituents' preferences and translate them into policies (McCubbins & Schwartz, 1984), the bottom-up policy bargains, which emerge as a result of fragmentation of authorities within the bureaucracy, provide a parallel mechanism that allows policymaking processes under authoritarianism to be inclusive of the regime's various constituents' preferences—although these "constituents" are not ordinary citizens but are functional divisions and territorial administrations. Consequently, it would appear that regimes with an elaborate bureaucracy are more attentive to the interests and demands of a broader group of players in society (Ahmed & Stasavage, 2020). The "developmental mindedness" of the Chinese state, along with those of other East Asian developmental states, therefore might be partly attributable to the region's history of pioneering the building of a modern bureaucracy over the past two millennia (Fukuyama, 2011; Wittfogel, 1957).

Of course, I do not wish to make a sweeping claim that bureaucracy is a panacea for pathologies associated with authoritarianism, only that fragmented bureaucracy can curb some of those pathologies. Indeed, where the ruler can easily govern with a centralized authority, bureaucratic fragmentation is unlikely. Thus there is more top-down control from the ruler in such areas, and the patterns of distribution will reflect the intention of the decision makers. In China, personnel appointments conform to this pattern. Unlike building high-speed railways, appointing officials does not require the expertise of technocrats from diversified backgrounds. The authority of appointment is therefore concentrated in the party's organization department (the human resource arm of the CCP), through which the party leaders appoint their followers to powerful positions (e.g., Shih et al., 2012). Thus, as many scholars have noted, patterns of patronage still remain common, unimpeded by bureaucracy. Further, as Chapter 6 will describe, the arena for competitions over policy resources among local officials that has arisen over high-speed rail might lead local elites to adopt risky bargaining strategies that could damage the regime's resilience. This fresh source of elite conflicts may ultimately be no less dangerous to those that have brought down other regimes. Instead, the system has transformed risks of political rivalries at the top into disputes over policy details at lower levels.

1.5 Chapter Overview

The remainder of the book consists of six chapters. Chapter 2 proposes the argument of localized bargaining, which posits that bottom-up bargains by territorial administrations shape the allocation of policy benefits. The discussions specify the institutional environment under which such a pattern of distribution would emerge. In particular, I examine how a central bureaucracy with fragmented authority limits top-down interference and makes bottom-up bargaining efforts by those local agents crucial determinants of policy outcomes. The chapter then describes the varying levels of bargaining power of local bureaucratic actors and the bargaining strategies they employ. It goes on to briefly discuss how localized bargaining supplements existing explanations in distributive politics. The chapter ends with a summary of testable hypotheses derived from the core argument.

Chapters 3 through 6 present empirical evidence to test the hypotheses laid out in Chapter 2. Table 1.1 presents a summary of the evidence and the hypotheses they test.

Chapter 3 begins with a description of the process a local government undertakes in seeking approval for its proposals for rail infrastructure in the locality. I describe the preferences and conflicts of relevant central bureaucratic actors involved in the process. The fragmented, interlocking nature of central bureaucratic authorities makes bottom-up solicitation by local governments a primary factor in explaining the variations in central allocative decisions. By studying the daily operation of localities' Beijing offices, the chapter then examines the strategies local authorities employ to solicit central policy benefits and the conditions under which such efforts succeed or fail. I find that local leaders' willingness and efforts, combined with localities' ranks in the party-state's hierarchy, are crucial determinants of the bargaining outcomes. The chapter ends with a survey of 893 Chinese local officials. Survey data on officials' perception of the role of bottom-up policy bargains in determining government resource allocation corroborates findings from the qualitative interviews.

Chapter 4 identifies the institutional sources of differential bargaining power across localities. It presents insights from an original data set on how prominently the documents created by the provincial governments feature cities and their policy proposals, most of which concern local infrastructure projects like railways. I find that concurrent appointments in the provincial decision-making bodies indicate greater institutionalized bargaining power.

Table 1.1 Observable Implications and Empirical Tests

Testable Hypotheses	Empirical Evidence
Chapter 3: (a) The fragmentation of decision-making authorities at the top creates opportunities for bottom-up bargaining by local policy recipients. (b) The allocation of policy benefits is a function of local governments' bargaining power and strategies.	– Qualitative analysis of the process of and the actors involved in the approval of high-speed rail projects at the central level. – Interviews with local officials on localities' strategies to elicit cooperation from central bureaucracies. – Survey of local officials on their perception of the role of bottom-up bargaining in allocative policies.
Chapter 4: Unequal representations in the party-state's hierarchies generate differential institutionalized bargaining power among localities.	– Analysis of 333 Chinese cities' policy presence in their respective provinces' 5-year planning documents.
Chapter 5: Localities where the officials have inherited greater institutionalized bargaining power within the bureaucratic hierarchies (the "cardinals") are more likely to procure favorable policy treatment from their superiors.	– Analysis of high-speed railway investment and construction data in different provinces and municipalities from 2004 to 2014.
Chapter 6: (a) Officials who lack institutionalized bargaining power (the "clerics") resort to extra-institutional sources of bargaining power such as the pressure of the masses. (b) Local authorities' superiors are more likely to concede to localities' demands when such demands are backed by popular pressure that poses a threat to regime stability.	– Case study of "consent instability" in China. – Survey experiments of local officials on the power of the masses in shaping policy decisions.

Cities whose leaders hold such appointments (cardinals) were able to insert a greater number of local proposals into the two recent waves of provincial five-year plans issued in 2016 and 2011. The chapter attributes the differences to these localities' enhanced abilities in influencing or even controlling their superiors' policy agendas through their positions. Unequal representation of localities in the party-state's decision-making bodies enables these localities to translate political privileges into tangible economic and policy benefits, often at the expense of those without institutional privileges, the cleric localities.

Building on the findings of Chapters 3 and 4, Chapter 5 unpacks the political geography of high-speed rails. Using an original data set describing the construction of high-speed rails between 2004 and 2014, I show that prov-inces and cities with leaders holding dual appointments at higher levels re-ceived preferential treatment from the central government. They were not only given faster permission to build their portion of the railway, but they were also connected to more lines and were allowed to build more stations within their jurisdictions. This empirical exercise also rules out "loyalty purchasing" and "technocratic solutions" as explanations. Local leaders' personal connections with top party leaders, and most of localities' socio-economic indicators, are not associated with favorable treatment from the center. These results lend support to the core argument that the allocations of policy benefits in issue areas with fragmented central authorities vary in local bargaining power.

Chapter 6 examines the strategies of cleric localities, whose peripheral positions within the party-state limit their voice and capabilities in procuring policy benefits through formal channels. In such localities, leaders seek help from actors outside of the party-state, and often through means that are less institutionalized than those cardinal localities use. Consent instability—tacit tolerance by local officials of mass mobilizations in which citizens demand policy benefits from higher government authorities—represents one such strategy. Based on the comments of local officials in interviews, I show that protests in the streets help send a costly signal to their superiors that ignoring the demand for resources will put social stability at risk. This logic has driven a dozen local "high-speed railway protests" across China in recent years. The chapter specifies the institutional conditions under which such a bargaining strategy emerges, using a detailed case study of an eastern county to flesh out the logic of "consent instability." Survey data on party cadres support the in-sight that popular pressure makes superiors more responsive to grassroots officials' demands.

Chapter 7 summarizes the main findings of the book and proposes sev-eral questions that are related to the subject for future studies. The argument and findings in this book prompt a reexamination of the sources of author-itarian resilience in China, and what recent changes to recentralize power in Chinese politics and the rise of popular localism mean for the future of China's policy process and development.

2

Bureaucracies and Localized Bargaining

2.1 Introduction

Politics is about "who gets what, when and how" (Lasswell, 1936). Political and policy decisions with distributive consequences are ubiquitous in everyday life. From where to build schools and roads, to which industry to subsidize or regulate, to which officials to promote, to which communities to provide better protection, political leaders make hard choices with limited resources. The decision to expand railway service is just another of these choices. In making such decisions, political leaders must prioritize issues, individuals, organizations, and regions. Unequal distribution of policy benefits across different segments of population and places is essentially inevitable.

In this chapter, I develop an argument focusing on the role of bureaucratic bargaining by policy recipients in shaping the allocation of policy benefits. Territorial administrations and their leaders, on whom the central leaders rely to implement various policies, have multitudes of incentives to gain access to greater policy benefits from their superiors. By navigating and forging consensus in a central bureaucracy with fragmented authorities, they may be able to secure favorable policy treatment. I call such actions by territorial governments *localized bargaining*. After laying out the main argument, the chapter highlights key differences between the localized bargaining argument and existing explanations of distributive politics, including the loyalty purchasing and the technocratic solution models, as noted in the introduction chapter. The chapter concludes by summarizing several empirical hypotheses derived from the argument.

Localized Bargaining. Xiao Ma, Oxford University Press. © Oxford University Press 2022.
DOI: 10.1093/oso/9780197638910.003.0002

2.2 Localized Bargaining

2.2.1 The Argument

Government is not a monolithic entity. It consists of numerous hierarchies and divisions. Tensions within the government have important implications for policymaking. This book argues that solicitation activities on the part of local governments importantly shape the allocative decisions of their superiors. While these local governments are agents of upper-level governments and are responsible for implementing their superiors' policy decisions, they also appear as the recipients of resources allocated by their superiors. The juxtaposition of political centralization and economic decentralization in China incentivizes local governments to pursue actions that try to sway their superiors' allocative decisions in their favor. In undertaking such actions, which I call *localized bargaining*, not all localities are created equal or adopt the same strategies of bargaining, however. Whether local requests for policy benefits successfully reach and convince their superiors depends on the bargaining power localities inherited within the regime or their respective bargaining strategies.

While the eventual recipients of most government policies are often citizens, this book pays attention to the "institutional recipients" and associated elites in an authoritarian context. They are powerful organizations or agents with whom the central bureaucratic agencies negotiate policy terms, such as territorial administrations, functional bureaucracies, or state-owned enterprises. Students of authoritarian politics have noted that regime insiders play a greater role in shaping policies than ordinary citizens (e.g., Svolik, 2012). There has also been a long scholarly tradition of treating organizations, rather than individuals, as the actors in elite bargaining.[1] Conceptually, these institutional recipients can be understood as members of the ruling coalition, who desire a share of policy benefits from the ruler (e.g., Bueno de Mesquita et al., 2005). Unlike individual elites, whose preferences are often "short-run" and subject to change, the interests of institutions "exist through time" (Huntington, 1968, p. 25).

The key outcomes of interest are policy decisions with distributive consequences. This book uses the terms *policy benefits*, *policy choices*,

---

[1] For examples of scholarly treatment of organizations as unit of analysis in elite bargain in Chinese politics, see Lieberthal (1992), Solinger (1996) and Cai (2014a); for example in the studies of former Soviet politics, see Kolkowicz (1970) and Stewart (1969).

allocative decisions, and so forth, interchangeably. Central policymakers typically allocate two types of policy goods with distinctive territorial implications. The first type are policies that affect all localities but are not attached to any specific one. Examples include the central banks' regulation of interest rates and currency exchange rates, foreign policies, or nation-wide environmental regulations. I call benefits associated with this type of policy *universalistic goods*. The second type are policies that benefit specific localities. Examples include transfers, subsidies, investments, permits, a special economic zone designation, or a redistricting decision that fiscally empowers some jurisdictions at the expense of others. I call this type *particularistic goods*. This book focuses on the allocation of particularistic goods, which targets specific institutional recipients at the local level.

In a unitary state like China, the line of authority typically flows along the bureaucratic hierarchy. The central decision-makers are at higher levels than the policy bearers, namely the territorial governments. In an ideal Weberian bureaucracy, the superiors possess greater power, and the localities are hence passive takers of the policy decisions made by their superiors. This book paints a different picture, one in which localities play a major role in shaping their superiors' decision-making in certain issue areas.

My argument has several elements. For convenience and clarity, I call higher-level authorities the "policymaker," and local authorities "policy recipients." Localized bargaining by policy recipients takes place because there is an over-concentration of policy resources in the hands of the policymaker. The policymaker consists of rulers and a central bureaucracy on which the rulers rely to make and implement policies. Fragmented authorities within the bureaucracy prevent rulers from allocating policy benefits at will, creating an opportunity structure for policy recipients to compete to gain access to resources. Despite similar incentives in getting more resources, policy recipients differ in their bargaining power, leading to various localized bargaining strategies that shape regional variations in allocation of policy benefits.

2.2.2 Concentration of Resources in the Hands of the Policymaker

The bottom-up solicitation of resources should only occur in cases of mismatch between policymakers' and policy recipients' resources and/

or responsibilities. If policy recipients possess resources commensurate with their responsibilities, they are unlikely to solicit additional resources. However, the policymaker may possess a majority of resources yet share few governance responsibilities, whereas policy recipients have responsibilities but few resources. The policymaker may purposefully design this situation as a way to control the policy recipients, who are often subordinates of the policymaker (e.g., territorial administrations and their leaders are subordinates of the central government in a unitary system).

At the same time, since the policymaker does not directly participate in local governance, he lacks knowledge as to which recipient most needs the resources. His need for information to increase the efficiency of resource allocation creates opportunities for the policy recipients to elicit a greater share of policy benefits for themselves than is optimal for the country.

Policy resources, however, are always limited at any given time. The zero-sum nature of resource allocation induces competition among the recipients. This is particularly intense with high-speed railway. The construction and opening of new railway lines bring various economic opportunities for localities. Local governments near the route thus all want to build stations in their jurisdictions. Yet, the technical requirements of high-speed railway entail that the railway cannot take detours or have too many stations within a short distance. This means that the placement of a station in one locale essentially means nearby locales will not have one. Thus placement becomes a political question, marked by fierce inter-jurisdictional competition.

Local governments thus must seek to make a strong case that they need a railway station more than the others do. In an authoritarian context where there are few institutionalized mechanisms to adjudicate competing claims among powerful political actors (e.g., deliberation in the legislature), the process of competition is often fraught with ad hoc bargaining and backdoor deals. The "winners" are often those most successful in this process rather than those with the greatest need.

Today the Chinese government system is a rare juxtaposition of both centralization and decentralization, which creates an ideal breeding ground for competition among policy recipients such as local governments for resources from policymakers, in this case central government agencies. The Chinese State Council, where most important social and economic policies are formulated and implemented, consists of only functional bureaucracies. Territorial administrations, as a result, are systematically excluded from day-to-day policymaking of the central government (e.g., Shirk, 1993).[2] In the 1980s and early 1990s, the provincial power had been on the rise vis-à-vis that of the center, so such disenfranchisement did not cause major problems for the local governments. The situation has changed since then, particularly after the tax-sharing reform in 1994, which enhanced the tax capacity of the center and created major gaps in resources and responsibilities on the part of the localities.

Measured by local fiscal responsibilities, China today is among the most economically decentralized countries in the world: local governments are responsible for more than 70% of overall government expenditures (Landry, 2008). Correspondingly, local governments have a high degree of autonomy over economic and social issues within their jurisdictions. In many regards, Chinese local governments govern like their central counterpart, with reduced scales at every level (Lieberthal, 2004; Maskin et al., 2000).[3]

Superiors empower local leaders but also hold them responsible for how they govern their jurisdictions (Cai, 2014b; Li & Zhou, 2005; Whiting, 2004). The Chinese Communist Party maintains the unity of this otherwise decentralized system by centralizing the power of personnel appointment and exerting top-down control of territorial leaders (Landry, 2008; Xu, 2011).

Besides personnel control, the central government controls a wide range of resources. Since tax-sharing reform was instituted in 1994, the central government has collected more than 50% of the revenue while having responsibility for less than 30% of the expenditure. The surplus is transferred back to the localities, which account for a significant portion of the local budgetary revenue (Wong, 2000). Poor localities rely on such transfers even to pay their civil servants and provide public services such as schools and hospitals (e.g., Liu et al., 2009; Lü, 2015). The central government also controls an army of state-owned enterprises, which have easy access to bank loans and aggressively invest in key sectors across the country. These firms have grown considerably in size over the past few decades, increasing the central government's ability to manage the economy (Huang, 2008).

---

[2] Provincial leaders (provincial party secretary and governors) are only invited to attend the Central Economic Work Conference that has taken place by the end of each year, which mostly discusses macroeconomic policies and broad plans for the next year instead of specific policies.

[3] The Chinese local governments have four levels: province, city, county, and township.

The central government also holds formidable regulatory powers. Central bureaucracies set numerous rules and regulations in their specialized fields, and local governments need to seek approvals or recognition when their undertakings fall in the jurisdiction of the central bureaucracies, ranging from permissions for investments to tax exemptions or designation of special regional status. Even if the localities are endowed with rich local resources and are not reliant on central transfers or investments, the central government's failure to approve some of their biddings can seriously hamper their ambitions to grow the local economy.

The combination of centralization and decentralization creates a strong incentive for the Chinese local governments to engage in bottom-up solicitation. On the one hand, local governments and their leaders continue to enjoy a considerable degree of delegation and are responsible for the development of their regions. On the other hand, the central government possesses a greater share of resources or policy instruments crucial for local development, especially after the tax-sharing reform in 1994. This has created a widening gap in resources and responsibilities between the central and territorial governments. A rational local leader seeking to maximize the opportunities for local development will try to obtain more resources from their superiors.

The juxtaposition of centralization and decentralization not only exists between the central government and the provinces; it also exists between different levels of local governments (i.e., provinces, cities, counties, and townships). As Lieberthal (2004) rightly notes, "[The] Chinese political system largely duplicates itself at each of the territorial levels" (p. 171). Provincial governments exert similar control over personnel, money, and policies of the cities as the center does over the provinces; and the cities exert similar control over the counties, and the counties over the townships. Provincial governments are "policy recipients" when they seek resources from the central government, and they become "policymakers" when cities under their jurisdictions approach them for preferential policy treatment. In China's multi-layered governmental system, a local government can play different roles in localized bargaining, depending on whether they seek resources from their superiors or are lobbied by their subordinate localities. The central government, however, as the ultimate policymaker, is always lobbied by members of all levels of local government. There are also occasions in which lower levels of government (e.g., cities or counties) circumvent their direct superiors and instead lobby the central government for policy benefits.

2.2.3 The Autonomy of the Resource-Allocating Bureaucracy

Having established that the policymaker is in control of a significant amount of resources, an additional question emerges: why does the ruler allow the recipients to compete for these resources? This would suggest that the ruler voluntarily forgoes the option of allocating the resources as he wishes. Conventional wisdom in distributive politics, such as the "loyalty purchasing" and "technocratic solution" models, assume that the ruler determines the allocation of the resources he holds. In the localized bargaining model, the ruler relies on a bureaucracy to make and implement distributive policies. Two features of the bureaucracy increase its autonomy and make intervention from the ruler difficult. The first is that, like most Weberian bureaucracies, it includes rational-legal institutions and professional expertise possessed by bureaucrats. The second feature is the fragmented authority within the bureaucracy.

Features of Weberian Bureaucracy. Weber (1978) characterized modern bureaucracy as an institution with a well-defined hierarchy and jurisdiction, staffed by bureaucrats with professional expertise, that operates and organizes itself under codified rules. In theory, the rational-legal institutions of the bureaucracy, along with professional knowledge of its members, should make bureaucracies effective agents of their political masters. In practice, these features actually increase the autonomy of the bureaucracy. In studying the 19th-century German bureaucracy, Rosenberg (1968) found that over time, the process of exercising the powers inherent in their office turned royal-appointed bureaucrats who had been "royal servants" into "servant[s] of the state" (p. 191):

> By subjecting the crown to certain binding rules, [the bureaucrats] curbed the powers of the absolute king, placed him under the law, reduced the personal element in government, and spurred the evolution of the official hierarchy into a self-centered political hierarchy. (p. 190)

Similar dynamics have been documented across places and history, including in imperial China (e.g., Kuhn, 1992; Qian, 1982), medieval Europe (González de Lara et al., 2008), and in modern democracies like the United States (e.g., Miller & Whitford, 2016).

As Rosenberg laid out with respect to 19th-century Germany, although the ruler could forcefully assert his will by dismissing or otherwise punishing the disobedient bureaucrats, the separation of political ministers—the top bureaucrats the monarch had appointed—and the remaining professional bureaucrats—who were recruited through a standardized civil service exam and who enjoyed relative career security (Rosenberg, 1968, p. 178)—further increased the autonomy of the bureaucracy. A yes-man minister who served nothing but the pleasure of the king still needed the cooperation of functionary bureaucrats to carry out policies.

In fact, politically appointed ministers who know very little about the professional business of the bureaucracy often find themselves dependent on career bureaucrats or even "taken hostage" by their subordinates. Naoto Kan, who served as the Minister of Health and Welfare in the late 1990s before becoming Japanese Prime Minister in 2010, recalled the day he arrived at the ministry as a freshman minister (Kan, 1998, pp. 76–77). The senior bureaucrats waiting in line at the lobby greeted him, and one of them handed him a piece of paper telling him that they had prepared a press statement for his use when he met the press later. On that paper was a list of policy tasks the ministry intended to accomplish. Thinking they were nothing more than political platitudes, Kan, who had no prior experience in public health and whose appointment was part of a political compromise between two ruling coalition parties, followed the bureaucrats' advice and read the statement in front of the press. He later found he had committed to a policy agenda the senior bureaucrats preferred, and that changing course when he had made a public commitment was impossible. These kinds of "initial traps" (Mabuchi, 2009, p. 276) are very common in systems like Japan's, where senior bureaucrats often possess more experience in their jurisdiction than their politically appointed superiors and thus can use various strategies to circumvent ministers' command and authority.

As illustrated in Kan's case, bureaucrats' power largely originates from their expertise and professionalism. Bureaucrats possess detailed knowledge in technicalities and know-how in their respective fields. Their expertise and knowledge are crucial to making the bureaucracy work. The political master (e.g., ruler) often "appears as a 'dilettante' before the expertise of the bureaucrats" (Miller & Whitford, 2016, p. 7). A ruler who attempts to command the bureaucracy often faces the hard choice between arbitrarily imposing his will and actually getting things done. Consultation with bureaucrats is the only way to have effective policies (Rosenberg, 1968). As in Naoto Kan's case, bureaucrats can obstruct and divert to obtain the policy outcomes they support. Rosenberg (1968, p. 193) described "inertia, chicanery, and sophistry" as key tools, "withholding facts or . . . supplying colored information" and, when they felt the occasion required, "cunning subterfuges, outright deception, and willful sabotage." Smart rulers were certainly aware that these actions were occurring, but they could do little to weaken bureaucratic autonomy. "In the midst of an odious atmosphere of mutual suspicion, distrust, and perpetual alertness," Rosenberg wrote, bureaucrats "exploited their powers of investigation and carried out unauthorized policies of their own by amending, undermining, or altogether emasculating royal directives."

Institutionalization also plays a role in bureaucrats' power. Bureaucrats are selected, trained, evaluated, and promoted on the basis of codified rules (Downs, 1967, p. 28; Tullock, 1965, pp. 16–19). These rules provide strong incentives that shape bureaucrats' behaviors. Those who perform their duties by following certain codes of conduct get rewarded and thus have little dependence on political leaders, which limits political leaders' ability to control and manipulate the bureaucracy as they wish.

Besides formal rules on paper, bureaucrats of the same agencies also share what North (1990) called "tacit knowledge" in running the bureaucracy. Ang (2016), for example, notes that the Chinese central government's policy guidance is rarely explicit, and that new programs are particularly ambiguous. This means that local officials in China must rely on their tacit knowledge to achieve their goals, especially in experimenting with previously untested policies, and, as Ang points out, they typically do (pp. 94–102).

These formal and informal rules, along with the shared knowledge of these rules, on the one hand increase the coherence within any given agency and reduce costs in coordinating tasks among its members (Coase, 1937). On the other hand, these elements also induce institutional loyalty among bureaucrats. They forge a sense of community and belonging among colleagues of the same institutions. Years of experience in climbing the professional ladders by following these rules create vested interests among bureaucrats in preserving the rules and institutions. Individuals who seek to break or bypass these rules often risk collective punishment by their colleagues (e.g., Lu & Ma, 2019). These rules and knowledge also create entry barriers, so that outsiders cannot easily replace experienced bureaucrats.

Fragmented Authority Within Bureaucracy . While we differen-
tiate the bureaucracy from its political masters, we should also be cautious not to consider bureaucracy per se as a coherent entity. Expertise
gives bureaucrats power and independence, and it also leads to divisions
of labor within the government. In modern states where governance
becomes increasingly complex and creeps into numerous aspects of social lives, bureaucracies also become more elaborate. Division of responsibility within the bureaucracy becomes necessary to increase efficiency.
Such division takes place among functional units of the same level, and
each agency specializes in one or a few policy domains. In states with a
vast territory, division of labor also takes place across territories and hierarchies. Central and local governments each take on different responsibilities in state governance.

Within each individual agency, bureaucrats with similar or complementary skills, expertise, or experience work together to achieve shared organizational goals. Cooperation between bureaucratic agencies often incurs
higher costs than cooperation within them. Different agencies have different
organizational codes, and their goals are not always aligned with each other.
Bureaucratic agencies with close or similar functions may become adversaries rather than allies (Downs, 1967). They may disagree about policies that
pertain to their overlapping jurisdiction; they may compete with one another
for scarce resources allocated by their superiors; or they might fight over who
should receive credit for policy success.

A ruler's ability to intervene in policymaking is further limited when he
delegates the resource-allocating power to a bureaucracy with fragmented
authority. The fragmentation means that the power to make and implement
policies is divided among multiple agencies, each of which oversees a specific
segment of the policy yet lacks jurisdiction over others. These agencies differ
in their specialties, organizational culture, interests, and so forth. Some of
the agencies even have competing interests on certain issues. Successful policymaking and implementation require consensus and collaboration among
these diverse agencies.

The ruler benefits from relying on a fragmented bureaucracy. First, governing alone is too great a task for one person, so bureaucratic delegation is
inevitable. Yet, delegation also breeds problems and risks, as those to whom
the ruler entrusts power might wish to challenge or replace him. Having
administrative power decentralized among a wide range of agents diffuses

the threat, as it increases the difficulty of collective action.[4] Of course, the increased security of the ruler comes at the price of reduced efficiency of the bureaucratic system.

Such fragmentation of decision-making often turns individual bureaucracies into "veto players" (Tsebelis, 1995) in policymaking and implementation processes. One agency's denial can result in policy paralysis. Reaching policy decisions therefore requires laborious consensus-building effort among these agencies. This requirement augments specialized agencies' regulatory influence beyond their professional purview. Thus it also creates an enduring stake among these agencies to collectively preserve the system. Their professional expertise helps them create technocratic justifications for cumbersome procedures, giving the system a legitimate façade.

The fragmentation of bureaucratic authorities also raises the cost of policy manipulation on the part of the ruler. A ruler who wants to shift the policy in his favor needs to bring on board bureaucrats from a range of specialized agencies, whose professionalism creates hurdles for the ruler to act at his will. The ruler might face less difficulty in forcing one agency to acquiesce once, but repeatedly forcing the bargain with multiple agencies will expend considerable political capital.

Therefore, the fragmentation of bureaucratic authority not only benefits the ruler who fears that his agents (i.e., the bureaucrats) might challenge and replace him, it also benefits the ruling elites, high-level bureaucrats included, who are fearful of the ruler. A credible power-sharing agreement between the ruler and his elite supporters is critical to the stability of authoritarian rule (Haber, 2007; Svolik, 2012). The fact that the power of an authoritarian ruler is often unchecked undermines the credibility of the ruler's promises to share power with elite members of the ruling coalition (Magaloni, 2008). Elites in the ruling coalition are not confident the ruler will not one day use the power they grant him to exploit their interests. Such suspicion and fear breed the seeds of elite rebellions in authoritarian regimes. By delegating his power to allocate resources to a fragmented bureaucracy, the ruler shows that his hands are tied and his ability to unilaterally break his promises regarding sharing power is limited. Such an arrangement is therefore conducive to the long-term stability of the intra-elite relationship in authoritarian polities. Thus the ruler does not allocate resources strictly according to his own will because his

---

[4] In the literature on the civil–military relationship, rulers' action to address this is also known as seeking to be "coup proof": the ruler cultivates multiple military forces to prevent any one of them from taking over. See Svolik (2012), pp. 131–132.

incentives, including preserving his own power, are aligned with delegation to the bureaucracy. Constraining the ruler's ability to unequivocally allocate resources based on his intention therefore creates an opportunity structure for the potential policy recipients to compete to gain access to these resources.

A remaining question is how the institutional arrangement of fragmented bureaucratic authority in China came about. So far, the discussion has adopted a functionalist narrative, which posits that the institutional arrangement is there because it performs certain functions (e.g., it mitigates the commitment problem between the ruler and the elites). Yet, this approach has limitations. If someone is powerful enough to engineer such a system, he can also use the same power to undermine it, and this institutional arrangement will also not be considered credible.

A more plausible explanation is that such an institutional arrangement is the result of numerous incremental changes over a long period of history. As Mertha (2006) notes, "dynamics exogenous to the bureaucracy" very often shape it (p. 299). No one event or individual could singlehandedly create the system. Instead, it was the accumulation of numerous, small changes on the margin, most of which lacked the intention of creating the final product. This historical path-dependence explanation also suggests that the system is difficult to change at once for any leader.

The contemporary Chinese state has its roots in the imperial Chinese bureaucracy, which dates back to the 7th century. China's bureaucracy at that time resembled its modern counterpart in many respects. It had sophisticated hierarchies and a professional system of recruitment, promotion, and specialization (Qian, 1982). The imperial bureaucracy and its strong capability to govern endured numerous dynastic cycles (Wittfogel, 1957) as part of "the oldest state apparatus in the world" (Tsai, 2017, p. 296).

Historians have noted a marked tension between the imperial bureaucracy and the emperors, the supreme rulers of imperial China (Kuhn, 1992; Qian, 1982). Qian (1982) characterized the monarch–bureaucrat relationship as the central theater of political contention in China's imperial history. On the one hand, the emperors needed the bureaucracy to rule the vast empire. On the other hand, the rigid and cumbersome routines of the bureaucracy created a check on the emperors' whims. Occasionally, the power of the prime ministers (*Zai Xiang*) even overshadowed those of the emperors. Many emperors were forced to abdicate, only to be succeeded by their own prime ministers. Although Chinese emperors had attempted to dilute the power vested in the positions of top bureaucrats, they were never able to get rid of the bureaucracy completely.

A notable feature of the imperial bureaucracy that has persisted into the contemporary age is the fragmentation of decision-making authorities. The imperial bureaucracy in the Tang dynasty (7th to 10th century CE), for example, was divided into three departments (*san sheng*), namely the central secretariat (*Zhongshu Sheng*), the chancellery (*Menxia Sheng*), and the department of state affairs (*Shangshu Sheng*) (Wechsler, 1979). Bureaucrats in these departments were recruited through merit-based imperial civil exams (*Keju*). A typical policymaking and implementation process involved the central secretariat first drafting a policy proposal, and then acquiring written approval from the emperor, followed by scrutiny and possible rejection by the chancellery, and finally implementation by the specialized ministries in the department of state affairs (Qian, 1982). No action could be taken without first achieving consensus among the three departments and the emperor. The chancellery rejected the proposals approved by the emperors with some frequency. The fragmentation of bureaucratic authorities further deepened in the dynasties following the Tang dynasty. In the Ming dynasty (14th to 17th century CE), Emperor Zhu Yuanzhang (in power 1368–1398) abolished the position of prime minister altogether and directly gave orders to the six specialized divisions of the imperial bureaucracy, furthering the fragmentation of bureaucratic power at the level below him.

Lieberthal (2004) documents similar fragmentation of authority in the contemporary Chinese bureaucracy.

> Despite the highly authoritarian nature of China's political system, actual authority is in most instances fragmented. There are numerous reporting lines throughout the system—through the party, through the government, to the territorial organs, and so forth. (p. 187)

He also writes:

> One consequence of the structure of the Chinese political administration is that important issues require the cooperation of officials who are in different bureaucratic domains and who therefore lack jurisdiction over each other. Construction of a major new steel plant, for example, may demand the active support of individuals in the Ministry of Commerce, the Finance Ministry, the State Development and Reform Commission, and the local government and party authorities (for road building, housing construction, sanitation, removing peasants from their land, and so on). If foreign

capital is involved, the People's Bank and others will also have to come on
board. (p. 189)

And he concludes:

Because of the general fragmentation of authority in the system, resolving a
matter below the center often requires building a consensus among an array
of pertinent officials. . . . Chinese policy making is, consequently, characterized by an enormous amount of discussion on bargaining among officials to
bring the right people on board. (p. 191)

The Soviet model also plays a role in shaping China's modern bureaucracy. To
implement a Soviet-style central planned economy, China established a central bureaucracy with numerous specialized divisions (i.e., ministries) aimed
at strengthening central control of different aspects of economic life. The 7th
State Council elected in 1978, for example, had more than 50 constituting
ministries.[5] The majority of the ministries were responsible for economic
planning. Their jurisdictions ranged from coal, petroleum, and textiles, to
railway, grain, and farm management. Although most of these specialized
ministries have been reorganized, merged, or abolished following the market
reform, some, including the railway ministry, continue to exist and defend
the interests of particular industries or sectors.

Market reform itself contributes to bureaucratic fragmentation in a different way. Officials' behaviors have become less value-based (i.e., less ideological), and are increasingly driven by economic interests. It has become
more difficult for the party to invoke revolutionary ideologies to mobilize
cooperation among officials in different bureaucratic domains (Shirk, 1993).
Instead, bureaucratic agencies strike bargains with each other for "personnel
assignments, funds, access to goods and markets, and so forth" (Lieberthal,
2004, p. 191) to determine policies and their implementation (Lieberthal,
1992; Lieberthal & Oksenberg, 1988; Mertha, 2006, 2009). These bargains
increase the cost of unilaterally manipulating policies for individual central
leaders, and facilitate a more inclusive policymaking process among relevant
actors.

Not all issue areas follow the same model in decision-making. In areas such
as personnel appointments, bank loans, and fiscal transfers, the party leaders

---

[5] In contrast, the 13th State Council elected in 2018 has 26 ministries.

have considerable control over the decision-making. Empirical studies of these areas find that central leaders use the resources, in a top-down manner, to benefit their associates or local clients (e.g., Jiang & Zhang, 2020; Shih, 2004, 2008; Shih et al., 2012). A single agency, or very few of them, hold the authority to make such decisions. For example, the party's organization department exclusively handles the appointments of government positions, and the People's Bank of China controls the distribution of bank loans, directly overseeing the commercial banks. This centralization keeps the ruler's cost of forcing or coordinating policy consensus among bureaucrats relatively low, which makes it easier for him to manipulate the policy according to his will.

Rulers face more difficulty to manipulate policies when the decision-making authority is fragmented among numerous agencies, as with constructions of steel plants, dams, airports, and other large-scale, cross-regional infrastructure projects. High-speed railway projects require coordination of numerous ministerial-level central agencies (e.g., National Development and Reform Commission, Ministry of Transport, China Railway Corporation, Ministry of Environmental Protection, Ministry of Land and Resources, Ministry of Housing and Urban-Rural Development, China Development Bank). As Chapter 3 describes, some of these ministries require the localities to get multiple rounds of approvals at different stages of implementation. These areas involve highly sophisticated and specialized knowledge, and therefore they need the input and cooperation of agencies with very different expertise. In this regard, bureaucratic fragmentation can also be considered a byproduct of modernization. The development of modern technologies brings increasingly complicated and technical-intensive issues into the realm of governance. These changes require specialization and division of responsibilities within the government (Weber, 1978). In contrast, a government ruling a largely agrarian, pre-industrial society would not be responsible for constructing high-speed railways, airports, or transcontinental grids, nor would it need the corresponding state agencies to perform or solve these tasks. Consequently, policymaking and implementation are less likely to be subject to the personal wills of individual leaders in modern states with elaborate bureaucratic authorities.

The argument presented in this section is summarized in Figure 2.1. An authoritarian ruler enhances the credibility of his commitment to sharing power by delegating the policymaking authority to a central bureaucracy. The bureaucracy's ability to insulate itself from the influence of the ruler

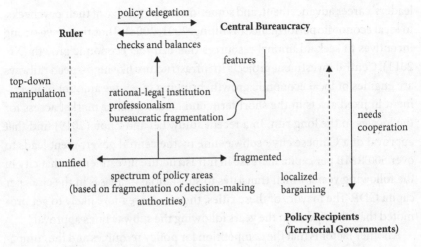

Figure 2.1 Summary of Key Arguments

relies partly on its expertise and adherence to professionalism. The credibility of delegation also crucially rests upon fragmented decision-making authorities within the bureaucracy. The ruler incurs a considerable cost to manipulate policies that are overseen by multiple bureaucratic agencies with non-overlapping authorities. The distributive patterns of government resources in these policy areas therefore should be less suggestive of the ruler's incentives or intention. The fragmentation of authorities in these issue areas instead creates opportunities for local authorities, whom the central bureaucracies rely on to implement their policies locally, to bargain for a greater share of benefits.

2.2.4 Highly Motivated Local Policy Recipients

Territorial governments are motivated both by formal and informal incentives to pursue more resources and preferential treatment from their superiors. As bureaucrats, they seek to maximize their departmental budget so that they can increase their salary and prestige (Niskanen, 1971), perform their respective functions, and retain power (Levi, 1988). Strong motivation to seek resources is essentially hardwired in their genes.

Formal institutions of the CCP increase localities' incentive to seek more resources as well. In China, the merit-based cadre evaluation system ties local leaders' career advancement, and sometimes even the size of their paychecks, to local economic performance (Whiting, 2001, 2004). Thus they have strong incentives to seek additional resources that can fuel economic growth (Xu, 2011). Central investment projects in infrastructure like high-speed railways are engines of local economic growth, bringing in a huge amount of investment in fixed assets in the short term and creating better market access for the locales in the long run. In a recent study, Lei and Zhou (2019) find that approval of a Chinese city's subway line by the central government leads to over 500 RMB per capita increase in infrastructure investment in that city in the following years, which translates to substantial increases in the city's per capita GDP. The mayors of these cities, they find, are more likely to get promoted than their peers in the years following the subway line's approval.

Another factor is that the competition for policy resources and the competition for promotion often take place among the same group of local leaders. While budget and technical limitations of infrastructure projects put proximate localities in competition with one another, the party apparatus generally selects among leaders in subdivisions of a single jurisdiction when looking to fill more prestigious positions (Lü & Landry, 2014). For example, candidates for high-level positions in a provincial government (e.g., deputy governors) typically come from the leaders of the cities within it. This confluence increases the intensity of competition. When they try to get more resources from their superiors, officials are simultaneously fighting for the future of their localities and for the future of their careers.

Of course, the possibility of promotion only plays a role among local officials interested in this possibility and convinced they can obtain it. But over 99% of China's local officials will remain in their departments until they retire, and they have little chance of promotion to leadership (Ang, 2016, p. 106). Thus they may have very different priorities than a handful of leading cadres who have a realistic chance of being promoted to a higher level. In a careful historical study of grassroots officials who were sidelined in local political competition, Zhang and Liu (2019) find that officials who meet the glass ceiling in their careers tend to pursue policies that could contribute to the material benefits of their local communities, their connected allies, or their own. Central policy benefits also serve such purposes well. In addition to the economic performance of their jurisdiction, the construction of new railway stations boosts the land prices nearby, and in turn increases the extra-budgetary revenue collected by local officials (Lei & Zhou, 2019). The extra-budgetary revenue from land sales is not subject to the same scrutiny as formal budgetary items, and local officials have greater discretion in determining the use of these funds (Whiting, 2011). In addition, the constructions of these central projects often lead to the creation of new employment opportunities and the hiring of local firms. The economic payoff for the local firms, with whom local officials often form close alliances (e.g., Zhang & Liu, 2019), is another incentive for officials to pursue such projects.

Structural conditions of the Chinese party-states also make localities better positioned to bargain with their superiors. Unlike in the Soviet system, where central ministries powerfully presided over the republics, the ministries and provinces enjoy the same political rank in the CCP's hierarchy.[6] Mao purposefully shifted economic power to the localities (i.e., provinces and cities), and local governments played a greater role in economic affairs than their counterparts in the Soviet Union, especially during the Great Leap Forward and the Cultural Revolution (Shirk, 1993, p. 13). Such decentralization has persisted in the reform era (Liu et al., 2018). These conditions give Chinese localities more leverage when they deliberate economic policies with the functional departments of their superiors.

2.2.5 Not All Localities Are Created Equal

The conditions this chapter has described thus far apply to all localities, and thus a vital question still remains: Why are some localities able to procure more favorable policy treatment from their superiors? Put another way, what determines the outcome of the localized bargaining this chapter has described as a product of multiple forces? Why do some local governments have greater bargaining power than others?

In her seminal work, *Of Rule and Revenue*, Margaret Levi (1988) defines bargaining power as the "degree of control over coercive, economic, and political resources" (p. 2). Such control enables rulers to shape fiscal institutions to their advantage. This may seem tautological: greater control provides greater control. However, Levi distinguishes between *types* of control: coercive, economic, and political. Thus her argument is that bureaucratic actors transform one type of resource (such as political resources) into others (such as economic resources). Variations in the ability to make

---

[6] Similarly, municipalities and provincial bureaus hold the same rank, as do counties, districts, and municipal bureaus also.

such transformations explain why only some actors are able to gain favorable terms in intra-bureaucratic bargaining that often involve multiple, similar competitors.

The term "bargaining power" describes a rather holistic feature of local government, instead of that of any individual leaders, even though idiosyncratic characters of individual leaders such as personality or connections could also affect the bargaining power of localities. This book argues that much of a local government's bargaining power is inherited from the past, and is institutionalized in the rules, norms, and hierarchies that have been governing local political dynamics irrespective of any particular leaders. A simple example is that provincial capitals in China, in most periods, receive more resources from the provincial government than other cities, regardless of the cities' party secretaries. This holistic definition provides a relatively stable (and institutionalized) basis for us to identify localities of differential bargaining power.

For conceptual clarity and reference, I make a rather stylized dichotomization of local governments with differential bargaining power. I label those with greater institutionalized bargaining power and influence within the regime as "cardinals" and those without strong influence as "clerics." I borrow these two terms from the literature on US congressional politics (Berry & Fowler, 2016), in which scholars examine why some congressional members are better at procuring earmarks for their constituencies than others—a context that bears some similarities to this study. They find that congressional members with committee leadership positions (cardinals) are better at gaining resources than those without (clerics). In this book, these terms describe the characteristics of a particular local government as a whole, not any specific leaders. Comparative research also finds that the power of office dominates the personal influence of officeholders, even in a context like post-Soviet Russia where charismatic leaders have played an important role in shaping politics (Baturo & Elkink, 2014). Below I discuss the institutional sources of bargaining power for the "cardinals" and the strategies the "clerics" might adopt to strengthen their bargaining power.

2.2.6 The Institutional Advantages of the "Cardinals"

Policymakers at higher levels tend to pay more attention to places with greater social, economic, and strategic importance. There are various factors that they see as signals of importance, such as size (in population), contribution to the national economy (in regional gross domestic product), contribution to the treasury (in fiscal revenue collection), role in the national economy (in terms of exporting more goods), and location (such as a port or a border city), and to this extent the technocratic solution applies to such decisions. But what really gives the cardinals durable leverage in competing with other locales and shaping policy choices are the *institutionalized arrangements* that consolidate their advantages and empower them *beyond* the aspects of their traditional strengths.

The one arrangement that appears most consistently among territorial administrations and functional bureaucracies is the "dual appointment" or "concurrent appointment" (Bulman & Jaros, 2019) system in which the head of a regional government or a bureaucracy also serves in the higher-level government. To understand why, we need to start with the ways in which Chinese bureaucracy is organized. The CCP has built a nomenclature system that effectively encompasses every state job in China (Ang, 2012; Burns, 1987; McGregor, 2010), including positions in the central and local governments, party organs, state-owned enterprises, and social organizations (such as public hospitals, schools, universities, and newspapers). These positions are organized vertically. Each has a rank in the hierarchy, and each is accountable to its supervisors one level up (O'Brien & Li, 1999). This rule applies to every organization and individual from central to local, with the one exception of the politburo standing committee, whose members are the top-ranked officials that technically answer to no one. In a dual appointment, one person has a role at one level and the level that supervises the first level.

Most dual appointments are fixed. The party secretary of a provincial capital city always sits on the provincial party standing committee, and the head of a city's public security bureau usually also holds the position of deputy mayor, or is a member of the city party standing committee. The chair of the largest academic department in a university might also be concurrently appointed as the vice president of the university.[7] This arrangement is an institutionalized recognition of the differential influence inherited by various bureaucratic units. For example, the provincial capital is important to the provincial authority as it hosts the provincial government and numerous other provincial-level institutions. The public security apparatus is critical

---

[7] For example, the dean of the medical school at Peking University has consistently been the vice president of the university, irrespective of who holds that position; the dean of the Marxism school at Renmin University of China, the first university founded by the CCP, is also appointed concurrently

in maintaining social stability—a top political priority for officials at various levels—which explains why the head of the public security bureau has a dual appointment (e.g., Wang & Minzner, 2015). The dual-appointment system remains a relatively stable arrangement, as the order of influence among localities and functional bureaucracy does not fluctuate frequently. Take Suzhou, an industrial hub in Jiangsu province and the gateway to Shanghai, for example; the city's party secretaries over the past three decades have been consistently given a seat in the provincial standing committee.[8]

Some scholars have viewed the dual-appointment system as a central government strategy to control local agents. Indeed, these appointments are not randomly assigned, and the central government may wish to exert more control over more important localities. Huang (1999) argues that the dual appointment helps reduce policy discrepancies between the central and local governments in a highly decentralized system. Local leaders who are "integrated" into the central leadership through the dual appointment may find their career prospects lie with the center rather than the localities they are assigned to, and therefore tend to follow central policy more closely. Sheng (2010, 2019) finds that integration of local officials in the central leadership helps curb localism in economically powerful regions, and increases these regions' policy and tax compliance.

The appointments might indeed serve the purpose of the central government, but, this book will argue, localities can also use the dual appointments to aid in their bargaining. Institutions can become "resources" for purposes other than the reasons they are created in the first place (Hall & Thelen, 2009; Hou, 2019). Indeed, in other domains of Chinese politics, scholars have found that individuals can benefit from institutions whose primary role is to maintain the party's control. For example, the local legislature—the local people's congress—is widely considered as a tool for the party to co-opt and control influential local economic elites (Zhang, 2017). Yet, local entrepreneurs effectively use their seats in the local legislature to protect themselves from government predation (Hou, 2019). In the case of dual appointment, even

as the vice president of the university. Regarding the latter, see Xu, L. Y. (2019, July 30). 为了"双一流"：人大副校长同时兼任学院党政"一把手." (To achieve first-class academic performance: Vice president of Renmin University appointed to school leadership position), weixin.qq.com, retrieved from https://mp.weixin.qq.com/s/qCTo4bhb7VpZrWoXz8RgGw.

[8] See, for example, Wang, H. P. (2014, June 24). 苏州市委书记高配格局再升级:由省委副书记兼任 (Further rise of Suzhou's status: Provincial deputy secretary appointed as the city's party secretary), Sina.com, retrieved from http://news.sina.com.cn/c/sd/2014-06-24/095430413154.shtml.

if the top local leader indeed becomes a loyalist to his superior, his deputies and functional bureaucrats in the local government can still use the locality's elevated status to procure more benefits from the upper levels.

Holding a position at one level above gives the leader and his office greater access to central government actors than their peers. Having superiors hear a request is a crucial first step to soliciting support. It circumvents the problem in which local information gets diluted and distorted as it travels across hierarchies of bureaucracy (e.g., Lorentzen, 2013; Oi, 1989; Solinger, 2001; Wallace, 2016).

The dual-appointment system also enables the appointees to promote and incorporate their local agenda into leadership decisions that have binding power over other subdivisions. This mechanism works similarly to the "agenda setting" argument in the congressional politics literature (e.g., Baron & Ferejohn, 1989; Romer & Rosenthal, 1978), where studies find that chairs of congressional subcommittees are able to dominate decision-making processes and make proposals with little input from rank-and-file members. Competition among adjacent jurisdictions for railway resources makes this particularly important for such projects. Localities with dual appointments can legitimately force their agenda among peer locales through mandates by upper-level leadership, and block the voices of peer localities that have competing demands.

These factors collectively give the localities with dual appointments enormous advantages in procuring policy benefits from above. If we compare the process of localized bargaining among locales to a race, cardinals not only start running much earlier than the rest, but they also play the role of a referee—they are able to change the rules in their favor when strong competitors appear. The distributive implication of such an institutional arrangement is therefore not hard to infer. Cardinals enjoy systematic advantages when they compete for resources within the bureaucratic system.

2.2.7 The Weapons of the "Clerics"

Despite similar incentives and efforts to solicit policy benefits, many localities are left behind due to their lack of institutionalized bargaining power. Places without strong influence in the regime often can do little but acquiesce to policy choices that are unfavorable to them. "Clerics" are bound by their positions in the hierarchy to accept policy mandates from above, even though some policies might disproportionally favor their peers. The two problems they face—the opposite of the advantages of the "cardinals" discussed above—are difficulties in having leaders above them hear their voices, and the lack of bargaining leverage to compete with their more powerful peers.

Clerics therefore seek to enlist support from those outside the bureaucracy. An important outside source of bargaining power is the demand of grassroots constituents. Although Chinese officials are not subject to electoral incentives, they do take public opinion seriously. Failures in responding to public grievances often result in sanctions of officials in charge (Edin, 2003). Local officials thus take a risk when they strategically tolerate the expression of public dissatisfaction to extract policy concessions from their superiors, whose superiors also expect them to quell dissent. When the demands of the population are congruent with local officials' agendas, the risk may be worth it.

In recent years, China has witnessed a growing number of local mass mobilizations that depart from our traditional understanding of local activism. These mobilizations center on local concerns but, rather than criticizing local policy, they criticize local officials' superiors for failing to give them the resources to address local concerns. A notable recent example is a movement in Linshui county, Sichuan province, which amounted to a reverse-NIMBY (not in my backyard) movement. In 2015, tens of thousands of local residents took to the streets to protest the provincial government's plan for the high-speed railway to bypass the county (Allen-Ebrahimian, 2015). Local officials demonstrated an unusual degree of tolerance during this mass mobilization. They turned a blind eye to the organization, development, and escalation of these mobilizations. There is even evidence that some local officials were in collusion with the people in the street to promote the messages to their superiors (Deng et al., forthcoming; Ma, 2019; O'Brien et al., 2020).

I term such mobilizations "consent instability." It is an informal yet effective alliance between the cleric officials and ordinary people. The public display of constituents' discontent, particularly those in the form of mass mobilizations entailing greater threats to the regime (e.g., protests), helps strengthen officials' bargaining power in soliciting policy benefits. Bottom-up mass mobilizations—with participants that are self-organized—serve as a credible piece of evidence of the existence of public dissatisfaction.

Public pressure becomes powerful leverage that officials can invoke to extract concessions from others, and when public pressure is aligned with the officials' desire, they have an incentive to let demonstrators act. The disruptive effect of mass mobilizations illustrates ex ante the grave consequences (i.e., social instability) of rejecting a locality's demand. Superior leaders recognize that the localities' constituents are primed to pose a stronger challenge to social stability if they do not comply. The people in the street help the clerics to get the attention of their superiors and give the clerics greater leverage.

The use of consent instability hinges upon the assumption that officials at different levels have different priorities. Local officials may be risking their own careers by tolerating the mass mobilization. Here again, the fact that they have a slim chance of promotion (Ang, 2016) arises. Many of them do not value career prospects as much as their superiors, but they do value the benefits of high-speed railway projects (or other policy programs) in their localities.

By circumstance and desire, some officials do not employ consent instability. Its appearance requires the alignment of several idiosyncratic conditions. First, it will only appear in cleric jurisdictions. Cardinals have other, stronger tools and a greater incentive to protect their career prospects, and thus do not resort to such risky methods of bargaining. Indeed, some cleric local officials will decide the risk is too high, based on their own weighing of the benefits and the costs. Thus the second condition is that the cleric official decides the risk is worth it. Third, local citizens must show interest in the same policy goal—high-speed railway service—that local officials want. While in most localities residents probably favor high-speed rail service, tacitly failing to discourage mobilizations is far less risky than prompting people to mobilize about a particular issue. Thus local officials have to hope people will show an interest. In addition, local officials must have the means to encourage protest without doing so openly. This depends on social organizations (e.g., local business associations) that can organize the mobilization, as it would be far too risky for the local officials to do it themselves. For these reasons, consent instability only appears sporadically across places and issue areas. Although not a systematic strategy, when successfully invoked, as Chapter 6 will suggest, consent instability does have power to shape policy choices by leaders at higher levels.

2.3 Comparing Localized Bargaining with Existing Explanations

The chapter so far proposes an argument that focuses on the role of local governments in shaping the making of policies that have bearing on them. This section compares the argument with existing explanations in distributive politics and highlights its theoretical contributions.

2.3.1 Loyalty Purchasing and Technocratic Solutions

The introduction chapter noted two groups of explanations of the political logic of distribution. The first is "loyalty purchasing." This line of argument is based on the intuition that authoritarian leaders, like their democratic counterparts, strategically distribute policy benefits to secure support of key constituents and to deter potential defection. The targets of such allocation are political and economic elites crucial for the survival of the regime, such as high-level officials, business tycoons, generals, tribal leaders, and so on (Bueno de Mesquita et al., 2005; Haber, 2007). This exchange, similar to clientelistic politics under electoral systems (Hicken, 2011), keeps elites aligned with the ruler, as those who attempt to defect risk losing such benefits. An implication of the loyalty purchasing argument is that allocations of policy benefits are often patterned on the elites' personal relationship with the incumbent rulers (e.g., Shih, 2004, 2008; Shih et al., 2012).

By contrast, the "technocratic solution" explanation posits that the ruler delegates decision-making power to a bureaucracy with expertise in the relevant areas. This bureaucracy is characterized by hierarchy, routinization, professionalism, and organizational coherence (Evans, 1995; Evans & Rauch, 1999; Weber, 1978). These features allow the bureaucracy to resist outside pressure and formulate policies based on their professional expertise (Gereffi, 1990; Haggard, 1990). The technocrats in the bureaucracy identify the strengths and weaknesses of the country's economy, make developmental plans that befit its comparative advantage, allocate resources based on planned priorities, and regulate market access to protect nascent domestic industries (Johnson, 1982). Under this analytical framework, the state's policy choices represent the technocratic solutions leaders adopt to solve pressing development issues. Sectors or territories that the technocrats deem more important to the growth of the economy receive preferential policy treatment. Scholars have attributed the successful economic development of many late-developing countries, including that of China, to governmental intervention in growing the economy (e.g., Gerschenkron, 1962; Glaeser et al., 2004; Haggard, 1990; Huang, 2008; Johnson, 1982; Naughton, 2007; Woo-Cumings, 1999).

Both the loyalty purchasing and the technocratic solution models adopt a top-down perspective in explaining variations in policy benefits, suggesting rulers (or bureaucrats) at the top determine the allocation of policy benefits. Compared with the localized bargaining argument, the top-down approach has three limitations. It does not address how decision-makers at the top acquire information that is necessary for formulating and implementing policies. It also neglects a potential commitment problem associated with distributive politics. Finally, it does not sufficiently address the issue of delegation within the state apparatus.

The Government's Acquisition of Information. The "loyalty purchasing" explanation assumes that the ruler has fairly good knowledge of whether elites are loyal. Yet, loyalty is not a readily observable characteristic. In authoritarian regimes, public expression of opposition to the ruler often results in brutal punishment or purge, and discontent toward the regime often festers quietly and only becomes public when the regime nears collapse (e.g., Kuran, 1991). The commitment to violently eliminate potential challengers paradoxically makes them difficult to identify. Scholars dub this paradox "the dictator's dilemma" (Wintrobe, 1998). In semi-competitive autocracies like Singapore or pre-2000 Mexico, elections mitigate the information problem. Elections and their results give an early warning of challengers and their potential, making it easier for autocrats to block them by, for example, buying off or containing oppositions when they are still in nascence (e.g., Magaloni, 2006; Magaloni et al., 2007; Tremewan, 1994). Numerous studies find that levels of electoral support have shaped the distribution of public goods both in new democracies (e.g., Min, 2015) and in electoral authoritarian regimes (e.g., Blaydes, 2010; Magaloni, 2006). Such studies find the allocation of key policy benefits, such as electricity, roads, and agricultural subsidies, are systematically associated with regional distributions of incumbent votes as well as electoral cycles, supporting the loyalty purchasing explanation (e.g., Shi & Svensson, 2006).

In places where competitive electoral institutions are weak or nonexistent, such as China, rulers rely on primordial or socially constructed characteristics of the subjects to gauge loyalty. Shared family ties (e.g., Tsai, 2007), ethnicity (e.g., Habyarimana et al., 2007), or political experiences (e.g., Shih, 2004; Shih et al., 2012;) become the basis on which leaders allocate critical resources. Elites who belong to the small circles knitted together by these ties often enjoy more policy benefits than others. However, these constructed characteristics serve, at best, as an information shortcut for leaders to identify likely loyalists among a sea of unknown subjects. Rulers do not know their subjects' true intentions or preferences. From Brutus in ancient Rome to Absalom in biblical Israel to Lin Biao in Mao-era China and Jang Songthaek in contemporary North Korea, history is not short of examples in which trusted family members, co-ethnics, and colleagues turned their backs on a ruler.

The technocratic solution explanation also requires policymakers to have access to information. Various theoretical and empirical work has found that government generally works better when policies are supplied locally instead of universally applied across the country, which means that technocratic solutions require highly specific local information[9] (e.g., Bardhan, 2002; Ostrom, 1990). Decision-making without a sufficient supply of local information could lead to disastrous consequences, even without particularly malicious intention on the part of the decision-makers (e.g., Kung & Chen, 2011; Sen, 1999).

Even in democracies, decision-makers have difficulty obtaining the information they need for technocratic solutions. Various institutions, such as legislature, media, and civil society, facilitate information flows from the bottom to the top, alerting policymakers at the center of local problems that require action and aggregating voter's individual preferences into policy demand (e.g., McCubbins & Schwartz, 1984). However, political capture often compromises this function (e.g., Bardhan & Mookherjee, 2006), giving certain groups of people more say in the process of policy deliberation. An effective bureaucracy therefore needs to find a nuanced balance between communicating with society and shielding itself from various social pressures (Evans, 1995).

In authoritarian states, of course, lack of democratic institutions that channel citizens' demands upwards, as well the non-transparent nature of authoritarian politics, creates a hindrance. Secrecy and non-transparency are hallmarks of non-democratic politics (Hollyer et al., 2011; Svolik, 2012).

---

[9] Evans (1995), for example, argues that the informal networks within the private sector allow bureaucracy to heed information from the market, and to facilitate cooperation between the state and business circles.

Withholding information helps the authority demobilize potential oppositions, and also frees authoritarian officials from being held accountable by the public or their superiors.

In China, local officials engage in a multitude of actions to deceive their superiors by manipulating or withholding local information. They routinely report inflated economic statistics (Wallace, 2016), cover up local problems (Lorentzen, 2014), conceal corruption (Pan & Chen, 2018), and repress citizens' grievances (Lorentzen, 2013). The policymakers at higher levels therefore face very mixed signals from below. The policies they make based on such poor information are therefore often far from utility-maximizing. Indeed, media coverage and discussions of the largely empty high-speed trains running in many parts of China (e.g., M.A., 2011; Spegele, 2011) suggest that rational, technocratic cost-and-benefit planning alone does not explain the decisions that led to the construction of these railways.

Yet the performance of the Chinese economy suggests that the government must be able to allocate resources with some efficacy. Recent studies on China have begun to pay attention to the institutions that supply local information to the center that have likely facilitated this success. Some scholars argue that institutions such as the People's Congress, which had been dismissed as rubber stamps, serve the function of collecting and channeling local information to the top (e.g., Manion, 2016; Truex, 2016). Some argue that the regime purposefully shows some restraint in controlling its media or in repressing citizens' critiques to get uncensored information on local governance (e.g., Chen & Xu, 2017; Lorentzen, 2013, 2014; Lu & Ma, 2019). Others have pointed to institutions of the digital age, such as the online message board or the "mayor's mailbox," as tools to deal with the information deficit (e.g., Chen et al., 2016; Distelhorst & Hou, 2017). While these studies contribute a great deal of knowledge to our understanding of how the Chinese regime overcomes the information problem, they describe primarily how the central government might learn about local grievances or official wrongdoing. It is unlikely that the People's Congress or the mayor's mailbox guides policy decisions that involve more technocratic consideration, such as how to prioritize the construction of roads, airports, or railways in different regions. Expressing desires for service in these outlets is not difficult, and it is hard to tell whose desire is most genuine. The demand for service is also just one factor among many to guide the best prioritization of different projects.

Localized bargaining is a process in which localities compete to feed superiors with information that would lead to desired policy decisions. Local governments adopt different strategies in doing so. Some use their elevated ranks (through dual appointments) to have the ears of decision-makers at higher levels; some use the power associated with their positions to sideline competing demands from nearby localities; and some tolerate citizen mobilizations to send costly signals of policy demand to the higher-ups. These actions create numerous streams of information flows within the government, based on which superiors make and adjust policy choices. Localities that are better at delivering such information to the decision-makers, either through institutional or extra-institutional channels, are more likely to acquire desired policy benefits. Although information generated through localized bargaining is far from perfect—in fact, they are fraught with distortions—localized bargaining nevertheless provides a regularized mechanism for the articulation of local interests in a political context that lacks formal institutions to facilitate it.

Commitment Problem. As the introduction chapter referenced, neither the loyalty purchasing explanation nor the technocratic solution approach address the commitment problem. In an authoritarian context without an impartial authority as the third-party enforcer, any contracts between the ruler and his subjects are unenforceable in the long run (North, 1990; North & Weingast, 1989; Williamson, 1983). Thus the ruler cannot make sure ex ante that the subjects given benefits will remain loyal after he invests in infrastructure, and subjects have no way to ensure the loyalty they provide after such an investment will be continually rewarded.

The commitment problem affects investment in infrastructure such as a high-speed railway differently from policy benefits such as social welfare, agricultural subsidies, and other financial aid. The effectiveness of using policy benefits to buy support hinges upon the idea that the fear of losing benefits in the *future* keeps the recipients in line with the ruler in the current term (Robinson & Verdier, 2013). Retracting benefits from infrastructure projects involves actually demolishing the benefit. Thus a rational ruler is unlikely to use infrastructure investment to secure the loyalty of his subjects, as doing so is hugely wasteful and ineffective in the long run.

Legislators from Japan's Liberal Democratic Party have used infrastructure projects to secure support in their own districts over five decades in which they have been in power (Saito, 2006). The practice has been so common that there is even a Japanese term for it: *Gaden Intetsu* (literally, pulling railway lines to my electoral base). Each time when election comes, politicians promise additional investments in railways to their constituents.

The practice has had a price. Excessive investment in remote areas with sparse populations led to growing debt and non-performing loans that crippled the Japanese economy, a situation that the CCP has been trying to avoid in China.

Without institutional arrangements that simultaneously help the ruler monitor the actions of his subordinates and tie his own hands such that they have confidence in his promises, loyalty purchasing is ineffective. Even in semi-democratic contexts where politicians and voters have more ways to hold each other accountable, scholars find that vote-buying (i.e., pay voters to get them to switch vote choices) is hard to enforce ex post, and politicians instead use money to buy turnout among supporters (Nichter, 2008).

The commitment problem also undermines the "technocratic solution" explanation. As explained in the introduction chapter, power delegation breeds sources of instability between the ruler and the bureaucrats. On the one hand, the ruler fears that the bureaucrats will one day use the power delegated to them to plot against him or even replace him. On the other hand, knowing that the ruler is suspicious of them, the bureaucrats also live in the fear that he will replace them, which makes his promise to delegate power to them not credible. The lack of trust makes the outcome both parties fear a self-fulfilling prophecy. A stable power delegation therefore requires an institutional arrangement that limits the ability by either the ruler or the bureaucrats to reverse the delegation.

Localized bargaining, as explained earlier, is the result of the ruler's delegation of decision-making power to a bureaucracy with fragmented authority. Such a structure mitigates the commitment problem by limiting the ruler's ability to unilaterally reverse bureaucratic delegation on the one hand, and by increasing the difficulty of coordinating opposition against the ruler among the elites (e.g., high-level bureaucrats) on the other. While localized bargaining does encourage competition for resources, it is conducive to regime durability in the long run by providing assurance for stability to both the ruler and the elites.

Delegation and Divisions Within the Government. The top-down approach assumes that politics have little role within the state itself. The loyalty purchasing argument assumes that the ruler is in total control of resources and makes decisions independently. This rarely occurs in the real world. First of all, the ability to control and allocate resources based on one's volition is the very definition of power (Pfeffer, 1981). If the ruler had total control of all critical resources, he would have no need to buy support by pleasing anyone else. Most autocratic leaders share decision-making authority with other elite members of the ruling coalition, rely on the expertise of technocrats and bureaucratic personnel, and delegate a substantial amount of administrative tasks to regional leaders (Boix & Svolik, 2013; Svolik, 2012), especially in a large country like China. Even in countries smaller than China, the ruler may be very powerful but nonetheless cannot make all decisions, and the task of governance is always tedious and complex. Once power-sharing takes place, the elites with whom the ruler shares his power also use the power to pursue their own agenda, and their personal interests and agenda are not always aligned with those of the ruler. Economists term the resulting dynamic "the principal-agent problem" (Ross, 1973). In elaborate bureaucracies like China's, delegations of power take place among multiple layers of hierarchies, and resource-allocating authority is often divided among several central agencies. Tensions arise not only among local jurisdictions vying for resources but also among central agencies who struggle to agree on certain policy issues.

The technocratic solution model similarly assumes that the bureaucracy works as a unitary and logically coherent actor, and overlooks the rich and complex compositions of the bureaucracy that often have competing interests. Scholars after Weber have repeatedly raised doubts about the logical coherency assumption of the bureaucracy, and argued that it is an institution full of "threats, exchange, and integrative relations" (Niskanen, 1973, p. 13).

Even in a politically centralized state like China, disagreements among various layers and segments of the government take place on a daily basis (e.g., Lieberthal, 1992; Lieberthal & Oksenberg, 1988; Mertha, 2006, 2009). While some of these inconsistencies might result in bureaucratic red tape or even policy paralysis, some others have paradoxically created crucial sources of incentives that spur economic growth. Take the division of authority between the central and local governments in China as an example (e.g., Jin et al., 2005; Montinola et al., 1995). The decentralization of authority gave local governments considerable autonomy in governing local economic issues, and allowed them to retain a portion of the profits generated from the growth they promoted. Local governments thus became ardent advocates of the market reform, which proved critical in preserving the market reform when the conservatives within Chinese central leadership attempted to reverse the reform in the early 1990s. Mertha (2006) also finds that redundancy in the authorities in enforcing trademarks in China created a "policy enforcement market," prompting bureaucracies with overlapping authorities to compete for the enforcement market to secure more financial resources, which resulted in better intellectual property protection.

The localized bargaining model, in contrast, fully recognizes the complex divisions and dynamics within the state apparatus. As articulated in earlier sections, it argues that the internal tensions within China's party-state shape policy outcomes.

2.3.2 Bottom-up Perspective of Lobbying

Compared with the top-down approach, the localized bargaining model has more similarities with the phenomenon of lobbying by interest groups. The literature on lobbying can be traced back to David Truman's (1951) seminal work, *The Governmental Process*, which defines interest groups by their shared attitudes, the fact that members have at least some degree of interaction, and their use of government institutions to make claims on other groups in society. Various types of organized interests play an important role in shaping policies in democratic settings (e.g., Almond, 1958; Truman, 1951). Cadot, Röller, and Stephan (2006), for example, find that investments in public transportation in France are systematically associated with the presence of large private firms. They argue that this is because these firms often draw on large pools of labor and therefore have incentives to lobby government for investments in transportation.

For a fairly long period of time, the literature on lobbying has focused exclusively on actions by firms, business associations, or other membership-based groups. Only in recent decades have scholars begun to treat local governments as another type of interest group (e.g., Cammisa, 1995; Wibbels, 2005). Recent empirical research shows that, under fiscal federalism, cities hire lobbyists to persuade state or federal policymakers to provide additional policy benefits (Goldstein & You, 2017; Payson, 2020a, 2020b). Research on intergovernmental lobbying under democracies is enabled by institutionalized mechanisms that accommodate interest articulation actions like lobbying and the corresponding information disclosures that provide researchers with a wealth of data. The equivalent process in authoritarian states, however, remains largely unknown, as they typically lack deliberative institutions that allow various groups to publicly express and assert their interests.

The scarcity of observable evidence, however, does not mean no interest groups are working to change policies in authoritarian states.[10] Even in a context like the Soviet Union, where scholars once believed that the governmental system was monolithic and free of conflict under the hegemonic control of the communist party, ample anecdotal evidence suggested that genuine conflicts took place because regime insiders proactively pursued their own interests (e.g., Kolkowicz, 1970; Skilling, 1966; Stewart, 1969). Djordjevic (1958), in observing Yugoslavian politics, found that various types of groups participated in governmental processes. These groups included "economic organizations and social institutions, those holding 'strategic positions' in the government system (such as the Leagues of Communists), and those representing the special interests of the citizens (such as unions or churches)" (Skilling, 1966, p. 444). Shirk (1993) notes that economic groups gain influence through the structure of Chinese government bureaucracy in the absence of elections, and that most lobbying is addressed directly to bureaucrats (p. 99). Cai (2014a), in another example, finds that monopolistic industrial firms with government connections (such as state-owned grid companies) are well positioned to shape public policies at the expense of less influential groups in China. It seems clear that under the façade of tight control of the ruling party, various underlying forces pursuing interests in the communist states are just as dynamic as those in the democratic context. Yet unlike in democracies, these forces do not push policy directions publicly or work as independent organizations. They often coalesce their shared interests around the existing state apparatus and operate behind closed doors.

Localized bargaining and intergovernmental lobbying share many aspects in common. Both focus on how local governments influence their superiors, and both are under the arrangement of fiscal federalism in which central (federal) governments share revenue and other policy resources with local authorities. There are also important differences. In localized bargaining, besides traditional methods of intergovernmental lobbying such as persuasion, localities also employ non-institutionalized methods to put pressure on their superiors, such as tolerating grassroots mobilization. While the targets of intergovernmental lobbying are often lawmakers or other politicians with decision-making power, localized bargaining targets bureaucratic agencies

---

[10] A notable scholarly work on lobbying in the authoritarian context is Kennedy (2009), which examines the politics of business lobbying in China, which takes place mostly in informal contexts.

and focuses on coordination of consensus among various bureaucratic actors.

2.4 Summary

The chapter began by laying out the institutional conditions under which localized bargaining takes place. It then discussed how localities of different types invoke institutional or extra-institutional sources of bargaining power in their competition to gain access to policy benefits from their superiors. The core components of the argument can be summarized in the following five points.

1) The fragmentation of decision-making authorities at the top creates an opportunity space for local policy recipients to solicit more resources for themselves.
2) The allocation of policy benefits by higher levels of government is a function of local governments' bargaining power and strategies.
3) The bargaining power of localities is largely determined by their institutional positions within the state hierarchies.
4) Localities where the officials have inherited greater institutionalized bargaining power within the bureaucratic hierarchies (the "cardinals") are more capable of procuring favorable policy treatment from their superiors.
5) Officials with relatively weak influence in the system (the "clerics") resort to extra-institutional sources of bargaining power, such as tolerating mass mobilizations that imply threats to regime stability.

The argument proposed in this chapter is different from existing explanations in several ways. First, it does not assume that the ruler has control of all the resources. Instead, the authority to make and implement policies is decentralized among numerous bureaucratic agents, which creates spaces for policy recipients to actively lobby for a greater share of benefits. It also does not assume the ruler has all the information for policymaking. It conceptualizes the bottom-up solicitation by local recipients as a process through which decision-makers acquire local information. Finally, it answers the question as to why such an arrangement mitigates the commitment problem and creates an enduring stake among the ruler and the ruling elites. The fragmentation of the decision-making authorities and the resulting bottom-up bargaining create a credible power-sharing relationship between the rulers and members of the ruling elites. The ruler is less concerned that those in whom he entrusts power will challenge him, and members of the ruling coalition are also more assured that the ruler's hands are tied such that he cannot unilaterally break his promises to share power and benefits with them.

Chapters 3 through 6 explore the empirical evidence: how the distribution of resources in China's high-speed railway program corroborates each of the argument's components outlined above.

3

Local Ambitions in Central Policymaking

This chapter addresses the following questions: What roles do central and local governments each play in building high-speed rails? What kind of tensions arise from the process? How does the structure of central decision-making in infrastructure investments affect the interactions between central government and territorial administrations, and in particular, how does that shape the spatial allocation of central policy benefits across different parts of the country? The chapter, drawing on rich archival and interview materials, shows that the fragmentation of central bureaucratic authorities in the process of approving high-speed railway projects necessitates action on the part of localities, making local bargaining efforts a crucial determinant of preferential central decisions. The chapter further asks what challenges localities need to overcome in their bargaining with the central bureaucracies, and identifies several factors that could affect localities' bargaining power through in-depth interviews with central and local officials. It also presents results from an original survey with 893 local cadres, which corroborate insights drawn from the qualitative evidence.

Section 3.1 describes the Shanghai Hongqiao Railway Station and explains why no other place has its equal. The case illustrates a central message this chapter seeks to convey: building high-speed rails is a daunting political task for local officials, as they have to navigate a labyrinth of central bureaucracies and convince them to support their proposals.

3.1 The One and Only Hongqiao Railway Station

On July 1, 2010, Shanghai unveiled the city's new train station, the Hongqiao Railway Station. Completed in less than two years, it is the city's third main terminus station after Shanghai Railway Station and Shanghai Southern Railway Station, located in the city's western suburb. At its time of opening, it was China's largest train station, with 16 operating platforms, 30 tracks, and a waiting hall of 11,340 square meters that can hold up to 10,000 passengers

Localized Bargaining. Xiao Ma, Oxford University Press. © Oxford University Press 2022.
DOI: 10.1093/oso/9780197638910.003.0003

at peak hours. The station is the terminus for two of the country's most traveled high-speed railways, the Beijing–Shanghai high-speed railway and the Shanghai–Kunming high-speed railway. A number of regional intercity high-speed railways also connect major metropolitan areas such as Nanjing, Suzhou, Hangzhou, and Ningbo in the Yangtze River delta region to the Hongqiao Railway Station. More than 270 electric-powered express trains depart the station every day. Two subway lines ran through it in 2010, and in 2017 it got another. Numerous viaducts conveniently transport more than 200,000 passengers in and out of the station every day.

Hongqiao Station quickly became the envy of other Chinese localities that tried to build their own high-speed railway stations. Unique among train stations in China at the time, Hongqiao Station is seamlessly integrated with a terminal of the Hongqiao International Airport, which was completed and started service a few months before the station opened. The station and Terminal Two were designed and constructed as one structure. Passengers getting off the trains at Hongqiao take a 15-minute walk through Level B1 of the station to check their bags at the airline counters. China Eastern Airlines, which operates its headquarters and a hub in the airport, offers a special pass, "air-rail connect (空铁通)," that allows passengers in the Yangtze River delta region who plan to fly via Hongqiao to buy a single ticket that covers the train rides between their homes and the airport, as well as airfare.[1]

In spite of the ambitions of other localities, the Hongqiao Railway Station still remains the only transportation complex of its kind. A handful of other places have some of its advantages. For example, railway stops are built into or near the airports in Haikou Meilan, Changchun Longjia, Zhengzhou Xinzheng, Wuhan Tianhe, Lanzhou Zhongchuan, and Chengdu Shuangliu. But none of them are terminus stations like Hongqiao, which typically accommodates more passengers. Most of them are small stops in the middle of train lines or terminuses for airport rail links.[2] None of them have the seamlessness of Hongqiao between air and rail travel, not least because none of them were built near-simultaneously with an airport terminal, as it was.

The absence of other transportation complexes like Hongqiao contrasts with Chinese localities' tendency to follow each other's examples and

---

[1] See China Eastern Airlines. (2014, December 24). 空铁通 (*Air-rail Connect*), ceair.com, retrieved from http://www.ceair.com/about/dhcpjs/t20141224_16925.html.

[2] For example, the Lanzhong railway is an airport link that connects downtown Lanzhou and Zhongchuan airport. Most Chinese cities' airport links are operated by the cities' mass transit system (e.g., subways or light rails). In these aforementioned cases, the airport links are operated by the Chinese national railway system.

invest in expensive infrastructure projects. The sprawling "new towns (新城)," also called central business districts (CBDs) that mirror the skylines of Shanghai Pudong or Beijing Guomao in numerous second- and third-tier cities, reflect this.[3] And many localities have indeed proposed plans to build comprehensive transportation hubs much like Hongqiao that combine high-speed railway stations and airport terminals. Ningbo, a port city located 200 kilometers south of Shanghai, proposed in 2018 to build an integrated structure for the city's West Station, a terminus for the proposed Shanghai–Ningbo intercity high-speed railway and its new airport Terminal Three.[4] Ningbo and other cities like it have funding and do not face technical challenges, as they could follow Hongqiao's model. Most of the localities with such proposals have also undertaken more expensive programs like subways or container ports. But the challenge is political.

Localities cannot build whatever their leaders have in mind. For large and crucial infrastructure projects like railways, airports, subways, and seaports, localities need to receive approval from the central government before construction can begin. This has a legitimate rationale: these large projects often have externalities. Letting localities build whatever they want might result in problems such as overcapacity, misallocation of investments, inferior construction quality, and unfettered competition among local governments. Back in the 1990s and early 2000s, some local leaders ordered the construction of such projects without notifying the central government, or proceeded before they got the approval in what was colloquially called "jumping the gun (抢跑)." The CCP increased the use of disciplinary measures to curtail these actions starting in the early 2000s, sanctioning and sometimes removing audacious local officials. The most famous case was the Jiangsu Tieben incident (铁本案) in 2004. Local officials in Jiangsu's Changzhou city pushed for a ten billion yuan investment in building a steel mill, without complying with the State Council's regulation and receiving its approval. Eight high-level local leaders, including the deputy director of Jiangsu Provincial Planning Commission and Changzhou municipal party secretary, ultimately received

---

[3] For example, it is reported that there were over 40 cities that planned to build CBDs in early 2000s. That number has only grown since then. See Liang, H. (2003, October 21). 县级市都在规划建CBD 中国能建这么多CBD吗？ (*Even counties are building CBDs, can China build this many CBDs?*), Sohu.com, retrieved from http://business.sohu.com/29/49/article214674929.shtml.

[4] See Lu, Y. (2018, October 18). 宁波西站最新规划：与机场航站楼无缝对接，实现 "空铁一体" (*The latest plan for Ningbo West Station seamlessly connects the airport terminal, integrate air travel with railway*), zjol.com.cn, retrieved from http://town.zjol.com.cn/cstts/201810/t20181018_8509620.shtml.

disciplinary punishment.[5] These actions had the desired effect, and local officials today generally comply with central government rules, waiting to start projects until they get approved.

The structure of authorities in the central government has made obtaining permission to build a transportation complex following Hongqiao's model nearly impossible because there are so many "veto points (Tsebelis, 1995)." Even getting permission to build a railway terminus is extremely difficult. It requires localities to present proposals and plans to, negotiate details with, and receive approval from at least six ministries: the National Development and Reform Commission, the Ministry of Transport, the China Railway Corporation (formerly the Ministry of Railways), the Ministry of Natural Resources (formerly Ministry of Land and Resources), the Ministry of Ecology and Environment, and the Ministry of Housing and Urban–Rural Development. Including an airport terminal in the proposed complex requires the permission of the Civil Aviation Administration, the People's Liberation Army (PLA) Air Force, the military region to which the locality belongs, and in some cases the PLA Navy.[6]

Each of these central or military institutions oversees a specific issue that pertains to the construction of the complex. For example, the National Development and Reform Commission decides whether the project is feasible or necessary at all; the Ministry of Natural Resources is responsible for scrutinizing a land requisition request for the construction; the Ministry of Ecology and Environment evaluates the environmental consequences of the project (such as noise or light pollution) and the effectiveness of any preventive measures; the Civil Aviation Administration evaluates whether the design of the terminal per se and the surrounding structures (i.e., the train station) meet the aviation safety requirement (e.g., airfield clearance); and the military authority assesses whether the changes in the existing parameters of the civilian airport affect the military-controlled airspace. Localities need to prepare and submit different files to each of these institutions. Some of them can be done simultaneously, while some need to be done in sequence,

---

[5] See Li, Y. (2004, May 13). 冷眼看江苏铁本事件 (*Examining the Jiangsu Tieben incident with a calm perspective*), Sohu.com, retrieved from http://business.sohu.com/7/0504/36/column220103 662.shtml.

[6] The PLA Air Force manages China's airspace. In those places where the PLA Navy also has airports for naval aviation, the locality needs to coordinate with the Air Force, the Navy, and the military region (战区) for all projects that pertain to civilian airports. See (2017, October 17). 中国空域应该谁说了算？ (*Who manages China's airspace?*), Sohu.com, retrieved from http://www.sohu. com/a/198673803_685248.

meaning that in some cases localities cannot apply to some institutions until they have secured permission from another. Any mistake in this process will result in delay or no project.

Getting permission from any individual ministry is generally difficult. Ministries like the National Development and Reform Commission have hundreds or even thousands of local proposals to evaluate, and for a given project there may be competing proposals from other localities. Projects can easily get sidelined by such competition. Beyond the sequencing of submissions, localities must fulfill particular regulations and requirements based on a given ministry's mandate. For example, a locality could propose a railway station with eight platforms and find that the National Development and Reform Commission or the China Railway Corporation determine that five platforms are sufficient, and prevent the project from going forward with eight. Keeping the original design will require lengthy negotiations and bargaining with the technocrats in the ministries. Localities do succeed in defending their original plans on occasion, but more often they make some forms of concession. However, ministries do not always agree with one another.[7] Changing the parameters of a project to fulfill the requirements of one ministry could contradict the requirements of another ministry. For example, the China Railway Corporation prefers to have grandiose stations, as many recently completed high-speed railway stations across China have evidenced. Yet, placing a huge station next to an airport terminal can easily violate the Civil Aviation Administration's regulation on airfield clearance. However, designing an underground station to satisfy the requirements of the Civil Aviation Administration may create a design that the China Railway Corporation or the Ministry of Ecology and Environment will not approve.

Some localities that aspired to a combined rail station and airport terminal like Hongqiao's have determined that building them separately is the only way to move forward. For example, only one year after Ningbo announced the plan to build its West train station together with a new airport terminal, the locality decided in 2019 that there would be several kilometers and an airport rail link between the airport and the train station. A local official in the city's transportation bureau told me that the city's leaders had made the

---

[7] Truex (2020) explains that such institutional division is frequently the cause of delays in national legislation in China.

change to expedite the process, as they expected an indefinite delay if they held to the original plan.[8]

The processes that localities face in seeking approval for their infrastructure projects reflect the fact, which many scholars of contemporary China have pointed out, that the Chinese government is not monolithic. Instead, there are overlapping and competing sources of authority within the bureaucracy, what scholars have called fragmented authoritarianism (e.g., Lieberthal, 1992; Mertha, 2009). Section 3.2 first provides a step-by-step roadmap that localities use in order to have their construction proposals approved in this context.

3.2 The Long and Winding Path to Approval

Figure 3.1 lists the steps a Chinese province usually needs to take before building a high-speed railway. I acquired the information through conversations with a senior staff member at the governor's office of an eastern Chinese province.[9] Steps are listed in chronological order, and relevant central bureaucracies involved in the steps are underscored.

The process can be divided into four phases. The first phase, steps 1 through 3, involve having local proposals acknowledged, in written form, by various agencies of the central government. The key product of this phase is the inclusion of a local government's railway proposal into the state's Medium- and Long-Term Railway Network Plan. The inclusion is akin to a message by the central government to the locality that reads "Hey, I noted your plan. I have put it on my agenda and will deal with it at a future point." The second phase, steps 4 through 8, lead to the approval of the project suggestion report. The main body of this report focuses on why undertaking the project is necessary and feasible. It also provides some rough estimates on technical issues and construction logistics. The approval of the report is the first formal permission issued by the central government for a particular project. With this permission, the localities and the railway authority can start concrete preparations (e.g., on-site investigation) for the project. The third

---

[8] Interview with an official at the airport section of the transportation bureau of Ningbo, July 7, 2019. As I submit the final book manuscript to the press in fall 2021, the plan has still not received approval. In an informal conversation, the same informant told me that the city's new party secretary, who took power in spring 2021, is considering a different design, which might further delay the process.

[9] Interview with a secretary to the governor of an eastern province, November 6, 2015.

1. Local government drafts a report requesting the construction of a new railway, and delivers the report to the China Railway Corporation*.
2. The China Railway Corporation sends the report to one of its subsidiary planning institutes (e.g., Siyuan Survey and Design Group) for research and evaluation.
3. The National Development and Reform Commission, the Ministry of Transport, and the China Railway Corporation agree in principle on the proposal, and include the proposed route in the Medium- and Long-Term Railway Network Plan.
4. A designing agency, chosen through a bidding process initiated by The China Railway Corporation, drafts the pre-feasibility report (预可行性研究报告).
5. China Railway Economic and Planning Research Institute (CREPRI) of the China Railway Corporation (铁总工程设计鉴定中心) conducts an internal review of the pre-feasibility report.
6. A third-party engineering consulting firm conducts an external review of the pre-feasibility report.
7. The China Railway Corporation and the local government jointly submit the project suggestion report (项目建议书) to the National Development and Reform Commission.
8. The National Development and Reform Commission approves the project suggestion report.
9. A designing agency, chosen through a bidding process, drafts the project feasibility report (项目可行性研究报告).
10. The CREPRI conducts an on-site investigation to determine key technical parameters of the project, and reviews and recommends changes to the project feasibility report.
11. The China Railway Corporation and the local government jointly submit the project feasibility report to the National Development and Reform Commission.
12. The National Development and Reform Commission, the Ministry of Transport, the Ministry of Environmental Protection, the Ministry of Land and Resources, the Ministry of Housing and Urban-Rural Development (if applicable), and the Ministry of Water Resources (if applicable) each evaluate and review the project feasibility report, particularly on the environmental impact evaluation (环评) of the project, and when necessary, demand changes to key parameters.
13. The National Development and Reform Commission approves the project feasibility report.
14. A designing agency, chosen through a bidding process, drafts the preliminary project construction design (项目初步设计), which is in turn reviewed and approved by the CREPRI and the National Development and Reform Commission.
15. Land taking and other preparations by the local government.
16. The China Railway Corporation chooses construction companies through a bidding process.
17. Construction begins.

*The China Railway Corporation was known as the Ministry of Railway until 2013). The chairman of the company is a minister-level official appointed by the state council. In June 2019, the corporation was reorganized into China State Railway Group Company (or "China Railway" for short). This book uses China Railway Corporation for consistency in spite of that change.

Figure 3.1 Bureaucratic Agencies in the Approval Process of High-Speed Railways

phase, steps 9 through 13, lead to the approval of the most important document for an infrastructure program, the project feasibility report. The report contains detailed parameters on all aspects of the project, including the scale (as defined by numerous technical indicators), the amount and the location of land required to finish the project, the environmental consequences and redress measures, the length of construction, and the amount of investment and possible sources of investment.[10] Once a locality receives approval for the project feasibility report, it can turn to phase four, steps 14 through 17, to clear some final hurdles (mostly logistics issues) before the construction can formally begin.

As shown in Figure 3.1, numerous central bureaucracies have jurisdiction over some aspects of the planning or construction of railways. Among them, three are key agencies in regulating investments in transportation infrastructure, and multiple others may be required to conduct a review. These bureaucracies differ in their specialty, expertise, and power.

China Railway Corporation. The state-owned China Railway Corporation was formed in 2013, following the dissolution of the former Ministry of Railways. As I write this book in fall 2019, the company just went through another round of reorganization and was renamed the China State Railway Group Co., LTD, or simply China Railway (as listed on the company's website). The company has inherited the majority of what used to belong to the Ministry of Railways, including 18 regional railway administrations (now regional railway corporations), 40 subsidiary companies and agencies (such as the China Railway Economic and Planning Research Institute [CREPRI] and the China Railway Investment Co., LTD), over two million railway staff members, and the authorities in planning, operation, and maintenance of the railway network.[11] The company's headquarters is located in what used to be the Ministry of Railways, and its chairperson enjoys the same rank as the former railway minister. The main difference between the company and the former Ministry of Railways is the National Railway Administration, which was created as a subordinate agency of the Ministry of Transport at the same time as the China Railway Corporation in 2013. The National Railway Administration is responsible for regulating and overseeing the operation of the railway corporation. Chapter 5 provides further details on the internal structure of the railway corporation and its role in the construction of new railways.

---

[10] See a National Development and Reform Commission document that approves the Beijing Daxing International Airport in 2014. National Development and Reform Commission. (2014, November 22). 国家发展改革委关于北京新机场工程可行性研究报告的批复 *(The National Development and Reform Commission on the approval of the project feasibility report for the Beijing New Airport)*, ndrc.gov.cn, retrieved from http://www.ndrc.gov.cn/gzdt/201412/t20141215_652148.html.

[11] For the current structure of the China State Railway Group, see China Railway. (2021, June 24). 组织机构情况 *(Organizational Structure)*, china-railway.com.cn, retrieved from http://www.china-railway.com.cn/gsjs/zzjg/.

National Development and Reform Commission. As well as the China Railway Corporation, the National Development and Reform Commission (NDRC) plays a pivotal role in every phase of determining a proposed plan's fate. As the successor to the State Planning Commission, the NDRC holds considerable regulatory power over economic and social activities in China (Yeo, 2009). The subdivisions of the NDRC are charged with duties ranging from macroeconomic policies to price control to national-level economic and social planning, to projects management, foreign investment management, and food and supplies management.[12] Owing to its wide-ranging power, the NDRC has been dubbed the "mini State Council (小国务院)" by the media. Most ministries have one person, the minister, who holds the rank of minister (正部级), and have one leader who sits in the CCP central committee. The NRDC has three deputy directors at the minister level and has been known to have four CCP central committee members simultaneously among its leadership because of its significant authority.[13] A State Council document issued in 2004 has 13 categories of investment that require the NDRC's approval, including railway. The document stipulates that railway projects longer than 100 kilometers or that involve more than one province need to receive approval from the NDRC.[14] Further complicating the NRDC's role in each project, the vetting process for proposals to bring railway to a locality falls in the jurisdiction of several bureaus of the NDRC, including the Development Strategies and Planning Bureau (发展战略和规划司), Fixed Asset Investment Bureau (固定资产投资司), and Infrastructure Development Bureau (基础设施发展司).

Ministry of Transport. The Ministry of Transport has a range of duties in overseeing the transportation sector, including coordinating the planning and development of different forms of transportation infrastructure (e.g., highways, airports, ports, and railways), regulating and managing the operation of different transportation systems, and proposing national-level

[12] For a detailed description of the Commission's duty, see NDRC. 职能配置与内设机构 *(Function and internal organizations)*, ndrc.gov.cn, retrieved from https://www.ndrc.gov.cn/fzggw/bnpz/?code=&state=123.

[13] The four central committee members were Xu Shaoshi (then director), Xie Zhenghua, Liu He, and Wu Xinxiong (then deputy directors), when they were appointed to the Commission's leadership in 2013.

[14] See The State Council Information Office. (2004, July 28). 政府核准的投资项目目录 *(The list for government approved investment projects)*, scio.gov.cn, retrieved from http://www.scio.gov.cn/xwfbh/xwbfbh/wqfbh/2004/0728/Document/327107/327107.htm.

budgets on transportation.[15] The railway authority previously remained largely independent from the Ministry of Transport, as it had its own ministry. Since the dissolution of the Ministry of Railways in 2013, although the railway authority still largely operates on its own (through the ministerial-level state-owned enterprise, China Railway Corporation), the Ministry of Transport now holds some regulatory power over the railway sector. For example, the inclusion of a locality's proposal into the Medium- and Long-Term Railway Network Plan would require consent from the Ministry of Transport. The Ministry's deliberation largely depends on whether the proposed railway would supplement (or compete with) existing or planned projects other than railways (e.g., highways). The ministry also has approval power of the budget for railway investments.[16]

Other ministries also evaluate and approve local proposals for railway service. If the proposed railway would require revising existing planning of urban space in major cities, the *Ministry of Housing and Urban–Rural Development* must review it, and if it will affect a major hydraulic facility (e.g., a reservoir), the *Ministry of Water Resources* must review it. The *Ministry of Land and Resources* must also scrutinize the draft of the project feasibility report to determine whether the proposed requisition of land for the project fits with its regulations. The local authorities I interviewed particularly emphasized the *Ministry of Environmental Protection* as a barrier. It requires the local government to perform an environmental impact assessment before it will greenlight the project. Economic considerations often conflict with environmental impact, and redesigning a project to conform takes time. To be sure, protecting a natural preservation area or avoiding increasing noise pollution in a densely populated neighborhood serves the public interest, but diverting a route can be costly, and a revised environmental impact assessment can take time. Obtaining environmental approval can require multiple versions of the environmental impact assessment. For example, local authorities in Beijing and Liaoning had to submit four versions of the environmental impact assessment report for the Beijing–Shenyang high-speed railway before it was approved, which caused a delay of three years.[17]

---

[15] For a detailed description of the ministry's responsibility, see Ministry of Transport. (2021, May 17). 主要职责 *(Main responsibilities)*, mot.gov.cn, retrieved from https://www.mot.gov.cn/jiaotonggaikuang/201510/t20151015_1902308.html.

[16] Ibid.

[17] Interview with a railway expert in Beijing, January 16, 2020.

There are particular reasons to follow the steps in Figure 3.1 in order. For example, the NDRC's review in step 13 requires a document showing the approval of the project suggestion report, which is step 8. Similarly, the review of the project construction design in step 14 cannot go forward without an approved project feasibility report, step 13.

Many projects stall at one phase or another. For example, Zhejiang and Shanghai proposed the construction of a track capable of running maglev trains connecting Hangzhou and Shanghai in the early 2000s. The project completed step 8, NRDC's approval of the project suggestion report in 2006.[18] The Hongqiao Station, which was designed in the same period, has space to this day for the platforms of this proposed maglev line. But the Ministry of Railways changed its view on maglev trains in the mid-2000s, considering them inferior to wheeled trains for the high-speed railway program. The project feasibility report was never approved. However, such dichotomous outcomes are in some ways better than the more common circumstance in which projects are mired in processes seeking approval from an agency seeking many revisions but never outright killing a project.

In addition to the central authorities' various ways of meeting their mandates, approvals can be mired in negotiations over investment. For example, the China Railway Corporation, the locality or localities involved, and sometimes other central institutions will all bear some expense, and each would like the others to take on a greater share. At the same time, NDRC and some other central institutions seek to limit the amount the local governments can levy through bank loans for their share of the costs, as many local governments are borrowing at a rate they cannot pay back in the future.

Negotiations over these details can draw out the approvals process, and no independent authority sets the clocks for these procedures. The dedication and strategies of localities play an important role in shaping the outcomes of these policy bargains. These interactions most often take place behind closed doors and therefore are hard to observe, let alone examine systematically. The establishment of numerous offices by localities in China's capital city to support these endeavors nevertheless suggests the prevalence of such exchanges, although in 2010 the central government ordered the closure of many.

---

[18] See Yue, D. L. (2006, February 26). 国务院通过沪杭磁悬浮项目建议书 (*The State Council approves the project suggestion report for the Shanghai-Hangzhou maglev rail*), zjstv.com, retrieved from http://www.zjstv.com/zcloud/730874.html.

3.3 The Functions of Beijing Offices

The Beijing offices are like domestic embassies for Chinese localities. This role can be traced back to the Han dynasty (206 BCE–220 CE), when regional authorities built *liudi* (留邸), literally *staying mansions*, to accommodate local officials overnight when they visited the Han capitals (Huang, 2010, pp. 17–20). During the Tang Dynasty (618–907 CE), territorial administrations and military governors (节度使) established as many as 56 *jinzouguan* (进奏馆), literally *reporting pavilions*, in the capital city of Chang'an (nowadays Xi'an; Huang, 2010, p. 22). During later periods, localities' capital offices also opened to civilians, becoming a place for social interactions among native officials, intellectuals, businessmen, and imperial civil service exams attendees (Belsky, 2005; Huang, 2010, p. 24).

The Inner Mongolia autonomous region established the first capital office in Beijing after the communist revolution in March 1949. Other regions quickly followed. On December 27, 1966, seven months after the beginning of the Cultural Revolution, the State Council ordered the closure of all Beijing offices, claiming they were "spy agencies" for local "counterrevolutionaries." The ban was lifted in December 1978, and the provinces reopened their Beijing offices (Huang, 2010, pp. 34–45). Since then, the number and activities of Beijing offices have drastically increased. By 2010, there were more than 10,000 Beijing offices as functional departments of local governments at different levels (e.g., local transportation bureaus, planning commissions), local state-owned enterprises, social organizations (e.g., universities, research institutes) and other organizations had opened them.[19] Among these, the 52 provincial-level Beijing offices alone employed more than 8,000 full-time staff.[20]

Most provinces and provincial capital cities have built or purchased entire buildings for their Beijing offices. These places are easy to identify on maps, which often bear the names of the regions they represent. For example, the Inner Mongolia autonomous region's Beijing office is located in the "Inner Mongolia Mansion (内蒙古大厦)," and Zhejiang province's Beijing office similarly is in a "Zhejiang Mansion (浙江大厦)." Much like the *liudi* of old,

---

[19] See Southern Metropolis Weekly. (2010, March 15). 驻京办怎么办? *(What should Beijing offices do?)*, sohu.com, retrieved from http://news.sohu.com/20100315/n270835394.shtml.

[20] The provincial-level offices include those of the provinces, deputy provincial cities (副省级城市), separately planned cities (计划单列市), special economic zones, Hong Kong, Macau, and the Xinjiang Production and Construction Corps.

these buildings include hotel-style accommodation and even restaurants for local officials traveling to Beijing, as well as office space.[21]

The Beijing offices of localities are formally a branch of those local governments, and the directors of these offices have the same rank as the heads of other local government departments.[22] Most of those who work under these directors are civil servants the localities have sent to work in Beijing. They perform a range of duties, but their key task is to facilitate exchange between central and local governments. According to a published document of Zhejiang provincial government's Beijing office, the duties of the office include the following[23]:

1. Enhance communication on governmental affairs between the province and central party and state apparatus and also the relevant departments of Beijing municipality.

2. Report important political information to the provincial party and government leaders in a timely manner.

3. Coordinate activities of provincial firms registered or doing business in Beijing, and provide necessary assistance and services to entrepreneurs, students, and citizens visiting Beijing.

4. Provide work guidance to the Beijing offices of the cities (of the province); facilitate and enhance their efforts to build uncorrupt government institutions (廉政建设). Manage and facilitate party building work among provincial party members in Beijing.

5. Provide services to provincial leaders visiting Beijing for business meetings, national conferences, or cadre training programs. Help organize large events initiated by the province in Beijing. Provide logistics service to provincial civil servants' business trips to Beijing.

6. Communicate and coordinate with the State Bureau for Letters and Calls and relevant departments of Beijing municipality, and handle petitioners and other problematic people that need to be addressed

[21] In fact, many of these hotels and restaurants are also open to the public, and the restaurants of the Beijing offices are popular destinations for local foodies and tourists, as they serve cuisine local to the localities they represent.

[22] For example, the director of the provincial Beijing office shares the same rank as the director of provincial bureaus, and the director of the municipal Beijing office shares the same rank as municipal bureaus.

[23] See Beijing Office of Zhejiang Provincial Government. (2021, March 11). 浙江省人民政府驻北京办事处2021年部门预算 (*Budget report for the 2021 fiscal year of the Beijing office of Zhejiang provincial government*), retrieved from http://www.zj.gov.cn/art/2021/3/11/art_1229278038_4530965.html.

and send them back. Cooperate with Beijing municipal government to maintain social stability in the capital.[24]

7. Keep in contact with central state-owned enterprises and research institutions that have cooperative initiatives with Zhejiang province, and provide services to enhance cooperation.

8. Keep in contact with state leaders who are of Zhejiang origin or have worked in Zhejiang, and academicians of the Chinese Academy of Sciences and the Chinese Academy of Engineering who are Zhejiang natives.

9. Manage and monitor the state-owned assets of the provincial Beijing office.

10. Undertake other tasks assigned by the provincial party committee, the provincial government, or the relevant central government agencies.

Fulfilling broad mandates such as "enhance communication on government affairs (做好政务联络)" can be complicated. This became clear in interviews in which two divisional chiefs (处长) in the Beijing office of a city N in eastern China described their jobs. The city is a major port and an industrial hub along the coast. Both divisional chiefs are responsible for communicating and coordinating with relevant central agencies for the city's transportation and energy projects. They frequently visit the NDRC, the Ministry of Transport, the China Railway Corporation, the Ministry of Housing and Urban–Rural Development, the Ministry of Natural Resources, and relevant central state-owned enterprises and research institutes for this purpose. These visits, as they summarized, have four functions: "reporting (汇报), soliciting (争取), coordination (衔接), and networking (联络)."[25]

3.3.1 Reporting

Reporting involves keeping relevant officials in the central ministries informed of the localities' work. For instance, they report the construction progress of a bridge or a highway that the ministry recently approved, and the conclusions from a feasibility study of a proposed railway or power plant.

---

[24] Beijing offices are tasked with monitoring and sending petitioners traveling to Beijing back to their home places.

[25] Interview with a divisional chief A in the Beijing office of a coastal city N, October 15, 2019; Interview with a divisional chief B in the Beijing office of a coastal city N, October 15, 2019.

Sometimes visiting local leaders whose portfolios cover these issues may be the instigators of such meetings.

The central ministries typically do not require such reports outright. Yet providing such reports gives local officials a legitimate reason to meet with key central bureaucrats who have the power and authority to make decisions. Their comments about this are aligned with the idea that the attention of central bureaucrats is what March and Olson called "a prime scarce resource" (1983, p. 292). They spend most of the time in these meetings in exchanging pleasantries and platitudes with central bureaucrats, but bureaucrats may in the process drop signs or clues about the directions central policymaking seems likely to take. Knowing about a proposed change in key policy parameters, a new central investment initiative in drafting, or a short-notice opportunity to apply for a small grant or subsidy disposed by a specialized bureau before other localities provides a first-mover advantage and vital time to prepare for when policy changes or opportunities become public. Localities that act preemptively on this information have advantages in getting future policy resources. These meetings also put a locality and its agenda on the radar of central bureaucrats, which might be beneficial to the locality in the future. One of the division chiefs explained: "If the ministries have plans or initiatives that need local participation, they would think of us first" because of the many meetings.[26]

3.3.2 Soliciting

Soliciting benefits for their localities is the most consequential task for officials at the Beijing offices. This might involve, for example, convincing a bureaucrat at the National Energy Administration that it should locate the new oil refineries it is planning to build to reduce the country's reliance on imported gas and chemical products in the locality, bringing jobs and other resources. Soliciting also involves presenting own proposals for new projects, including railway projects, and seeking central ministries' approval and support. An interviewee explained that the documents presenting such proposals must demonstrate necessity (必要性), including real societal demand for the project; urgency (紧迫性) (e.g., why the lack of it becomes a bottleneck for local development); and technical and financial feasibility (可行性). They should

---

[26] Interview with a divisional chief A in the Beijing office of a coastal city N, October 15, 2019.

also demonstrate that the locality is better suited than other places to host the project and that it has importance (重要性) in the sense of a positive impact on society that will benefit the region and beyond over the long run.[27] Interviewees described the elements and formality required for a persuasive report as not difficult to learn. Almost all localities can present their version of the story with coherent arguments, compelling data, and meticulous feasibility studies to demonstrate these points. They obtain these data either from their own research institutes or commercial institutions they pay to produce evidence to support the arguments they wish to make. Such documents will later become the basis upon which local governments draft the project suggestion reports for the NDRC's approval. However, central bureaucrats are well aware of the source of the data, and seemingly persuasive documents do not necessarily secure favorable treatment.

In this environment, top regional leaders may pay personal visits to central bureaucracies to show their sincerity, frequently couching their visits as reports (汇报工作). Interviewees described fierce competition between different localities for formal meetings as well as private discussions with central bureaucrats, and long lines for meetings. Governors and deputy governors can be found waiting in line to present themselves, humbly, in front of an office of a divisional chief at the more powerful ministries like the NDRC, even though they vastly outrank the divisional chief in the party-state's hierarchy.[28] While the activities of such officials at the local level receive high-profile coverage by the local party's mouthpieces, their visits to ministries are kept private because failure to obtain their objective would pose an embarrassment. At the same time, since paying visits by regional leaders has become the new normal in project solicitation, its effectiveness as a strategy is diluted.

3.3.3   Coordination

Coordinating different central ministries and local governments also requires meetings, sometimes sequences of them. When a policy issue spans

---

[27] Interview with a divisional chief B in the Beijing office of a coastal city N, October 15, 2019.

[28] See Yan, Y. L. (2015, May 30). 发改委被指越改革权力越大:副省长不敢反驳处长 *(The Reform and Development Commission is accused of being more powerful as reform goes on, deputy governors do not dare to disagree with a divisional chief in the commission)*, Sina.com, retrieved from http://finance.sina.com.cn/china/20130530/082015636012.shtml.

the jurisdictions of several agencies, they may disagree about certain aspects of the issue. Employees at the Beijing offices must exert pressure on these agencies to obtain a resolution and move the project forward, which requires studying what each party wants and the substance of their disagreements. They also need to weigh their own interests against these different positions. Occasionally, they prefer the position of one agency over another's, and they can use the position of the first agency to sway the second in their own favor. According to interviewees, bureaucrats are often not very proactive on these matters, so local officials must present official documents from their counterparts, signed and sealed, to confirm the position, especially if it represents a change. While it could be in the remit of bureaucrats to work together, local officials have far greater incentive to facilitate such coordination.

All of these activities require detailed documents that state the situation and proposed solutions to the problem. Beijing office staff might need the party secretary, governor, or mayor to present these documents in person. Sometimes they will seek the attention of even higher-level leaders (e.g., vice premiers) for a resolution if this fails.[29]

3.3.4 Networking

The extent to which Beijing office staff can achieve the tasks mentioned above depends in part on whether they have good personal connections with the central bureaucrats involved. Since they generally have very little in common with the minister of any central authority, who outranks them significantly,[30] networking largely pertains to relationships with lower-level bureaucrats in the ministries, such as divisional and sectional chiefs. With these officials they report and negotiate policy details. And in fact, rank-and-file bureaucrats can be enormously valuable, as they may serve in their positions for decades, which is rare with ministers. They are also the experts in their fields, serving as gatekeepers in screening, revising, or rejecting policy proposals before they reach the eyes of the ministers. Lacking their favor almost certainly guarantees the failure of policy solicitation, which

[29] Interview with a divisional chief B in the Beijing office of a coastal city N, October 15, 2019.
[30] Some exceptions might apply if the ministers happen to be connected with local officials in some other contexts, such as attending the same university or coming from the same place.

is why local leaders as powerful as provincial governors are so deferential to them.

Most networking takes place in informal settings. Interviewees described meals, drinks, and karaoke with central bureaucrats. They call such gatherings "connecting emotions (联络感情)." Some Beijing offices even operate their own bars and karaoke boxes, as the demand is strong.[31] They also give out gifts on holidays or invite central officials to visit their localities.[32] The bills for meals, drinks, karaoke, and local visits are, of course, charged to the locality. News reports reveal that the Beijing offices of Xuchang (许昌) and Luohe (漯河), two municipalities in Henan, spent 660 thousand yuan at once for expensive Chinese liquor, Moutai, for such activities.[33] Some Beijing office workers become brokers between local entrepreneurs and central officials, helping the former to get access and policy perks from the latter. These interactions, not surprisingly, often involve bribes, abuse of power, and other illicit activities.[34]

A good relationship with central bureaucrats can pay handsomely. The ministries receive hundreds and thousands of reports, requests, applications, and proposals from all levels of governments on a daily basis. This creates a scarcity of attention, and knowing someone in the ministries, especially those functionaries that handle these materials, can help a document move up in priority. In his detailed study of Beijing offices, Ma (2009) interviewed a local official who acknowledged that the time to get approval for a project that would otherwise require ten months of waiting was cut in half thanks to "relationship building (疏通感情)" with ministerial officials by the locality's Beijing office (p. 39). Such expedited treatment had significant economic implications for localities, which were in fierce competition with other places to generate faster growth (p. 42).

[31] See *Zhong Guo Ji Jian Jian Cha (Chinese discipline inspection)*. (2017, September 6). 变味的"驻京办"是这样被清理的 *(This is how some corrupted Beijing offices get cleansed)*, zgjjjc.ccdi.gov.cn, retrieved from http://zgjjjc.ccdi.gov.cn/bqml/bqxx/201709/t20170907_106742.html.

[32] Interview with a district commerce bureau official from Guangdong, January 15, 2020.

[33] See Li, D. M. (2009, April 13). 驻京办买777瓶茅台酒请谁喝 *(The Beijing offices purchased 777 bottles of liquor for who?)*, people.com, retrieved from http://opinion.people.com.cn/GB/9118919.html.

[34] For example, the deputy director of Yangzhou city's Beijing office charged a local entrepreneur half million yuan for introducing him to a National Energy Administration official. Both officials were later charged for corruption. See (2016, August 1). 扬州驻京办原副主任行贿获刑4年 向别人索贿50万 *(The former deputy director of Yangzhou's Beijing office is sentenced to serve 4 years for demanding bribery of half million yuan)*, xdnyzz.com, retrieved from http://www.xdnyzz.com/jjrd/1003.html.

Even more than reports, informal interactions may give local officials access to information. Ma (2009) documents two episodes that vividly illustrate this point (p. 36). In one case, a staff member of a city's Beijing office learned from a bureaucrat at a ministry with whom he had a good personal relationship that the State Council was considering putting local land use under central regulation and requiring local governments to obtain central approval for all new land purchases. With this intelligence, the city purchased enough land for the city's construction plans for the next 20 years before the order was issued, which was a huge advantage over localities with no advance warning of the order. In another case, a city was able to prepare documents that would allow a county that had once been a revolutionary base area (革命老区) to apply for a poverty alleviation subsidy as soon as a central authority announced such areas would have preferential status in such applications. The ultimate result of having such documents ready before other municipalities due to the close relationship between a city staff member in Beijing with a member of the Poverty Alleviation Office of the State Council (国务院扶贫办) resulted in the doubling of aid.

These two cases preceded January 2010, when the general office of the State Council issued a document ordering the closure of Beijing offices by entities below the municipal level.[35] The order allowed provincial-level units (i.e., provinces, deputy provincial cities, special economic zones, Hong Kong, Macau, and the Xinjiang Production and Construction Corps) to keep their Beijing offices. These offices were formally registered under the National Government Offices Administration (国务院机关事务管理局). For municipalities that had already opened their Beijing offices, the State Council document required them to receive approval from their respective provincial governments and register under the Development and Reform Commission of Beijing municipality to continue operating their offices. Also, these municipal Beijing offices were no longer called "Beijing offices." They were "downgraded" to "communication sections (联络处)," putting them under the jurisdiction of their provincial Beijing offices in formality. In practice, the communication sections still operate independently and answer to the municipal leaders. The Beijing offices of counties, districts, and

---

[35] See The State Council of People's Republic of China. (2010, January 29). 国务院办公厅关于加强和规范各地政府驻北京办事机构管理的意见 (*The opinion of the general office of the State Council on enhancing management and regulation of local governments' Beijing offices*), gov.cn, retrieved from http://www.gov.cn/zwgk/2010-01/29/content_1522398.htm.

functional departments of all levels of governments (including provincial bureaus) had to close within six months. Over 500 county Beijing offices were eventually closed.[36]

3.4 Beijing Offices Since 2010

The State Council's action was a response to a series of scandals surrounding Beijing offices involving corruption, abuse of power, and misuse and waste of taxpayer money, and criticism that the operation of these offices lacked oversight from their home governments. It was estimated that at its height, the annual operation cost of all Beijing offices amounted to 10 billion RMB.[37] A record shows that back in the early 1990s, the Jilin provincial Beijing office paid over 7,000 air and train tickets annually for provincial officials traveling to Beijing, and that number had only grown larger since then (Ma, 2009, p. 30). Another province hosted more than 1,300 visits by its provincial leaders and 4,600 visits by provincial bureau leaders in 2008 alone (Ma, 2009, p. 24). While a handful of Beijing offices could profit from their restaurants and hotel services, most of them would require local government subsidies to sustain operation.

The State Council's action has consequences for localities. Counties and districts are affected the most, although some of their offices turned to underground operation. The demands that gave rise to Beijing offices still exist. Local officials still need to gather information from the central government, they still need to solicit projects and policy benefits from the ministries, and they still need to take care of their leaders visiting Beijing from time to time and to send back aggrieved petitioners. With their offices closed, the former county Beijing offices' staffs rent apartments or stay in hotels to accomplish these tasks. A big challenge for them is their titles and personnel affiliations (人事关系). With Beijing offices being banned, they could not stay on the government payroll as Beijing office workers. They have to find new titles. Many of them have been assigned to other county bureaus, and they present themselves as being on "long-term business trips" to Beijing while continuing their past activities. The

---

[36] See Southern Metropolis Weekly. (2010, March 15). 驻京办怎么办? *(What should Beijing offices do?)*, sohu.com, retrieved from http://news.sohu.com/20100315/n270835394.shtml.
[37] Ibid.

central government also launched follow-up campaigns to try to root out these underground Beijing offices. Some counties opened offices in nearby Langfang or Tianjin, and conduct their business by long hours of commuting.[38]

The functional departments of local governments were also among those forced to close their Beijing offices. Departments in the provincial or municipal governments can move their Beijing offices' staff into their respective province's or municipality's Beijing offices. These staff keep their original personal affiliations with the departments but work as members of the localities' Beijing offices. For example, the divisional chief I interviewed in city N's Beijing office was sent by the city's transportation bureau, which used to have its own Beijing office. He is on the transportation bureau's payroll and is mainly responsible for communicating on issues related to the city's transportation development, but he now works in the city's Beijing office.[39]

The dissolution of many Beijing offices has consolidated the advantage of local governments that are already powerful. The change limits the voice and presence of localities down the hierarchy who were forced to close their offices. It has distributive implications for local development, as the fundamental dynamics of central–local relationship stays unchanged. The central government still controls a vast amount of resources, and communications with agencies that control these resources can benefit localities. The Beijing offices per se are not the root of the problem. Their existence is a testament to the fundamental institutional configurations that give rise to such interaction between the central and local governments. One former county Beijing office director from Hebei commented in a newspaper interview, "the fundamental problem is still the fiscal allocation between the central and local governments . . . [the establishment of Beijing offices] shows that grassroots governments now have their own "consciousness (主体意识)" (instead of being the subordinates of their superiors). They actively participate and try to influence central government's policymaking."[40]

---

[38] Ibid.

[39] Interview with a divisional chief B in the Beijing office of a coastal city N, October 15, 2019.

[40] See Southern Metropolis Weekly. (2010, March 15). 驻京办怎么办? (What should Beijing offices do?), sohu.com, retrieved from http://news.sohu.com/20100315/n270835394.shtml.

3.5 Why Are Some Localities More Successful than Others?

The story of the Beijing offices suggests that localized bargaining is a common practice among Chinese localities. This raises the question as to what determines the varied outcomes of their activities. Why do some localities get swift approvals from the central government while other, similar places are denied permissions or stuck in endless gridlock? The divisional chief at city N's Beijing office pointed to three dimensions that might play a role.[41]

3.5.1 Leaders' Commitment

The divisional chief feels that some local leaders do not expend enough effort. The frequency with which local leaders visit central bureaucracies to negotiate policy details varies significantly. Some launch campaigns in local government to direct funds and staff to the project's application, and some do not. He also described significant variation in the mobilization of informal resources, including personal connections, to achieve the intended goals. The dedication of the local leader's attention and efforts is not only a signal to the ministries of a locality's sincerity and seriousness; it also helps reorient the local bureaucracy to commit additional resources to the issues in question. It is therefore not surprising that local leaders' effort makes a significant difference.

The importance of a local leader's priorities and attention raises the question as to what determines their level of commitment. Chinese local leaders govern like the heads of state in their jurisdictions (Zhou, 2016). They are responsible for all aspects of local governance, including promoting economic development, maintaining social stability, protecting the environment, and ensuring the quality of health care and recreational activities including sports and cultural activities (Ang, 2016, p. 123). Getting an infrastructure project approved by the central government is one task among many they must complete. Given the obstacles to success, some may not see railway projects as a worthy expenditure of their time and resources. In some cases, local transportation or development bureaucracies may play a decisive role in securing the commitment of local leaders. Thus local bureaucracies have to undergo

---

[41] Interview with a divisional chief B in the Beijing office of a coastal city N, October 15, 2019.

a process not unlike the lobbying that local leaders committed to a project must direct at the central authority. Nor are infrastructure projects the only subject of such local-level lobbying, as departments can seek the attention of the local leader to request funds or other resources for myriad purposes.

Political considerations also affect whether leaders want to exert efforts on a certain project. If the current leader's predecessor initiated the project, this may have an impact. If the predecessor was horizontally transferred to serve in another place or does not belong to the same political faction as the current leader, the current leader has very little incentive to press the project forward. The predecessor will likely take much of the credit from the project. Likewise, if the predecessor was removed from office or demoted through disciplinary action, the incumbent will seek distance from the disgraced predecessor, including any associated projects. For example, after Chen Liangyu was removed from his office as the party secretary of Shanghai in 2006, his replacement, Han Zheng, called off several construction programs proposed during his tenure that had been considered Chen's "showcase projects (面子工程)."[42] Chinese officials do not decide or anticipate the length of their own tenure (their superiors do), which leads to many unfinished proposals and projects when the office changes hands. Such projects have incurred huge waste in fiscal resources and bureaucratic effort.

At the same time, it sometimes behooves local leaders to continue projects in process. If the predecessor was promoted and became the locality's direct superior or belongs to the same faction as the incumbent leader, then it might benefit the incumbent's career to carry through on the predecessor's legacy. Likewise, picking up an existing proposal that already has some foundation laid can be easier than starting from scratch, and completing a project can offer political points. Sometimes the leader who revives a project and achieves it gets more credit than the one who initially proposed it. One way to make it easier to capitalize on this is to repackage the project (e.g., giving it a new name or changing some key features). In recent years, the CCP has also called on local officials to increase the continuity and coherence in local policymaking following leadership turnover.[43]

---

[42] See, for example, (2007, January 12). 陈良宇面子工程上海摩天轮停建 (Chen Liangyu's Showcase project the eye of Shanghai was suspended), Sohu.com, retrieved from http://news.sohu.com/20070112/n247564496.shtml.

[43] See, Zheng, J. M. (2016, August 10). 新官理旧事是责任担当 (Dealing with old business is the responsibility for newly appointed officials), xinhuanet.com, retrieved from http://www.xinhuanet.com/politics/2016-08/10/c_129217273.htm.

The fate of a planned high-speed railway to Shanghai by city N illustrates both the importance of local leaders' willingness and efforts in bottom-up policy solicitation and how a transfer of power can affect outcomes.[44] The city first proposed the railway in 2008, but local leaders had low expectations of achieving it any time soon. The city had just completed a highway to Shanghai, and they recognized that the central government was unlikely to grant the city another large transportation project so quickly. The city's provincial and national people's congress representatives and people's consultative conference delegates submitted motions and suggestions on this project virtually every year, but from 2008 to 2015, three consecutive party secretaries did not make it a priority. The section chief of city N's Beijing office accompanied the directors of the city's transportation bureau to the ministries numerous times, but these visits made very little difference without the support of the party secretaries. There were also disagreements within the city about how the project should proceed. Two counties under the city each argued that the proposed railway should have a station in its jurisdiction. With this unresolved, the city could not finalize a plan to send to the ministries. During the same period, several nearby cities had proposed similar railway projects, and two of them got approved and began construction. The divisional chief of the Beijing office, who spent much of his time following the project, lamented that the city "started the earliest yet finished the last (起了个大早，赶了个晚集)."

The situation changed in 2016 when a new party secretary took office. The new secretary announced in a meeting with the city's bureau directors and county (and district) executives that the proposed railway project would become the city's "Number One Project (一号工程)," and he would be directly responsible for it. The city's transportation bureau director also made a public pledge that the bureau would make the passage of the "Number One project" its number one priority.

He only served for a year, but, as the section chief of the city's Beijing office told me, that secretary visited the China Railway Corporation three times, meeting with the chairman and deputy chairman of the corporation and negotiating details of the project, including key issues such as the division of the project's financial responsibilities between the corporation and the local

---

[44] The case is based on interview with a divisional chief B in the Beijing office of a coastal city N, October 15, 2019.

government. The party secretary also used his authority to settle the city's internal disagreements on the proposed route and location of the stations.

The party secretary's efforts paid off. In 2017, months before the party secretary left office and was promoted to serve elsewhere, the proposed railway was finally included in the Medium- and Long-Term Railway Network Plan , which acts as an official birth certificate. It was also listed as a part of the national 13th five-year plan (2016–2020), which the State Council announced in the same year. Inclusion in the five-year plan means that the project needs to start construction no later than the end of 2020. This gives the city a favorable bargaining position when it negotiates details with the relevant ministries. At the time of this writing, the railway has passed the preliminary feasibility study and started on-site prospecting. The approval for the project feasibility report seems assured. The party secretary's efforts have clearly made a tangible difference, but it also seems likely that he made a good choice in determining when to push.

3.5.2 Political Status of Localities

While there may be unevenness in the effort local leaders put in, the fact that many local leaders want high-speed rail projects and are willing to put in the effort required raises the question as to what determines the outcomes of competition among localities whose leaders are equally motivated. The answer lies in the CCP hierarchy. The Chinese party-state, or the *nomenklatura*, encompasses various levels of government organizations, state-owned enterprises, and some nominally private entities, and organizes them into an elaborative and coherent hierarchy (Burns, 1987; McGregor, 2010). There are ten different ranking levels of leaders laid out in the Civil Servant Law of the People's Republic of China.[45] As shown in Table 3.1, the ranks of local leaders are primarily determined by the types of territorial administrations they govern. For example, governors rank higher than mayors, as provinces are above municipalities. But there are cases where the distinctions are less straightforward. Mayors, for example, can hold vastly different ranks depending on the types of cities they administer (Chung & Lam, 2004). The mayor of a centrally administered city has the same rank as a provincial

---

[45] See Article 18, Chapter 3, Civil Servant Law of People's Republic of China, approved by the Standing Committee of National People's Congress, April 27, 2005.

Table 3.1 Hierarchies and Positions in the Chinese Party-State

Rank	Positions (examples)	
State Level (正国级)	General Party Secretary, President, Premier, Politburo Standing Committee Members	
Deputy State Level (副国级)	Politburo Members, Vice Premiers, Supreme People's Court Chief Justice	
Provincial/Ministerial Level (省/部级)	Provincial Party Secretaries, Governors, Party Secretaries, and Mayors of Centrally Administered Cities	Ministers
Deputy Provincial/Ministerial Level (副省/部级)	Deputy Provincial Party Secretaries, Deputy Governors, Provincial Party Standing Committee Members, Party Secretaries, and Mayors of Deputy Provincial Cities	Deputy Ministers
Municipal/Bureau Level (地/厅级)	City Party Secretary, Mayors	Ministerial/Provincial Bureau Directors
Deputy Municipal/Bureau Level (副地/厅级)	Deputy City Party Secretaries, Deputy Mayors, Municipal Party Standing Committee Members	Deputy Directors of Ministerial/Provincial Bureaus
County/Division Level (县/处级)	County Party Secretaries, County Executives	Municipal Bureau Director, Ministerial Division Chiefs
Deputy County/Division Level (副县/处级)	Deputy County Party Secretaries, Deputy County Executives, County Party Standing Committee Members	Deputy Directors of Municipal Bureaus, Deputy Chiefs of Ministerial Divisions
Township/Section Level (乡/科级)	Township Party Secretary, Township Leaders	County Bureau Directors, Municipal Section Chiefs, Ministerial Section Chiefs
Deputy Township/Section Level (副乡/科级)	Deputy Township Party Secretary, Deputy Township Leaders, Township Party Committee Members	Deputy Directors of County Bureaus, Deputy Chiefs of Municipal Sections, Deputy Chiefs of Ministerial Sections

governor, while the mayor of a county-level city is equal to a county executive and is the subordinate of a municipality mayor.

Even the leaders of the same type of territories do not necessarily share the same rank. Some hold concurrent appointments at a higher level (Bulman & Jaros, 2019); an individual's highest position determines his or her rank. For example, a municipal party secretary who is concurrently a member of the provincial party standing committee is considered a deputy provincial-level cadre, and he or she is the superior of other municipal party secretaries that do not have a concurrent appointment.

A higher rank confers tangible advantages on localities in procuring policy benefits from higher levels. The central government's campaign in 2010 to regulate Beijing offices—local governments' primary institutions in facilitating policy bargains with the central bureaucracies—reflects this. It was highly discriminatory against lower-level authorities. Provinces and deputy provincial cities were allowed to preserve their existing Beijing offices, whereas municipalities and counties were forced to downscale or close their offices. But this only increases the weakness of the lobbying capacity of lower levels of governments that existed before. In addition, with a few exceptions (such as the targeted poverty alleviation program), most central policies and allocation of resources need to go through levels of territorial administrations to reach the grassroots. This means that regional administrations of upper echelons (e.g., provinces) might enjoy some discretionary power over the allocation of central benefits to their subordinates (e.g., municipalities, counties). Finally, the uneven ranks of the same type of territorial administrations (i.e., among horizontal units), mostly caused by the concurrent appointments of local leaders, give certain localities an unfair advantage in competing with their horizontal peers. It makes a locality simultaneously a referee and a participant in the race for acquiring resources, and the outcome of such a race is not difficult to infer. Chapter 4 provides more detailed discussions on how concurrent appointments translate into policy advantages.

A local leader's rank also directly affects the process of interactions between local and central bureaucracies.[46] Whereas the party secretary of city N was able to travel frequently to Beijing and meet with the ministers, most local leaders have difficulty getting audiences with the most powerful

---

[46] Interview with a divisional chief A in the Beijing office of a coastal city N, October 15, 2019; Interview with a divisional chief B in the Beijing office of a coastal city N, October 15, 2019.

members of the ministries. While the schedules of the ministerial leaders play some role in determining this outcome, the ranks of the local leaders are generally determinative.[47] The official exchanges between different bureaucratic entities in China follow the norm of reciprocity, something similar to what heads of states practice in international diplomacy. That is, a leader is only obligated to deal with his or her exact counterpart (in position or rank) from another bureaucracy (e.g., Ma, 2017). This means that if a provincial party secretary or a governor visits a ministry, the minister has an obligation to meet with him or her. The only exception would be if the minister's schedule is previously booked (e.g., the central leaders have summoned the minister), in which case it would be appropriate for the deputy minister to host the provincial leaders instead.[48] If a municipal party secretary or mayor visits the ministry, the ministry only needs to send a bureau director to meet with the visitor (see Table 3.1 for the ranks of the two positions).[49] In practice, when receiving party secretaries—the top leaders in their regions from below the provincial level—the ministry would send someone just above the rank of the guest to show courtesy, or to "give face (给面子)" in Chinese. For example, when the party secretary of a deputy provincial city visits, he or she might be able to meet with the minister, but the minister is not obliged to take the meeting. Similarly, a municipal party secretary might sometimes be able to meet with a deputy minister if his or her schedule allows. If the locality sends a deputy (instead of its top leader), the ministry is likely to provide a meeting with someone with commensurate rank.

The rule of respect means that by design, localities with higher ranks have greater access to more powerful figures in the ministries. This has consequences for the bargaining outcomes. Meeting the minister can help produce meaningful progress on the issues. Local and ministerial leaders both know that for most technical issues, the ministers have the authority to call the shots, and it would appear disingenuous for a minister to further defer a decision to another actor. In contrast, if a municipal leader meets with a bureau director or a deputy minister, the host might not have the authority to decide on the issues in question and instead must consult his or her superiors. Even if a person does have the authority, he or she can still use

[47] Interview with a researcher in the provincial government policy studies center of an eastern province, June 24, 2016.

[48] In some rare cases, a provincial party secretary can concurrently hold a deputy state-level position (e.g., a politburo member). In these cases, the provincial leader ranks above the minister, and the minister must meet with the provincial leader.

[49] Interview with a district commerce bureau official from Guangdong, January 15, 2020.

his or her relatively inferior position as an excuse to avoid making a commitment. Opportunities to meet with top ministerial leaders also save localities the costs of coordinating consensus among subdivisions of a ministry. Once a minister commits to an action, his or her ministry has some burden to mobilize cooperation and reduce tension between ministerial bureaus with conflictual interests, or between his or her ministry and other central authorities. Thus the coordination task that Beijing office staff described to me largely falls to localities of lower ranks, who go through painstaking negotiations with heads of ministerial departments to achieve cooperation in the absence of greater support.

A simple illustration: Imagine that two nearby cities have competing proposals on the location of a railway station, and the railway ministry has to choose between them. One of the cities is a deputy provincial city, and its party secretary was able to secure a meeting in person with the minister and plead the case for the city. The other city is just a regular municipality, and its party secretary got to meet with a deputy minister (or in a worse scenario, only a bureau director). It is not difficult to determine which city will get the station.

3.5.3 Idiosyncratic Factors

Systematic factors such as ranks or efforts might not explain every successful case. Some local governments have secured favorable central policy treatment because of factors or situations that cannot be replicated in other places. That is, they were lucky. Some of these factors were personal, and others were circumstantial.

Knowing the right person can be helpful in easing many of the challenges in policy solicitation. As noted earlier, localities mostly rely on their own efforts in building closer relationships with officials in the central bureaucracies. In some cases, local leaders might have already cultivated a good relationship with central officials in their prior positions. For example, transfers of officials between central bureaucracies and territorial administration have been common practice (e.g., Li & Zhou, 2005). Local leaders who worked in the central ministries can mobilize their previous connections to serve the local interests. The city N's incumbent party secretary used to serve as a bureau director under the NDRC. The city benefited tremendously from this experience, as the party secretary knows almost every bureau director very well. These directors would also "care for the dignity (照顾面子)" of their former colleague when he made requests for the city.[50] The reversal of this situation can also benefit localities. If a local leader is transferred to serve in the ministry, then local officials (e.g., directors of functional bureaus) enjoy the advantage of knowing someone well in the central bureaucracy when they lobby for policies. Some leaders have spent their entire careers in local governments but have created close relationships with certain ministries through prior communication and cooperation on projects that are in the jurisdictions of the ministries. When they are transferred to other places, these previously forged connections also become valuable assets, especially when these places need similar projects that the officials have accomplished in their earlier positions.[51] Some local leaders might happen to have been in the same cohort with a central bureaucrat in the cadre training programs of the Central Party School or similar cadre training institutions (Shambaugh, 2008). Such alumni connections may later save the localities some effort in approaching high-level officials in ministries where the bureaucrat serves.[52] But localities cannot anticipate or engineer these connections, as local leaders are appointed by superiors. They have no information in advance as to who will be appointed as their leaders or what kind of resources and connections they will bring.

Local leaders are not the only ones that might have the ears of central bureaucrats. Localities can also benefit from local socialites who have special channels to reach powerful figures in Beijing. The role of Pao Yue-kong in helping Ningbo achieve the status of separately planned city (计划单列市) is a good example. In the early 1980s, Ningbo was only a minor city. Cities with much greater national influence and higher status, such as Nanjing, had sought this status. Pao was at the time a shipping magnate and the richest man in Hong Kong, who became a close friend with Deng Xiaoping. China was desperately in need of overseas capital, and Pao was among the first overseas Chinese to invest in mainland China. Deng had also cultivated him because he sought the support of Hong Kong local elites during and after the negotiation with the United Kingdom on the handover of Hong Kong. The two's close relationship was manifested by numerous visits Pao paid to Beijing in the 1980s, and Deng invited Pao and his family

[50] Interview with a divisional chief B in the Beijing office of a coastal city N, October 15, 2019.
[51] Interview with a professor of public administration at Tsinghua University, July 17, 2015.
[52] Interview with a professor of political science at Tsinghua University, July 17, 2015.

to his home on occasion (Yu, 2012). In 1986, when local leaders of Ningbo, Pao's birthplace, wanted to elevate the city's status to achieve greater policy autonomy, they turned to Pao for help. Pao proposed to elevate Ningbo to a separately planned city during a family dinner with Deng, and Deng readily agreed.[53] Ningbo formally achieved the status in 1987 ahead of many other, more eligible cities because of Pao's intervention. Pao's personal connection with Deng was the only reason Ningbo was able to get ahead in this competition.

Similarly, when the Chinese central government announced a plan to build a railway from Beijing to Shenzhen (京九铁路) in the late 1980s, it was said that local governments in Jiangxi went to Beijing and met with the surviving member of a couple who had been founding revolutionaries of the People's Republic. She had been born in the Ji'an city of the province, and they persuaded her to use her influence to lobby for the railway to go through the city.[54] Ji and Ma (2021) also find that counties where retired revolutionaries were born can capitalize on their influence in lobbying the central government for railway benefits. However, many localities do not have such connections, and those who do may not be enterprising enough to identify and mobilize such resources.

Circumstantial factors that are exogenous to the parties involved can also affect the fate of infrastructure projects. For example, there may be sudden pressures from outside or a change in the macroeconomic environment. These factors might inadvertently empower certain parties in the bargaining or make their counterparts or competitors more vulnerable. Ministries are usually in a dominating position vis-à-vis localities; the localities want something from them in the form of scarce policy resources, and the ministries usually do not want anything from the localities. But these dynamics can change. For example, a ministry could have committed to certain policy goals (e.g., building a certain length of roads in certain areas of the country), but are found short at the end of the planning period. The ministry would need the cooperation of localities to meet their deadline. This would lead bureaucrats to speed approvals. The localities are also more likely to extract some policy concessions from a ministry at such times (e.g., the

---

[53] See (2018, November 16). 百年包玉刚 殷殷桑梓情 (*A hundred years of Yu-kong Pao, deep emotions for his hometown roots*), zhxww.net, retrieved from http://www.zhxww.net/zhnews4073/mskd/mskd_news/201811/20181116095628-2.asp.

[54] Interview with a bureau staff member in Shenzhen municipal government, October 6, 2015.

ministry may pay for a greater share of construction costs or loosen the regulation on a key parameter of the project).[55] In some other situations, the locality is tasked with a project that has an impending deadline imposed by the higher authority (i.e., the central government). The local government can strategically peg their own projects to that central project and use the deadline for the central project as a bargaining tool to force the ministry to expedite approvals. For example, in 2015 Hangzhou became the host city for the 19th Asian Games, which will take place in September 2022. Since then, the municipal government has initiated a massive infrastructure campaign, proposing the construction of more than a dozen subways, a new railway station (the Hangzhou West Station), and a new airport terminal with an underground train station. The municipal government packaged these projects as the "auxiliary projects (配套工程)" for the Asian Games, despite the fact that they will require investment exceeding those of the actual facilities of the games several times over.[56] These projects all received swift permissions to allow the construction to complete before the Asian Games. Such advantages have been the major incentive for local governments to bid for international events like the Asian Games. Most local governments actually lose money by hosting such events, but realizing large infrastructure projects makes them worth it.[57]

Although idiosyncratic factors are hard to study systematically, they do create more possibilities in the process of bottom-up policy solicitation. The outcomes of bargaining are not determined only by the relative political status and power of the participants. Instead, variables such as whether localities are endowed with exclusive access to key central decision-makers, whether they are adept in detecting timings during which their superiors are susceptible to pressure, and whether local leaders can entrepreneurially hedge against bureaucratic gridlock through political resources in hand, might produce outcomes that dramatically differ from people's expectations. Such possibilities explain why many localities, despite being structurally placed in a disadvantaged position in the hierarchy, still actively seek approvals for their projects.

[55] Interview with a bureau director of Development Research Center of the State Council, July 19, 2015. Interview with a deputy director of the general office of a district in Zhejiang province, August 20, 2015.

[56] Interview with a staff member at the Zhejiang Provincial Planning and Research Institute, December 24, 2016.

[57] Interview with a deputy director of the development and reform commission of a deputy provincial city, July 17, 2019.

3.5.4 Why the Hongqiao Station Got Built

The Hongqiao Station illustrates the importance of many of the factors this chapter has described. Shanghai is a centrally administered city. It enjoys the same political rank as a province. The city's party secretary is a member of the politburo, the CCP's top decision-making body. Built as a part of the Beijing–Shanghai high-speed railway program, Shanghai municipal government also dedicated a significant amount of effort to ensure the successful completion of the station.

Shanghai also benefited from personal and circumstantial factors. First, the project benefited from the 2010 Shanghai Expo. It was a six-month-long international exhibition that attracted more than 70 million visitors from all over the world. The only event that rivaled it as an opportunity to showcase China's economic development was the 2008 Beijing Olympic Games. The Chinese central government started preparation for the event in 2001. It appointed the party secretary of Shanghai as head of the preparatory committee. The secretary made the Hongqiao complex part of a list of "tribute projects (献礼工程)," and the ministries had no choice but to give "special treatment under special occasion (特事特办)" and expedite the required processes to meet the deadline.

Another non-negligible factor was the role of Liu Zhijun, who served as the railway minister between 2003 and 2011. Although Liu was arrested and removed from office under corruption charges in early 2011, he was widely credited as the "father of Chinese HSR (high-speed railway)" (e.g., Ma, 2011). During his reign at the Ministry of Railway, China started and completed the construction of more than 10,000 kilometers of high-speed railways. The annual investment in railway construction grew from 51.6 billion yuan in 2004 when he started his term to over 700 billion yuan in 2010 (Kato, 2011). Liu was infatuated with the construction of high-speed railways. He got the nickname "Leapfrog Liu (刘跨越)" for proposing that Chinese railway should embrace "leapfrog style development (跨越式 发展)." To achieve that goal, he employed an unorthodox style of leadership.[58] He was known as a "dictator" who did not welcome any questioning of his opinions. Unlike most officials at his level, he was also willing to

---

[58] See Dai, X. H. (2013, May 20). 铁道部窝案：多面刘志军 (*The Crimes in the Railway Ministry: the multiple faces of Liu Zhijun*), capitalweek.com.cn, retrieved from <IBT> http://.www.capitalweek.com.cn/2013-05-20/76213491.html.</IBT>

take responsibility for his decisions. He liked to make aggressive targets and often pushed his subordinates to work very hard. An official who had worked for him recalled, "If he wanted to see the results by a certain date, you had no other choices."[59] Liu was able to command deference in the ministry despite his ruthlessness, partly because he worked even harder than his subordinates. He often held meetings about details of a project at midnight. He always stood at the front of the train when a newly completed railway line had its first trial operation. Even when he realized he might be in trouble, he used the short period before his arrest to inspect over 7,000 kilometers of completed high-speed railways.[60] His dedication even earned him recognition from his critics. Some compared him to Sogo Shinji, the former president of the Japanese National Railway and the father of Shinkansen, the first modern express railway (Kato, 2011).

A charismatic and uncompromising leader, Liu paid a great deal of attention to the Hongqiao project. He saw the station, which would be the largest in the country, as his signature project. He visited the construction site twice in the spring of 2010 alone, and gave instructions on small details of the construction.[61] Liu was also a close friend with Yu Zhengsheng, who had become party secretary of Shanghai in 2007 and, like his predecessor, was the chairman of the preparatory committee for the Expo. Yu had been the party secretary of Hubei province (2001–2007), Liu's home province. One of the earliest high-speed railway projects, the one that connects Wuhan (the capital city of Hubei) and Guangzhou, was also approved and began construction during Yu's time in Hubei and under Liu's term as the railway minister.

The Hongqiao complex is a product of Liu, reflecting his unusual ambition and character. Liu's successors, in contrast, are poker-faced bureaucrats who follow the norms. Without an aggressive ally like Liu in the Railway Ministry, other places pursuing similar projects face much greater challenges in cutting through regulations and gridlock imposed by various ministries.

[59] Ibid.
[60] Ibid.
[61] See The Central People's Government of People's Republic of China. (2010, April 26). 刘志军：高标准、高质量建造百年不朽的精品工程 (Liu Zhijun, building a project of a century by upholding high standards and high quality), www.gov.cn, retrieved from http://www.gov.cn/gzdt/2010-04/26/content_1592633.htm.

3.6 Dynamics at the Sub-provincial Levels

So far the discussions have revolved around localized bargaining between the central and local governments. The fragmentation of decision-making authorities in the central bureaucracies allows local governments to take an active role in influencing the allocations of important policy benefits and produce varied outcomes. Superiors and subordinates of territorial administrations act much like the central bureaucracy and the localities. The structure of local governments in China generally replicates that of the central government (Lieberthal, 2004, p. 171). The functional departments of the local governments, like the central ministries, also hold regulatory and allocative power over their subordinates. For example, the provincial governments receive quotas for land conversion—an important mechanism for urbanization and local economic development (Whiting, 2011)—from the central government, and then disaggregate the quotas to municipalities, and the municipalities further disaggregate theirs to the counties (Cai, 2012, p. 26). Upper tiers of local governments (i.e., provinces, municipalities) also approve smaller projects (such as roads and factories) within their jurisdictions. Counties and municipality leaders similarly need to lobby the municipal and provincial bureaus respectively to procure more benefits. Although counties are no longer allowed to have Beijing offices, they establish offices in the capital cities of their provinces instead. The emergence of these "provincial capital offices" provides evidence that similar dynamics exist at the subnational levels.

There are also important distinctions at lower levels. The lower a government in the party-state's hierarchy, the greater is its responsibility for implementing policies rather than making decisions (e.g., Cai, 2008; Lee & Zhang, 2013). The township governments, which sit at the bottom of the party-state's hierarchy, are responsible for implementing all directives from the central to the county levels. The Chinese expression "A thousand threads from above, one needle point below" (Lee & Zhang, 2013, p. 1482) suggests the burden that falls on the lowest level of government. In these local-level governments, the divisions of specialty and duties among functional departments become blurred. Officials from different departments are often mobilized on an ad hoc basis to accomplish tasks assigned by superiors (e.g., Zeng, 2020). At medium levels such as cities, where the boundaries of functional departments are more solidified, local leaders form "leading small groups (领导小组)" to coordinate actions among different departments to implement policies or accomplish policy tasks assigned by superiors. The central bureaucracies, in this regard, are distinct from their local counterparts. Except on a few occasions when the central leadership has launched campaigns to mobilize the ministries to accomplish certain policy objectives (e.g., construction of the Three Gorges Dam), the ministries are not under significant pressure to cooperate or to make compromises. The few commissions (such as the National Security Commission) and central leading groups that aim to provide overall policy coordination over broad issue areas could not overcome the challenges of multiple lines of authorities when it comes to tackling a real problem in everyday governance (e.g., Lampton, 2015). Such fragmentation of authorities provides an ideal environment for the cultivation and consolidation of departmental interests, and also creates conditions for localities to influence central policymaking.

3.8 Measuring Attitudes of Chinese Local Officials

The analyses so far have produced two takeaways. First, the allocation of policy benefits by higher levels of government is a function of bottom-up, localized bargaining by territorial agents. Second, localities with greater bargaining power are more likely to secure policy benefits from superiors. In this section, I employ a survey of local officials to test whether the conclusions drawn from qualitative evidence are consistent with what Chinese local officials perceive on a daily basis.

3.8.1 The Respondents

Government officials differ from ordinary citizens in many dimensions. Crucially for my purposes, many of them are actually in a position to make decisions about infrastructure projects, or at least be involved in the decision-making process. They also have a better understanding than outsiders of the implicit rules or norms that govern interactions among different government units.

To recruit a sample of government officials, preferably those with decision-making authority (i.e., cadres), I worked with five official training institutions across China between Summer 2016 and Spring 2018. The names of these institutions are not disclosed to protect the identities of

Table 3.2 Descriptive Statistics of the Subjects (N = 893)

Variable	Mean
Male (1=male, 0=female)	0.62
Age	39.44
College degree or above (1=yes)	0.88
Party experience (years)	14.83
Length of service in government (years)	16.72
Rank at or above section chief (1=yes)[1]	0.55
Rank at or above deputy section chief (1=yes)[2]	0.79
Hold leadership position at work unit [单位] (1=yes)	0.50

1. Positions at the rank of section chief [科级] include: township executive, county bureau chief, and section chief in the bureaus of municipal government.

2. Positions at the rank of deputy section chief [副科级] include: deputy township executive, deputy county bureau chief, and deputy section chief in the bureaus of municipal government.

both the survey participants and those who helped implement the survey in these institutions. These schools host official training programs, and local governments regularly send young or mid-career cadres and officials to these programs. I distributed my survey questionnaires in the classrooms of these training programs and collected answers from the class participants. The faculty at the institutions verified that the classes where I distributed my survey questionnaires are attended exclusively by government officials.

The resulting sample includes 893 officials. The descriptive statistics are shown in Table 3.2.

This convenience sample, of course, does not perfectly represent Chinese officials. The composition of the sample depends on who happened to sit in that classroom when I distributed the questionnaires. Since it is nearly impossible to construct a representative sample of Chinese officials (perhaps the only organization capable of doing so is the Central Organizational Department), most surveys of officials as their subjects employ re-randomization within the sample to test causal hypotheses, as I do here.

Given the parameters, the quality of this sample appears to be reasonably good. Respondents came from 17 provinces, and they represent five out of China's six main regions, with only the northeast not represented.[62]

[62] These 17 provinces are Beijing, Tianjin, Shandong, Hebei, Zhejiang, Guangdong, Guangxi, Hainan, Hunan, Chongqing, Ningxia, Guizhou, Sichuan, Yunnan, Tibet, Qinghai, and Xinjiang.

Table 3.3 T-test of the Difference Between the Control and the Treatment Groups

Variable	Control	Treatment	p-value
Male	0.61 (0.49)	0.53 (0.48)	0.71
Age	39.12 (8.73)	39.71 (8.75)	0.33
College degree or above	0.88 (0.32)	0.88 (0.33)	0.71
Party experience	14.98 (7.93)	14.71 (7.63)	0.62
Length of service in government	16.40 (10.21)	17.00 (9.82)	0.39
Rank at or above section chief	0.53 (0.50)	0.56 (0.50)	0.49
Rank at or above deputy section chief	0.78 (0.42)	0.80 (0.40)	0.52
Hold leadership position at work unit	0.51 (0.50)	0.50 (0.50)	0.90

Standard errors in parentheses

More than 79% of those in the sample are officials at or above the rank of deputy section chief, and over 50% report that they hold leadership positions within their work units. The average work experience in the government is 16.72 years, much longer than the 10-year average in the benchmark study of this kind in the field (Meng et al., 2017). There are good reasons to believe that these officials have sufficient experience and knowledge on the ways in which government units operate to provide the insights I seek.

3.8.2 Survey Design and Results

Like all other modern governments, the CCP government claims that it uses sophisticated, well-calculated rationales to drive its policies, and the policies always put the interest of the people first. It is thus socially undesirable and politically risky for officials to admit that officials manipulate the policymaking process in order to serve their narrow departmental interests. To deal with such social desirability bias, I use an unmatched count technique (also known as the "list experiment") (Ahart & Sackett, 2004) to solicit genuine responses from the officials. I randomly divided the officials into two groups: the control and the treatment groups. Table 3.3 shows the descriptive statistics for the two groups and the p-value of the two-tail Pearson t-test for the group difference. The difference between the two groups is statistically indistinguishable across all variables, suggesting a satisfactory randomization.

To test the first hypothesis, which posits that the allocation of policy benefits by higher levels of government is a function of bottom-up solicitation by local agents, I asked the control and the treatment groups to answer the following question. The *italic* part only appears in the treatment prompt. Each respondent was asked to answer one of the prompts, and had no idea of the existence of a different prompt.

Question A

When planning and constructing large infrastructure projects (such as high-speed railways and highways), what factors should upper levels of government [上级政府] consider? Below is a list of factors. You do not need to point out which factor(s), but please choose the total number of factor(s) you think is(are) important.

A. *Whether the local government [地方政府] is actively lobbying for the project*
B. short-term cost of construction
C. long-term social and economic return
D. the demand of the local population

0 factor	1 factor	2 factors	3 factors	4 factors[63]

As we can see from the question, the only difference between the control and the treatment group is the inclusion of the key (sensitive) item in the options for the treatment group. If no one in the treatment group believes this item matters, then the answers from the control and the treatment group should have identical means. Conversely, if everyone in the treatment group thinks that item counts, the treatment condition should produce a mean one higher than the control condition.

---

[63] In the control prompt, the maximum number to choose is three factors.

To estimate the magnitude of the treatment, I regress the outcomes (i.e., number of factors that matter) on whether the respondents belong to the control or the treatment group. The coefficient of the result can be interpreted as the percentage of the sample who thought item A—the sensitive experimental item that many may be reluctant to admit through direct questioning—is an important factor.[64] The results are as follows (Table 3.4):

Table 3.4 The Role of Bottom-Up Solicitation

	Estimate	Std. Error	*t* value	Pr(>|t|)
(Intercept)	2.60741	0.08996	28.984	<2e-16 ***
Treatment	0.72125	0.05402	13.352	<2e-16 ***
Class fixed effect	Yes			

As the result suggests, an overwhelming majority—about 72.1% percent—of the sample respondents thought whether there is active local lobbying would influence the planning and construction of large infrastructure projects by the upper-level government. The result is statistically significant. The coefficient for the intercept is 2.6, which represents the average answer for the control group. This means that the respondents also consider the three factors in the control group, which reflect the typical technocratic calculation.

The second hypothesis predicts that localities with greater bargaining power are more likely to secure policy benefits from the above. To test this hypothesis, I ask the control and the treatment groups to answer the following question, where the *italic* part only appears in the treatment prompt:

Question B

In the development of a locality (or a department), we often face the problem that the leaders at the upper level of government *do not give enough attention or policy support* [上级领导重视不够，政策扶植力度不强]. Here we list some factors. How many of them do you think will affect

---

the level of support from upper levels of government to a locality (or a particular department)?

A. the development potential of the locality (or the department)
B. *whether there is an aggressive [强势] leader*
C. the quality and ability of the officials
D. the demand of the local people to the upper levels

0 factor	1 factor	2 factors	3 factors	4 factors[65]

The results are shown below (Table 3.5):

Table 3.5 The Role of Bargaining Power

	Estimate	Std. Error	*t* value	Pr(>|t|)
(Intercept)	2.46792	0.10006	24.665	< 2e-16 ***
Treatment	0.69911	0.06034	11.587	< 2e-16 ***
Class fixed effect	Yes			

More than two thirds, 69.9%, of the respondents thought that whether a locale or a department has a leader aggressively pursuing local interest would affect the level of support from upper levels of government. The term "aggressive" used here is a rather vague expression. It could indicate certain leadership styles, or it could also refer to the general power or influence of a department. Due to the limits of the survey design, we cannot clearly separate these two aspects. However, the results of the survey do echo some general points from the analyses made earlier in this chapter.

3.9 Conclusion

To briefly reiterate, the construction of high-speed rails involves complicated interactions between the central and local authorities. The fragmented

---

[65] In the control prompt, the maximum number to choose is 3 factors.

structure of authorities at the central bureaucracy produces bargaining space among the localities. Evidence from case studies, interviews, and surveys suggests that both systematic and idiosyncratic factors explain whether localities would succeed in their pursuit of acquiring preferential policies from their superiors. Chapter 4 will focus on factors that systematically set localities apart in their bargaining power.

4

The "Cardinals" and the "Clerics"

4.1 Introduction

Chapter 3 established the fact that bottom-up interest articulations are pervasive among Chinese localities. It also shows that most localities spare no efforts in asserting their interests. These findings raise the question as to whether there are factors that systematically predict which localities will succeed in their efforts to influence policymaking at higher levels.

This chapter turns to the administrative configurations of the party-state for answers. Within the CCP's Leninist hierarchies, the leaders of some localities (or functional departments) are appointed concurrent leadership positions at one rank above themselves (the cardinals). These localities with institutional representation at a higher level enjoy a wide range of advantages in localized bargaining. As Chapter 3 indicated, this includes easier access to decision-makers and bureaucrats at the top. This chapter explores another advantage: they have the institutionalized abilities to influence and even control upper-level policy agendas that directly affect resource allocation among themselves and their competitors. The cardinal localities are thus not only better connected than the cleric localities, but also better able to use their empowered positions to get resources. It is as if the cardinal localities were both player and referee in the same game, and cleric localities, who are only players, suffer the consequences.

Administrative status within government systems has long attracted scholarly attention in explaining variations in regional development outcomes. For example, De Long and Shleifer (1993) find that European cities ruled by absolutist princes had significantly less population than cities without an absolutist government between 1000 and 1800. They attribute this gap to the higher rates of taxation imposed by absolutist rulers and its chilling effect on population and economic growth. Bai and Jia (2019) find that prefectures gaining or losing the status of provincial capitals was associated with increase or decline of population and levels of urbanization in imperial China. They argue that provincial capitals have greater economic development than other

Localized Bargaining. Xiao Ma, Oxford University Press. © Oxford University Press 2022.
DOI: 10.1093/oso/9780197638910.003.0004

cities because of public employment and superior transportation systems. Campante and Do (2014) find that voters in U.S. states where the political capital is not in the biggest city have more difficulty holding politicians accountable, and that local corruption is greater and public goods provision is diminished. In the seminal use of "cardinals" and "clerics" analogy for members of the U.S. Congress, Berry and Fowler (2016) reference administrative status in describing how cardinals, who are chairs of appropriation subcommittees, divert more funding to their constituents than clerics, who are only members of congressional committees.

China scholars have also examined the impact of regional hierarchies and concurrent appointments at higher levels. For example, Huang (1999) finds that provinces whose leaders hold concurrent positions in the national leadership are under greater top-down control by the central government and thus more likely to faithfully execute policies desired by the central authority, such as inflation control. Sheng (2010, 2019) finds a similar pattern of increased local compliance with central mandates among localities whose leaders are integrated into party's central leadership. Other scholars have disputed the political control function of concurrent appointments (e.g., Bulman & Jaros, 2019; Lam, 2010). Bulman and Jaros (2019), for example, develop a typology that distinguishes economic and political functions of concurrent appointments among officials in China. The economic dimension refers to whether concurrent appointments advance the economic interests of the superiors or those of the localities. The political dimension refers to whether concurrent appointments increase superior control of subordinates or grant localities more policy autonomy. Based on these two dimensions, Bulman and Jaros construct a typology of four intergovernmental dynamics under concurrent appointments: control, co-optation, compromise, and concession. Analyzing a panel data set of Chinese municipalities, coupled with detailed case studies of three Chinese cities, they find little evidence that the central government more effectively controls those whose leaders have concurrent appointments. Instead, concurrent appointments might "function as a softer form of co-optation, whereby higher-level authorities offer lower-level units expanded resources and political voice in exchange for their support of higher-level priorities, or even as a concession to powerful local actors" (Bulman & Jaros, 2019, p. 235).

In light of others' findings, this chapter examines the role of concurrent appointments in localized bargaining. Overall, I find that concurrent appointments empower the localities to assert local interests in higher-level policymaking. Employing an original data set of two waves of provincial five-year plans—a crucial policy document that determines resource allocation at the provincial level—I find that cities whose leaders hold dual appointments in the provincial leadership team on average receive more policy attention in these provincial documents. This correlation remains robust after accounting for a series of social, economic, and political factors that might also explain variations in policy attention at the sub-provincial level. In addition, I find that provinces where there are more cities other than the provincial capital that are represented in the provincial leadership team tend to have a more decentralized, and less pro-provincial-capital policy plan. From this finding I conclude that a key reason concurrent appointments confer advantage is that they make it easier to restrain competitors for resources in higher-level policy deliberation.

The chapter proceeds as follows: I first discuss the dual appointment system of the Chinese party-state and how that affects localities' bargaining power in section 4.2. Section 4.3 then introduces provincial five-year plans, and present the main hypothesis along with a discussion of politics in the plan drafting process. Then I detail the empirical strategy and the data in sections 4.4 and 4.5. Sections 4.6 and 4.7 lay out the results of the analysis. The chapter concludes with implications of the finding beyond provincial five-year plans.

4.2 Concurrent Appointments: The Making of the "Cardinals"

As described in Chapter 3 and laid out in Table 3.1, the CCP has built an elaborate system of hierarchies that encompasses all party and state organs, territorial administrations, state-owned enterprises, social organizations (such as public hospitals, schools, universities, and newspapers), and even some nominally private entities (Ang, 2012; Burns, 1987; Manion, 1985; McGregor, 2010). Each organization and its leaders are assigned a rank in this system, from the state level all the way to the township. The assignments of power and privileges increase with rank. Officials at lower levels answer to their superiors in the same functional domain.

As noted in Chapter 2, concurrent appointments are ubiquitous in almost every domain of the party-state. For example, the director of a region's public security bureau, the main apparatus tasked with maintaining social stability and public safety, almost always carries a concurrent appointment at the higher level (Wang & Minzner, 2015). The provincial capital's party secretary is always a member of the provincial party standing committee. Leaders of territorial administrations or functional departments have concurrent appointments if they are also assigned another leadership position at the next level up. Figure 4.1 presents a simplified version of the hierarchies among territorial administrations. Places listed in bold font have officials who hold concurrent appointments. The party secretary of province 1, for example, concurrently holds a seat in the central leadership (most likely a seat in the politburo); the leader of city 1 in province 2 is concurrently a provincial-level leader (i.e., a member of the provincial party standing committee, a deputy governor, or vice chairperson of the provincial people's congress or people's political consultative conference); the leader of county 3 of city 2 in the same province is also a member of the city's leadership (i.e., a member of municipal party standing committee, deputy mayor, or vice chairperson of the municipal people's congress or people's consultative conference); the leader of township 2 in the same county is simultaneously a county leader (i.e., a member of county party standing committee, deputy county executive, or vice chairperson of the county people's congress or people's consultative conference).

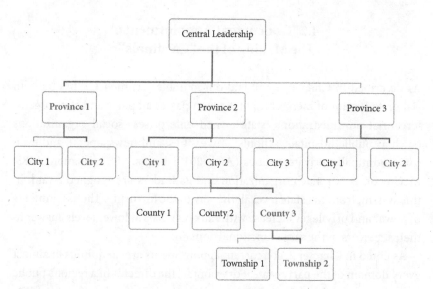

Figure 4.1 Concurrent Appointments of Territorial Leaders

Generally, the holder of concurrent appointments is the top leader of a region (e.g., party secretary). Occasionally, the second in line (usually the head of the government) has a concurrent appointment as well. For example, in the 1980s, the party secretary of Beijing held a seat in the politburo (as he still does), and the mayor was concurrently a councilor of the State Council, a deputy state-level position. Likewise, both the party secretary and the mayor of Shenzhen were members of the Guangdong provincial party standing committee from 2000 to 2005 (both offices turned over once in that period, but the appointments remained the same).

Concurrent appointments reflect the CCP's roots in the Leninist party system as well as dynastic Chinese rule. The party secretaries of Moscow sat in the politburo of the Soviet Communist Party, and the party secretaries of Ha Noi and Ho Chi Minh City are concurrently politburo members of the Vietnamese Communist Party (Malesky, 2008). Likewise, many regional governors in the Ming dynasty (1368–1644) received the concurrent title of "censor in chief," which allowed the governors to indict officials in their jurisdictions (Guy, 2017, p. 42). The reign of the Yongzheng Emperor (in office 1722–1735) of the Qing dynasty (1644–1911) established a tradition of giving governors the concurrent titles of senior vice president of the Censorate and members of the Board of War, both of which were elite positions in the imperial court (Guy, 2017, p. 59). Some regional governors, such as those of Guangdong, also held the concurrent position of salt commissioners (Guy, 2017, p. 311).

Scholars of contemporary China have explored the strategic functions of concurrent appointments. Some argue that the central government uses them to enhance its top-down control (e.g., Huang, 1999; Sheng, 2010, 2019). Economic reform has ushered in an era of decentralization, which gives rise to rampant localism (Jaros, 2019; Landry, 2008). Officials with dual appointments at the central level may find their careers lie with the center rather than with the localities they serve, and therefore are more likely to enforce costly central policies (such as inflation control or revenue remittance) in their jurisdictions. Yet, institutions often serve purposes that their founders do not foresee (Hall & Thelen, 2009; Hou, 2019), and Chinese localities are not only passive takers of central arrangements. Institutions that are established to strengthen central control can also become resources or channels for localities to influence their superiors. Comparativists have also found that inclusion of territorial actors in national institutions is a mechanism that allows localities to push central policy course in their favor (e.g., Tarrow, 1994; Wibbels, 2005).

Before I discuss the benefits associated with concurrent appointments, I should mention that the assignment of these dual appointments is not random. Officials in places or departments with political, economic, or strategic importance are more likely to be dually assigned. For example, the party secretaries of provincial capitals are ex officio members of the provincial party standing committee, and the city with the largest economy (other than the provincial capital) in a province typically also holds a seat in the provincial leadership (for example, the party secretary of Suzhou is a member of the Jiangsu provincial party standing committee). The prominence of these localities would affect their ability to obtain resources such as railway stations. The concurrent appointment is essentially an institutionalized recognition of these places' importance. However, superiors also use concurrent appointments to strategically give underlings greater capacity. For example, the fact that Hubei province has only one sub-provincial center (the provincial capital, Wuhan) has long hampered the province's economic development. The provincial authority granted the party secretary of Xiangyang, a city in the northern part of the province, a seat in the provincial party standing committee in the hope of developing the city into a sub-provincial center (Bulman & Jaros, 2019). Similar logic also applies to functional departments. The directors of public security bureaus at different levels, for example, were routinely given the concurrent title of the law and politics commission chairperson—an ex officio member of the party standing committee at various levels—when Zhou Yongkang, a now disgraced domestic security chief, attempted to strengthen the influence of the police apparatus within the regime (Wang & Minzner, 2015). As this chapter will explain, having representation at a superior decision-making body makes a big difference for localities or departments seeking to gain more policy resources from their superiors.

Chapter 3 explained that the dual appointments grant the localities easier access to the ears of decision-makers at higher levels. Having one's request articulated and heard is the first step in getting something from others. An appointment at a higher level provides local leaders platforms and qualifications (as discussed in Chapter 3) to communicate with their superiors, who hold the power in allocating resources. Yet the multilayered hierarchies of the party-state often cramp or distort flows of information, particularly those from the grassroots (Lorentzen, 2014). This chapter discusses a more powerful source of influence that also attends dual appointments.

Directly participating in the decision-making process, which concurrent appointments make possible, proves a more important source of influence than having the ears of those who make decisions. Superiors make decisions that affect their subordinates such as allocation of resources among subdivisions, and promotion, removal, and transfers of junior officials. While local officials might appear proactive in competing with their peers, they have little space to maneuver when it comes to following the mandates of superiors. Leaders of regions who have a concurrent membership among their superiors have the power to act on behalf of the province (or other superior levels), but the incentive to act on behalf of their own localities at the expense of competitors for resources. As I have established, competition for policy resources can be fierce, and such resources are often scarce. It creates a situation akin to the "conflicts of interest" in many professional settings. On the one hand, the leader is now empowered to make many important decisions that would affect a larger group of subordinate localities. On the other hand, the leader's interests are also tied to one of these localities that his decisions would affect. The "conflict of interest" arises when a local leader is able to make a jurisdiction-wide decision but in the meantime still prioritizes the interests of one of the subdivisions of that jurisdiction that he directly governs.

If the attempt to gain policy resources is a race, territorial leaders who have dual appointments get to start earlier, by having the ear of decision-makers, and essentially act as referees of the race. They can arbitrarily declare themselves as the winners, while other participants must simply watch. In the following section, I test this theory by examining provincial five-year plans, to discover whether municipalities with representation in the provincial leadership gain an upper hand in policy bargaining.

4.3 Measuring Policy Bargaining: The Provincial Five-Year Plans

Measuring the process and outcomes of policy bargaining requires surmounting numerous challenges. First, most bargaining takes place in closed-door meetings, and their content is not available to the public. The outcomes of these bargains are only selectively observable. Local governments tend to boast about successful outcomes but not to mention unsuccessful attempts, and thus their own accounts reflect bias. It is also very difficult to compare bargaining outcomes across issue areas. For example, policy bargains might include permission for a local project and the designation of a national special economic zone, and it is difficult to compare the outcomes of these two disparate situations. To overcome these challenges, this chapter uses provincial five-year plans to capture the dynamics of policy bargains among municipalities. The formulation of five-year provincial plans involves intense bargaining among localities seeking to insert their policy preferences into the document. They are also among the most important policy documents at the provincial level, guiding policy actions for the provincial government and all of the tiers below it (e.g., cities, counties). The text within them reflects the provincial government's view of policy priorities. They are also readily compared, as all Chinese provinces issue them, in a similar format, at around the same time. Finally, provincial plans are also digitized and easily accessible to the public, making them an ideal subject for scholars to study intra-provincial policy dynamics. The document, therefore, serves as a good, observable outcome of localities' bargaining efforts.

The tradition of five-year plans for social and economic development is a legacy of the planned economy era. The first national five-year plan was initiated in 1954, and provinces, cities, and counties made their own five-year plans at that time. These plans set binding targets of production for firms and localities. Since the 1990s, the nature and content of five-year plans at different levels began to change. They became a combination of both goals and guidance, with less emphasis on binding targets of production for officials to fulfill (Naughton, 1996). The provincial five-year plan is like the national five-year plan but with a reduced scale. A provincial five-year plan typically has the following components: a brief review of the achievements during the past five years; a lengthy statement of governing philosophy for the next five years; overall development goals, including targets for key social-economic indicators; and more detailed goals and plans for specific areas of governance, such as economic restructuring, regional balance, urbanization, rural development, transportation, trade, social welfare, and environmental protection. Unlike the national plan, which only references general principles, the provincial plans give the details of specific policy actions. For example, a provincial five-year plan will list individual infrastructure projects in highways, railways, airports, subways, and ports planned for the province, including the total amount of investment in these areas and the expected timeline of each project.[1]

The plan drafting process at the provincial level is similar to that of the national plan (Heilmann & Melton, 2013, p. 593). Provincial governments first rely on the reports of functional bureaucracies (i.e., provincial bureaus) and territorial authorities (i.e., city governments) to compile a list of policy priorities at the provincial level. This is a good chance for technocrats who have different domains or lines of reporting to assert their interests. The provincial authorities then aggregate these requests into coherent documents. They coordinate among sub-provincial territorial administrations and provincial bureaus to ensure that the finalized plans not only represent local and departmental interests but also reflect the developmental priorities that the provincial leaders seek to pursue. Cutting or adding is necessary in the coordination process. Projects or plans that contradict provincial leaders' vision or are considered redundant are removed or downplayed. Bargaining, trade-ups, and concessions take place between the provinces and the local units on which parts should be left out and which parts should be expanded.

Many China observers might question the utility of the five-year plans—to what extent do local governments treat them seriously? Some scholars and pundits often dismiss the plans as nothing more than "wish lists." It is true that policy goals are often not accomplished on time. Localities also sometimes vastly outdo the goals set by the plans. But scholars have contended that these documents play a crucial role in coordinating policy actions among different segments and layers of government. For example, Heilmann and Melton (2013) argue that these plans provide localities "an official authorization of local development ambition and discretionary policy-making power" (p. 592). Provincial governments establish institutions to conduct annual and mid-term evaluations of lower levels of governments' implementation of the plans based on binding or suggestive targets that become a part of the evaluation of local officials' performance (Heilmann & Melton, 2013, p. 603). Local officials have greater policy leverage when they advocate for projects that appear in the provincial plans to receive permissions from functional bureaus of the provincial government and loans from banks. Even unwilling bureaucrats may comply. Projects included in the provincial plans also qualify for subsidies from provincial governments. Thus, provincial plans,

---

[1] For example, see Section 1, Chapter 8, "Building a Modern, Comprehensive Transportation System" in the *13th five-year plan of Guangdong Province*, pp. 96–101.

like other institutions that might seem useless in authoritarian contexts to those who understand them as democratic mechanisms (such as a constitution), serve as a focal point that allows authoritarian elites to coordinate collective actions, especially those against rulers' transgression of the power-sharing agreement, which in turn contribute to the stability of authoritarian rule (Boix & Svolik, 2013; Myerson, 2008; Svolik, 2012). This applies to high-speed railway projects much as it does other projects, and in fact, provinces must apply for these projects rather than cities. Having a project included in the provincial plan signals provincial willingness in undertaking the project to the center, and also shows that the province has reached a basic consensus internally. As a result, individual sentences in provincial five-year plans can be the subject of intense lobbying by localities, functional bureaucracies, and other organizations (Naughton, 2005, p. 8).

The provincial party leadership plays a central role in the plan drafting process. A "special committee" or "leading group" under the supervision of the provincial government assembles the initial draft.[2] At the national level, the National Development and Reform Commission takes the lead in drafting the national five-year plan (Shirk, 1993). At the provincial level, the provincial development and reform commissions are responsible for the bulk of the work.[3] This begins with a wide consultation process. The commission elicits input and suggestions from city officials, members of provincial bureaus, state-owned enterprises, social organizations, private entrepreneurs, scholars, and leaders of the democratic parties. The procedure of enlisting suggestions from outside the government might make the drafting process appear neutral and technocrat-driven, but politics play a pivotal role. In an interview at the Zhejiang Urban and Rural Academy of Planning and Design, a staff member told me that despite being a nominally independent entity from the government, his agency always seeks the opinions of the local government leaders first when tasked to formulate plans for local development projects. Then they calibrate the ideal plans to meet the demands of the leaders. While an outsider might not be able to identify bias in the final product, the visions of local leaders shape the plans from the very beginning.[4]

---

[2] Interview with a staff member in the provincial government policy studies center of an eastern province, June 24, 2016.

[3] Interview with a researcher in the provincial government policy studies center of an eastern province, June 24, 2016.

[4] Interview with a staff member at the Zhejiang Provincial Planning and Research Institute, December 24, 2016.

Once the consultation process concludes, the provincial party committee holds the ultimate authority over the plan. Procedurally, the provincial party committee is supposed to convene once, following a deliberation among the provincial government's executives, to discuss and finalize the draft. But in fact, administrative records show that there are many pre-meetings, and most details are likely settled before the official meeting. The annual meeting of the provincial people's congress reviews the plan at this point and typically rubber-stamps it.

Provincial leadership prepares and approves the plan, which would likely give local leaders with dual positions in provincial leadership advantages in asserting their interests. This suggests the following main hypothesis:

> *Policies related to a city will be disproportionally represented in the provincial five-year plan when the city's leader is concurrently a member of the provincial leadership.*

This hypothesis does not assume that in a counterfactual world without political manipulations, policy proposals would be uniformly distributed among cities within a province. Cities in China vary considerably in size, which means that their needs differ and that the cost/benefit analysis of providing resources to a particular city will also differ. Thus, I assume that in an environment without political interference, the provincial government makes policies based on each city's endowments, as predicted by the technocratic solution model. The variations in policy attention therefore should be associated with indicators such as the size of each city's economy, population, and revenue. Cities that generate more economic activities, have a larger population, or collect more revenue should receive more policy attention from the provincial government. The residual variations—those that the technocratic rationale cannot explain—reveal the impact of political bargaining.

The prominent status of provincial capitals in China provides a compelling point of evidence to this hypothesis. In every province, the party secretary of the provincial capital city is an ex officio member of the provincial party standing committee. In the meantime, these cities receive disproportional policy favors from the provincial government. Take the capital city of Shaanxi, Xi'an, as an example. Although the city only accounts for 22.8% of the province's population and generates 30.9% of provincial GDP (2014 data), my own analysis shows that 40.6% of all policies related to cities in the province's 13th five-year plan (2016–2020) related to Xi'an. Likewise, Jaros's research shows that provincial governments' launch of large-scale infrastructure projects, implementation of new policy experiments, and attempts to find a host city for major foreign investments have consistently prioritized provincial capitals (Jaros, 2019).

In many provinces, particularly in inland provinces, the provincial capital is the only city where the city party secretary has a provincial dual appointment. In these provinces, the capital city tends to dominate the policy agenda of the provincial government. Prominent examples include Sichuan, Shaanxi, Hubei, Hunan, Gansu, Yunnan, and Anhui. Table 4.1 presents a list of cities with concurrent appointments in 2010 and 2015, the years before the

Table 4.1 Cities With Concurrent Appointments at the Provincial Level (2010 and 2015)

Province	Cities	Province	Cities
Hebei	Shijiazhuang, Tangshan, Qinhuangdao (2015)	Hunan	Changsha
Shanxi	Taiyuan	Guangdong	Guangzhou, Shenzhen, Zhuhai (2015)
Inner Mongolia	Hohhot, Baotou	Guangxi	Nanning
Liaoning	Shenyang, Dalian	Hainan	Haikou, Sanya
Jilin	Changchun, Yanbian	Sichuan	Chengdu
Heilongjiang	Harbin	Guizhou	Guiyang, Zunyi (2015)
Jiangsu	Nanjing, Wuxi, Suzhou	Yunnan	Kunmin
Zhejiang	Hangzhou, Ningbo, Wenzhou (2015), Zhoushan (2015)	Tibet	Lhasa, Shigatse (2015)
Anhui	Hefei	Shaanxi	Xi'an, Yan'an
Fujian	Fuzhou, Xiamen	Gansu	Lanzhou
Jiangxi	Nanchang, Ganzhou	Qinghai	Xi'ning
Shandong	Jinan, Qingdao	Ningxia	Yinchuan, Guyuan (2015)
Henan	Zhengzhou, Luoyang	Xinjiang	Ürümqi
Hubei	Wuhan, Xiangyang (2015), Yichang (2015)		

Note: The rule for selection is that a city party secretary held a provincial leadership position (members of the provincial party standing committee, deputy governors, or deputy chairpersons of the provincial people's congress or people's political consultative conference) for at least six months in any of the given years. The year in parentheses means that the city's leader only had a dual appointment for that year. Cities without a note had dual appointments in both years.

publication of the 12th (2011–2015) and 13th (2016–2020) five-year plans, respectively. The first city in each province is the provincial capital. Chinese netizens call attention to this, mockingly, by referring to these provinces using the name of their capital. For example, they call Sichuan the "Chengdu province."[5]

There are also many provinces where cities other than the provincial capital are represented in the provincial leadership. These include the five separately planned cities (计划单列市)—Dalian, Qingdao, Ningbo, Xiamen, and Shenzhen.[6] Other provinces incorporate leaders of sub-provincial economic centers (other than the provincial capital) into the provincial leadership. In Jiangsu province, for example, the party secretaries of Wuxi and Suzhou have long been ex officio members of the provincial party standing committee, along with the provincial capital Nanjing.[7] Places with historical or political importance might also receive special treatment. The party secretaries of Ganzhou (where the Jinggangshan revolutionary base is located) and Yan'an (which housed the CCP headquarters from 1935 to 1947) all sit in their respective province's party standing committees. In these provinces, the capital cities are no longer the only ones represented in the provincial leadership. They have to share policy spoils of the provincial government with localities that have an equal institutional footing in the provincial leadership, and are less likely to dominate the resulting provincial policymaking agenda. In other words, the distribution of policy benefits is expected to be more decentralized in these provinces.

This leads to the second testable hypothesis, an extension of our main hypothesis:

In provinces where cities other than the provincial capital have leaders with dual appointments, provincial capitals receive less advantage than in provinces where the provincial capital is the only one.

To be clear, the assignment of dual appointments to non-capital cities is unlikely a result of political capture (i.e., localities use their own resources to

---

[5] For an example, see 怎么看待"四川市成都省"？ *(How should we think about "Sichuan City of Chengdu Province?")*, zhihu.com, retrieved from https://www.zhihu.com/question/275077466.

[6] The separately planned cities enjoy considerable economic autonomy in their respective provinces. They report directly to the central government on many social and economic issues, such as revenue, finance, and customs. These cities enjoy a formal rank as sub-provincial cities.

[7] Since 2019, the party secretaries of Wuxi have not been made provincial party standing committee members.

exchange [or lobby] for leadership positions in the province). Likewise, it is not the case that provincial leaders groom leaders of places that have already received many policy benefits for leadership positions. Provincial leaders and their deputies are known as the "centrally managed cadres (中管干部)" in the CCP's personnel system. Central party leaders, not provincial leaders themselves, appoint the members of provincial leadership.[8] In fact, members of leadership groups at every level are selected by those above their level, not the top leader of that unit.[9] It is however true that the center tends to appoint party secretaries from economically more prosperous cities into the provincial leadership lineup (Bulman & Jaros, 2019), the same cities that technocratic decision-making might favor. Thus I take city-level characteristics into consideration when comparing policy influence. Some cities with dual appointments are small, in fact: The party secretaries of Zhoushan, which has the smallest GDP of any city in Zhejiang, carried the concurrent title of deputy provincial governor from 2012 to 2015.[10] Such cases make it easier to examine whether dual appointments confer policy advantages in addition to those naturally awarded to large and/or economically significant cities.

4.4 Measuring Distribution of Policy Attention in Provincial Five-Year Plans

I use the number of city-related policies in the recent two waves (12th and 13th) of five-year plans (2011–2015, 2016–2020) to measure the degree of policy attention each city receives from its provincial government. The more a city gets mentioned in these documents, the more likely it is that it will receive policy resources from the province in the planned period.

There are usually three occasions where provincial five-year plans mention cities. The first is in connection with planned cross-regional development. For example, the Zhejiang provincial 13th five-year plan (hereafter "Zhejiang plan") referenced a plan to expand four metropolitan areas that include four

---

[8] The provincial party committee does typically recommend candidates for vacancies in the provincial leadership. The center can reject them and appoint its preferred candidates, however.

[9] This corresponds to the CCP's system in which each level is accountable to the party organ at one level up (O'Brien & Li, 1999).

[10] The concurrent appointment for Zhoushan's party secretary during this period was likely driven by the city's designation as a national-level new area (i.e., the Zhoushan Archipelago New Area) in 2011. The concurrent appointment allowed the city to mobilize provincial resources to support the development of the new area.

core cities (Hangzhou, Ningbo, Wenzhou, and Jinhua-Yiwu) and five satel-
lite cities (Shaoxing, Huzhou, Jiaxing, Zhoushan, and Taizhou). The Zhejiang
provincial government also referenced a plan to build a "grand corridor of
technology and entrepreneurial innovation" in the west part of Hangzhou
(杭州城西科创大走廊), an ambitious urbanization project aiming at repli-
cating Silicon Valley in Zhejiang. The second occasion for mentioning cities
is in relation to projects within particular cities. These are projects proposed
and executed by individual city governments that appear in the five-year
plan to enrich the lists of the provincial plans (i.e., allowing provinces to take
credit for cities' development). The Zhejiang plan referenced the construction of new lines of the Hangzhou, Ningbo subway systems, and the expansion programs of the Ningbo–Zhoushan Port and the Hangzhou Xiaoshan
International Airport. The third type of reference involves projects or plans
proposed by the province or the cities that would require permissions or
investments from the central government. These are usually large-scale infrastructure projects controlled or regulated by relevant central bureaucracies. The provinces usually file the application on behalf of the cities, for
permissions needed for these projects from the central government. The
Zhejiang plan referenced projects to construct the Hangzhou–Taizhou and
Hangzhou–Wenzhou high-speed railways. In sum, the frequency with which
a city's name appears in these documents corresponds to the overall policy
attention the city receives from the provincial authority.

I tally the mentions of China's 333 municipalities in the plans of 27
provinces and autonomous regions.[11] I then calculate the total number of
mentions by each province, and divide the number of each city by the provincial total. It is formalized in the following equation:

$$Share_i = \frac{NM_i}{\sum_1^P NM_i}$$

NM_i denotes the number of mentions for each individual city i, and $\sum_1^P NM_i$
denotes the total mentions of P cities in a province. In this way, each city's

---

[11] These do not include plans by the four centrally administered cities (Beijing, Shanghai, Tianjin,
and Chongqing), which formally enjoy the status of provinces. They negotiate their policies directly
with the central government.

policy treatment is standardized to a score ranging from 0 to 1, with 0 indicating the city receives no attention at all from the provincial government, and 1 indicating that the city completely dominates the provincial policy platform to the extent that the plan mentions no other cities in the province.

The average share across the country is 8.1% (or 0.081) per city for both waves of plans. This is consistent with the fact that each province has on average 12.3 cities. There are nonetheless huge variations across cities. A handful of cities receive zero mentions in their province's plan, and some cities receive as many as more than 60% of all mentions in their provincial plan. The standard error of the national average is 0.079 for the 12th plan and 0.081 for the 13th plan.

The contrast between the cities with and without a seat in their provincial leadership is stark. Figure 4.2 shows the kernel density distribution of proportions between these two groups of cities in the two waves of plans. An overwhelming majority of cities without a seat in the provincial leadership (as shown in the solid line) receive less than 10% of the total mentions in their provincial plan, whereas most cities with a seat in the provincial leadership (shown in dashed line) on average receive more mentions than the former. The average share for cities without a provincial leadership seat is 6.0% (with a standard error of 3.8%) for the 12th plans and 5.7% (with a standard error of 3.4%) for the 13th plans. The average share for cities with

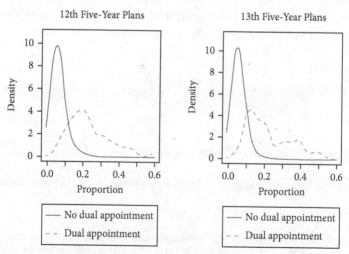

Figure 4.2 Comparison Between Two Types of Cities

a seat in provincial leadership is 23.3% (with a standard error of 12.1%) for the 12th plans and 22.7% (with a standard error of 12.2%) for the 13th plans. A simple two-tailed t test suggests that the difference between the two groups is statistically significant at the 0.001 level for both waves.

4.5 Estimating the Power of Representation in Provincial Leadership

To explain the variations in policy attention from the provincial government, the main explanatory variable is a dummy of whether the party secretary of a city holds a concurrent appointment at the provincial level (1 if yes, and 0 otherwise). These positions include members of the provincial party standing committee, deputy governors, or deputy chairpersons of the provincial people's congress or people's political consultative conference. Table 4.1 presents the names of cities with provincial dual appointments in 2010 and/or 2015. The two years are chosen because they are the years before the announcement of the respective 12th and 13th five-year plans, and most bargaining regarding the details of the plan should be taking place during that time. For leadership turnovers that took place in the middle of these two years, I adopt a rule of six months (i.e., I treat those who held the dual appointment for at least six months in that year as having it). This coding strategy yields 50 cities for the year 2015 and 41 cities for 2010. Of the 27 provinces, 17 have at least one city beyond the provincial capital that is represented in the provincial leadership team, and some provinces (such as Jiangsu, Zhejiang, and Hubei) have as many as three cities represented in provincial decision-making bodies.

Cities represented in the provincial leadership teams are clearly distinct from those that are not. In line with the greater likelihood that cities that are large in population, GDP, or fiscal revenue have officials with dual appointments, Figure 4.3 shows the kernel density distributions of GDP, population, and revenue data from both years between two groups of cities. As evidenced in the plot, the distributions for cities without seats in provincial leadership (solid line) are highly skewed toward the left (i.e., smaller values), whereas the distributions for cities with representations in provincial leadership (dashed line) are much less skewed to the left.

To determine whether dual appointments provide localities a political mechanism that can be separated from their size, I control for GDP,

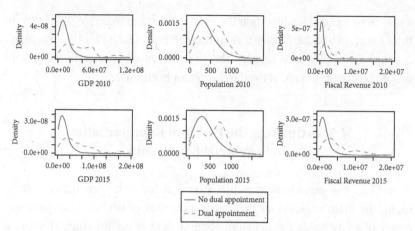

Figure 4.3 Comparison of Socioeconomic Indicators Between Two Groups of Cities

population, and fiscal revenue in analyzing the data.[12] Because we are comparing the overall influence of cities, I choose to use the aggregated numbers instead of the per capita measures of GDP and fiscal revenue. To ensure that the data is normally distributed, I take natural logarithms of these indicators.

In addition to these three indicators, I also include a dummy variable indicating whether the city is a provincial capital city. This control rules out the possibility that the provincial capitals, which are often the largest cities in Chinese provinces, solely drive the dynamics identified.

The outcome variable—the share of each city's policy attention in relation to the provincial total—depends on the number of cities in a province. Cities in a province with very few cities could have artificially large shares of mentions despite that policy attention is relatively equally distributed among the cities. To account for this bias, I also include a control variable that indicates the number of cities in a province. This variable does not vary among cities in the same province.

Finally, I also include provincial dummies to account for unobserved heterogeneities at the provincial level.[13] These heterogeneities could include but are not limited to factors such as whether a province is a coastal province,

---

[12] The socioeconomic indicators are from 2010 and 2015, the year before each wave's announcement, and are acquired from China Data Online.

[13] In the model specification where I include provincial dummies, I drop the variable that counts the number of cities in a province, because both variables do not vary within a province and therefore cannot be accommodated in a same model. The provincial dummies, however, do capture the variations in number of cities.

whether the province is economically more developed, whether the province as a whole receives more policy benefits from the central government, and whether the province might have a different plan drafting process than the others. Scholars of China have cautioned against direct comparison of cities from different provincial contexts (e.g., Hurst, 2006, pp. 468–469). The inclusion of provincial fixed effects reduces noise when we compare cities from different provinces and allows us to focus on within-provincial variations.

This leads to the following model specification:

$$Share_i = Dual\ Appointment_i + Controls_i + Provincial\ Dummy + \varepsilon_i$$

in which $Share_i$ is the share of policy attention each city receives in their provincial plans; $Dual\ Appointment_i$ is a dummy indicating whether the city party secretary is concurrently a member of the provincial leadership; $Controls_i$ denotes an index of control variables at the city level that accounts for social, economic, and other political factors that might also explain the variations on the left-hand side. $Provincial\ Dummy$ accounts for unobserved variations at the provincial level.

4.6 Baseline Results

I employ ordinary least squares (OLS) models to estimate the correlates of policy attention. Tables 4.2 and 4.3 present results for the 13th and 12th five-year plans respectively. For each wave, I present seven different model specifications. The first model only has the key explanatory variable, namely whether the city's party secretary sits in the provincial leadership. The second through the fourth model each add a socioeconomic indicator as a control variable. The fifth model further controls for whether the city is a provincial capital. The sixth model controls for the number of cities in a province, and the seventh model replaces that control with provincial dummies that account for unobserved provincial-level heterogeneities.

The key explanatory variable is positively and significantly associated with the outcome across all seven specifications in both waves. This lends strong support to the hypothesis that positions within the provincial leadership give cities an advantage in procuring policy support from the province. The magnitude of the effect is also substantial. Based on the fully specified model with

Table 4.2 13th Five-Year Plans

	Dependent variable: share of each city's mention						
	(1)	(2)	(3)	(4)	(5)	(6)	(7)
Appointment in Provincial Leadership	0.169*** (0.009)	0.180*** (0.011)	0.179*** (0.011)	0.173*** (0.011)	0.095*** (0.013)	0.079*** (0.012)	0.053*** (0.010)
GDP (logged)		−0.006 (0.005)	−0.003 (0.006)	−0.031** (0.013)	−0.026** (0.011)	−0.015 (0.010)	−0.010 (0.011)
Population (Logged)			−0.006 (0.006)	−0.002 (0.006)	−0.007 (0.006)	−0.003 (0.005)	0.001 (0.005)
Revenue (logged)				0.026** (0.011)	0.021** (0.009)	0.015* (0.008)	0.034*** (0.010)
Provincial Capital					0.138*** (0.015)	0.138*** (0.013)	0.107*** (0.011)
Number of Cities						−0.006*** (0.001)	
Constant	0.057*** (0.003)	0.100*** (0.032)	0.116*** (0.035)	−0.060 (0.081)	−0.012 (0.071)	0.061 (0.065)	−0.344*** (0.077)
Provincial Fixed Effect	No	No	No	No	No	No	Yes
Observations	333	282	281	281	281	281	281
R²	0.531	0.564	0.566	0.575	0.678	0.738	0.852
Adjusted R²	0.529	0.561	0.561	0.569	0.672	0.732	0.834

Note: *p<0.1; **p<0.05; ***p<0.01

a provincial fixed effect (model 7), being represented in the provincial leadership is associated with a 5.3% greater share of mentions than cities that are not represented in the provincial leadership in the 13th five-year plan (Table 4.2), and a 3.3% increase in the 12th five-year plan. The magnitude of the increase is large, as the average share of mentions is about 8.1%. In addition, this effect already accounts for economic and political factors such as the provincial capital dummy, suggesting an average, non-capital city could also enjoy a huge boost in policy attention if its party secretary gained a seat in the provincial leadership.

Among the three socioeconomic indicators, only revenue is positively and significantly associated with the outcome in the fully specified model (model 7) for both waves. A one-unit increase in logged revenue is associated with a 3.4% increase in the 13th plans, and a 2.7% increase in the 12th plans. The size of GDP and population are not correlated with the outcome. This set of

Table 4.3 12th Five-Year Plans

	Dependent variable: share of each city's mention						
	(1)	(2)	(3)	(4)	(5)	(6)	(7)
Appointment in Provincial Leadership	0.173*** (0.009)	0.183*** (0.011)	0.181*** (0.011)	0.177*** (0.011)	0.097*** (0.016)	0.081*** (0.015)	0.033*** (0.012)
GDP (logged)		−0.007* (0.004)	−0.005 (0.005)	−0.021 (0.013)	−0.019* (0.012)	−0.009 (0.011)	0.003 (0.011)
Population (Logged)			−0.006 (0.006)	−0.003 (0.006)	−0.007 (0.006)	−0.002 (0.005)	0.0004 (0.005)
Revenue (logged)				0.014 (0.010)	0.016* (0.010)	0.010 (0.009)	0.027*** (0.010)
Provincial Capital					0.117*** (0.017)	0.116*** (0.016)	0.102*** (0.013)
Number of Cities						−0.006*** (0.001)	
Constant	0.060*** (0.003)	0.177** (0.071)	0.163** (0.072)	0.212*** (0.080)	0.196*** (0.075)	0.169** (0.067)	−0.336*** (0.080)
Provincial Fixed Effect	No	No	No	No	No	No	Yes
Observations	333	282	282	282	282	282	282
R^2	0.518	0.550	0.552	0.555	0.617	0.693	0.825
Adjusted R^2	0.517	0.547	0.547	0.548	0.610	0.686	0.804

Note: *$p<0.1$; **$p<0.05$; ***$p<0.01$

results can be interpreted in two different ways. The first is that GDP data is not as reliable as fiscal revenue data, as many studies have found rampant manipulations in Chinese local officials' reporting of the data (Wallace, 2016). Therefore, the non-robust coefficient of GDP can be interpreted as a result of measurement errors. The second and related explanation is that provincial leaders value revenue more than GDP, as revenue is tangible and harder to manipulate (Lü & Landry, 2014), and therefore tend to divert more policy attention to localities that are able to collect more revenue.

The provincial capital dummy is positively and significantly associated with the outcome. Being a provincial capital helps boost a city's share of mentions by more than 10% (based on model 7) in both the 12th and 13th provincial plans. This result has already accounted for whether a city has its party secretary in the provincial leadership (i.e., the key explanatory variable). This means that in a province with multiple cities holding seats in the provincial leadership, the provincial capital on average still stands out as the clear winner in the race for policy favors. This result supports claims of a "capital bias" in China's political economy (Bai & Jia, 2019). Unlike many other countries, including the United States, where political capitals (be it national or subnational) are often geographically separate from economic centers, China is known for having political centers that are also hubs of economic activity. This phenomenon is closely related to the fact that the Chinese government plays a central role in the national economy (Huang, 2008; Pei, 2016).

4.7 Multiple Dual Appointments and Within-Provincial Decentralization

The analyses so far lend support to the core hypothesis that cities whose leaders hold concurrent provincial appointments receive more policy attention in the provincial plans. This association is indicative that special positions in the hierarchy allow the cities to advance their interests by controlling provincial policymaking agenda. To lend further support to this intuition, we test the extension of the core hypothesis, which predicts that the provincial policy platform will be less biased to favor the capital city—whose party secretary is always a member of the provincial party standing committee—if party secretaries from other cities also sit in the provincial decision-making bodies. The underlying idea is that if other cities also hold the same rank in the provincial leadership, they will likewise use that power to solicit a share of the policy spoils from provincial government, and their success will constrain the ability of the provincial capital to dominate the provincial policymaking process. Thus we should expect more decentralized distribution of policy attention in provinces with more cities with officials with dual appointments.

To test the extended hypothesis, I create a measure that looks at the distribution of policy attention among major cities in a province. The measure is the share of mentions of the provincial capital divided by the share of the most-mentioned city other than the provincial capital. It is represented in the following formula:

$$Ratio = \frac{s_{capital}}{s_{MMC}}$$

in which $s_{capital}$ represents the share of the provincial capital, and S_{MMC} represents the share of the most-mentioned city other than the provincial capital. Since in almost every province, the capital city receives the most mentions,[14] this measure is also equivalent to the ratio between the most and the second most-mentioned cities. This measure aims to capture the dynamics of competition between the provincial capital and its closest competitor. A ratio close to 1 suggests a relatively equal distribution of influence between the provincial capital and its competitor, and, as the ratio increases, it suggests that the provincial policy platform is more tilted to favor the provincial capital.

Provincial capitals clearly enjoy advantages. For the 13th five-year plans, the nationwide average ratio is 2.05. This means that, on average, provincial capitals are mentioned twice as often as the second most-mentioned cities in each province. Only three provinces have a ratio smaller than 1, and their ratios are either around (Shandong) or above 0.9 (Hebei, Inner Mongolia). This suggests that even in provinces with very weak provincial capitals, the amount of policy attention the provincial capitals receive is not very much different from that of the cities that receive the most attention. The remaining 24 provinces have a ratio greater than 1, 13 have a ratio greater than 2, five have a ratio greater than 3, and one has a ratio greater than 4. In Sichuan province, the provincial capital Chengdu is mentioned 4.6 times more than the second most-mentioned city, Deyang. For the 12th five-year plans, the nationwide average ratio is 1.83. The province with the greatest ratio is Yunnan. The provincial capital, Kunming, is mentioned four times more often than the second most-mentioned city, Qujing.

The unit of analysis here is province, and China only has 27 provinces,[15] which does not give me much degree of freedom in statistical analysis. I choose instead to compare the means of these two measures between

[14] There are a few exceptions. For example, in the 13th plans the capital cities of Hebei, Shandong, and Inner Mongolia did not receive the most mentions.

[15] This number includes provinces and autonomous regions. It does not include centrally administered cities (Beijing, Shanghai, Tianjin, and Chongqing), since no cities are under their administrations. It also does not include Hong Kong, Macau, or Taiwan.

Table 4.4　Comparison Between Two Types of Provinces

	Type 1 Provinces	Type 2 Provinces
Ratio (13th plans, 2016–2020)	1.81	2.47
Ratio (12th plans, 2011–2015)	1.41	2.22

provinces where the only city with dually appointed officials is the provincial capital, where there are more than one. The comparison is presented in Table 4.4. Type 1 provinces correspond to those where at least two cities have representation in the provincial leadership. Type 2 provinces are those where only the provincial capitals are represented in their provincial leadership. For the 13th five-year plans, there are 17 type 1 provinces and 10 type 2 provinces. For the 12th five-year plans, there are 14 type 1 provinces, and 13 type 2 provinces.

As shown in Table 4.4, provinces in which the provincial capital is the only city represented in the provincial leadership have a clear "capital bias." The ratio between the capital and the most-mentioned city other than the capital is much larger among the type 2 provinces (the difference is on average 0.66 for the 13th plans and 0.81 for the 12th plans). Despite the small sample size (N = 27), the difference between the ratios of the two groups is statistically significant at the 0.1 level for both waves. This comparison provides suggestive, although in no way conclusive, evidence that the incorporation of multiple cities in the provincial decision-making bodies dilutes the provincial capital's ability to dominate the provincial policy platform.

This exercise also provides a sneak peek into the trends of recentralization that have occurred since Xi Jinping took power in 2012. Decentralization, or empowering the local authorities, has long been hailed as the hallmark of China's reform and opening-up (Landry, 2008; Montinola et al., 1995; Xu, 2011). Since 2012, the party center has taken a series of measures to tighten its control over local authorities (Heilmann, 2018). Measures include enforcing stricter intra-party disciplines, sending out local inspection teams, and cracking down on local initiatives that occurred without higher-level authorizations. This campaign seems also to have caused centralization within provinces (Lu & Tsai, 2019). Concentration of power in the hands of provincial authorities naturally leads to the rise of provincial capitals, where most provincial institutes and headquarters of province-owned enterprises are located. As shown in Table 4.4, the ratios between the capital and the most-mentioned city other than the capital increase conspicuously from the 12th to the 13th plans, regardless of whether the province has more than one city represented in the provincial decision-making bodies. In other words, Chinese provinces have witnessed a significant policy shift toward building larger provincial capitals over the past decade or so.

Numerous anecdotes suggest that the central government initiating tighter control over the localities explains the shift. In 2018, an inspection team sent by the Central Disciplinary Commission criticized the Jiangsu provincial party committee and government for "not enabling Nanjing (the provincial capital) to fully perform its capital function."[16] Nanjing ranked third in terms of GDP within the province for a long time. It recently surpassed Wuxi but still stands far behind Suzhou. In a response letter submitted four months after the inspection, the Jiangsu provincial party committee promised the central authority that it would redirect provincial resources to strengthen the development of Nanjing. It listed detailed steps, including further enhancing infrastructure development in subways, railways, airport, and the port in Nanjing.[17]

In the age of rising superior control and reducing local initiatives, institutional representation in provincial decision-making bodies becomes even more important for local development. As shown in Tables 4.2 and 4.3, a seat in the provincial leadership is associated with a 5.3% increase in the proportion of mentions in the 13th plans and 3.3% in the 12th plans (which were formulated before Xi took power), after accounting for the effect of provincial capitals. Cities without representation at higher levels (the "clerics") have few other means but to bow to the "cardinals" in this recent wave of recentralization at the provincial level.

4.8 Conclusion

This chapter tries to understand how localities' relative positions in the party-state's hierarchies affect their bargaining power. To do so, it exploits variations in the amount of policy attention Chinese cities receive from their respective

[16] See Wang, J. (2019, October 26) 被巡视组点名"作用发挥不够"，这两个省会城市公布整改进展 (Being criticized by the inspection team for not fully performing the provincial capital functions, these two cities announced how they plan to improve,) sohu.com, retrieved from http://www.sohu.com/a/271430639_260616.

[17] Ibid.

provincial governments. As the evidence suggests, economics alone does not determine the distribution of policy resources, at least as signaled in the provincial five-year plans. The positions of the cities' officials within the party hierarchy also play a role. Those with simultaneous appointments in the provincial leadership tend to receive policy attention from the provincial government that other factors do not explain.

The analysis provides a perspective on how formal institutions and informal bargaining over policy favors interact with one another in the context of China. Past research on the distribution of policy favors in China has focused exclusively on the informal aspects, such as traits and behaviors of individual leaders in charge (e.g., Shih, 2008; Shih et al., 2012). The institutional context of these leaders (i.e., their positions, ranks) has received little attention.[18] Studies in other contexts, such as the US congress (e.g., Berry & Fowler, 2016) and post-soviet Russia (e.g., Baturo & Elkink, 2014), find that the positions held by individual leaders play an important role in politics. In fact, even in contexts like post-Soviet Russia, where charismatic leaders have significantly eroded the authority of institutions, research finds that the power of office still dominates the personal influence of officeholders (Baturo & Elkink, 2014). This study substantiates the power of institutions in behind-the-door bargaining by investigating the relationship between localities' positions in the party-state's hierarchies and the policy treatments they receive.

The findings in this chapter help us to understand the widening inequality among Chinese localities, despite continuing central and local efforts in promoting egalitarian development across regions. In the book *Beyond Beijing*, Yang (2002) identifies that the cleavages of regional inequalities do not only develop along the east–west or the costal–inland dimensions, but also grow within each province between central and marginal cities. Recent scholarship has also given a greater amount of attention to within-province variations in development (e.g., Bulman, 2016; Jaros, 2019; Zhang & Liu, 2019). While some provinces have achieved egalitarian development among their cities, others have witnessed the rise of provincial capitals as megacities, and a widening gap in economic development within provinces (Jaros, 2019). This chapter considers the provincial power structure, in particular the variations of localities' positions in the hierarchies of the party-state, a rather

---

[18] A notable exception is Huang (1999).

time-invariant characteristic, as one of the primary causes for widening intra-provincial inequality.

The empirical analysis in this chapter has several limitations. The primary concern is the measurement of policy treatment, which is the number of times each city appears in its provincial five-year plan. First, I treat each appearance as qualitatively the same, and lump together mentions of localities under different occasions or policy areas. But different areas may reflect differing advantages. Second, appearances in government planning documents do not always translate into real policy actions. The implementation of policy plans is also a process involving significant bargaining. As shown in earlier chapters, being included in the superior's plan is only the first step among many in the long journey leading to the completion of a high-speed railway project. The very factor examined in this chapter could also exacerbate the gap among localities during the policy implementation process. To deal with these problems, I look at the construction of high-speed railways directly, in the chapter that follows.

5

The Political Geography of High-Speed Railways

5.1 Introduction

This chapter offers empirical evidence on the core hypothesis advanced in the theory chapter, which attributes the local variations in central investments in rail infrastructure to the differential bargaining power of territorial administrations. I argue that the CCP does not function, at least with respect to disbursing resources to localities, as a unitary, strategic actor. Thus a bottom-up perspective illuminates how numerous local bureaucratic entities—each with the incentive to maximize its locality's share of resources (Levi, 1988; Niskanen, 1971)—compete with one another to solicit investment from the center. Those with greater bargaining power exploit their advantageous positions within the regime to project their demands to leaders at higher levels, and also exclude the voices of those agents with competing demands. They are, therefore, better positioned to secure preferential policy treatments from above.

I draw on a host of evidence to test this argument, using an original, monthly data set on the start and end dates of construction for 54 high-speed railways from 2004 to 2014. In line with Chapter 4, simultaneous appointments serve as a proxy for institutionalized bargaining power within the bureaucracy. Findings show cardinals—provinces and municipalities with leaders with simultaneous appointments—are able to secure a project from the center and start construction earlier than clerics. This association is robust after accounting for two competing explanations, namely the "loyalty purchasing" and "technocratic solutions," in the analyses at the provincial level. I establish this by including a series of controls such as whether the provincial leaders have connections with the party's incumbent general secretary, whether they are children of revolutionary veterans ("princelings"), the economic and population size of each province, the size of local revenue, and the previous railway passenger volume of each province. Cardinal cities are

Localized Bargaining. Xiao Ma, Oxford University Press. © Oxford University Press 2022.
DOI: 10.1093/oso/9780197638910.003.0005

not only among the first to construct the high-speed railways; they are also permitted to build more stations within their jurisdictions. At the same time, the association with speedy completion of projects is much weaker. Projects take several years, and they can exceed the average tenures of party secretaries. In such cases a new secretary has less ability to claim full credit, as the project began under their predecessors, and they may be less eager to exert effort. Another crucial finding is that personal ties with top party leaders and princeling status do not correlate with apparent advantage in obtaining resources for a locality. These null findings support one of the core implications of the book's theory. That is, in policy arenas with fragmented authorities, central leaders have limited ability to manipulate policies to their associates' favor. Instead, localized bargaining between local authorities and central bureaucracies govern the distribution of policy benefits. Those with greater institutionalized bargaining power can secure more favorable policy treatment from their superiors.

The chapter proceeds as follows. Section 5.2 provides background information on the empirical test—the central–local interactions in the construction of high-speed railways. Then I briefly review the core argument and hypotheses advanced in the theory chapter. Section 5.4 introduces the data and estimation strategy. Section 5.5 presents the empirical tests and results. Section 5.6 concludes the chapter.

5.2 Central–Local Interactions in the Construction of High-speed Railways

The unveiling of the Medium- and Long-Term Railway Plan in 2004 marked the beginning of China's high-speed rail era. In that year—which is the 40th anniversary of the world's first high-speed rail, the Japanese Shinkansen, began service between Tokyo and Osaka—the per capita gross domestic product (GDP) of China was 1,508 US dollars (US$). According to the World Bank, China became the first country with a per capita GDP below US$ 7,000 to invest in developing a high-speed rail network (Lawrence et al., 2019, p. 1). China's late entry did not prevent its rapid rise to leadership in the high-speed rail sector. By the end of 2018, China had opened over 29,000 kilometers (km) of high-speed lines, with design speeds ranging from 200 km/hour to 350 km/hour, longer than those in every other country combined. The high-speed lines carried 2.005 billion passengers in 2018 alone, accounting for 60.4% of all passengers using nonurban rail networks in that year. By the end of the first quarter of 2019, the Chinese high-speed lines had transported over ten billion passengers in total.[1] As of this writing, it undoubtedly exceeds the 11 billion passengers the Japanese Shinkansen carried in its first five decades.

Policy analysts attribute China's success in building and using high-speed rail to the country's long-term planning and close cooperation between the railway authority and the local governments (e.g., Lawrence et al., 2019). This assumes that the center and local share a division of labor in which the center specializes in planning, while the local focuses on implementation and construction. As Chapter 3 explained, the National Development and Reform Commission, the Ministry of Transport, and the China Railway Corporation jointly formulated the Medium- and Long-Term Railway Plan and must each approve all changes to it. However, such changes do occur. When it was first published in 2004, the plan proposed the construction of 12,000 km of passenger-dedicated high-speed railway tracks by the end of 2020. The plan then went through two waves of revisions. The first revision occurred in 2008, and the goal of construction by 2020 increased to 16,000 km. The second revision took place in 2016, which further increased the length of tracks by 2020 to 20,000 km. The 2016 plan also proposes a goal of 38,000 km by 2025 and 45,000 km by 2030. Instead of binding local actions, the plan functions as a fluid institutional recognition of local ambitions to pursue more rail infrastructure. With each iteration, individual localities engage in heated lobbying for references to projects they desire that amount to a couple of sentences at the most.

The Ministry of Railways was the primary target for such lobbying until its dissolution in 2013. Founded in 1949 following the Soviet example, the ministry was, according to both Chinese and English-language media, an "independent kingdom."[2] In addition to internal departments that oversaw the investment, construction, and operation of railways, the ministry supervised an independent police force, a court and procuratorate system, universities, middle and primary schools, research institutes, hospitals, publishers, newspapers, finance institutions, and numerous subsidiary companies and

---

[1] See Yang, J.G. (2019, May 14). 中国高铁累计运输旅客超百亿人次 (Chinese high-speed rails carried 10 billion passengers), Peoplerail.com, retrieved from http://www.peoplerail.com/rail/show-435-406000-1.html.

[2] See, for example, Lian, Q. C. (2013, March 14). 铁道独立王国的覆灭 (The collapse of the railway independent kingdom), cn.nytimes.com, retrieved from https://cn.nytimes.com/china/20130314/cc14lianqingchuan/.

institutes. It had 18 regional railway administrations managing daily operations and services on the ground, and the directors of these regional administrations held the same rank as municipal party secretaries. At its peak, the ministry employed over two million staff.[3] By the early 2010s, it was one of the last vestiges of the planned economy era in the State Council, the smaller-scale but nonetheless Soviet model Ministry of Aerospace Industry, Ministry of Coal Industry, and the Ministry of Radio, Film and Television having been reformed and transformed into firms or other semi-independent entities decades earlier.

There were several attempts by central leaders to dissolve the ministry before 2013. The most recent one was in 2008. Policy insiders widely circulated a proposal to merge the railway ministry with the Ministry of Transport before the 2008 ministerial reform.[4] It was a part of a larger reform program to reduce the number of ministries and streamline the administrative structure at the center. Worrying that they would lose their autonomy, officials of the ministry began to lobby central leaders in late 2007 to prevent the merger, successfully convincing them that the railway system was too important to be put under the jurisdiction of another ministry.[5] Practical considerations also hindered the reform. The need to manage and fund the ministry's numerous subsidiary entities and its two million employees constituted a big liability for any institution seeking to merge with it. The central leaders also worried that drastic changes could induce repercussions (i.e., instabilities) among the ministry's staff, and such concern in turn reinforced the bargaining power of the ministerial officials who resisted reform. The reform of the ministry eventually did not work out in 2008. The longevity of the Ministry of Railways signaled the enormous amount of vested interests associated with it. But in spring 2011, Railway Minister Liu Zhijun was arrested on charges of corruption. Several high-level bureaucrats within the ministry were also removed at the same time. Replacement of ministerial leadership by officials from outside weakened the internal resistance to reform. A high-speed train crash in Wenzhou a few months later also gave opponents of the ministry the opening they needed.

---

[3] See (2013, March 11). 建行行长：铁道部200万员工都发了信用卡 (*Chairman of Bank of Construction: We issued credit cards to the two million railway employees*), Sina.com.cn, retrieved from http://finance.sina.com.cn/money/bank/credit/20130311/051114783757.shtml.

[4] See Li, W. (2012, July 22). 铁路改革回顾：三道难坎 三次流产 (*Review of railway reforms: three hurdles and three failures*), news.sohu.com, retrieved from http://star.news.sohu.com/20120722/n348748114_2.shtml.

[5] Ibid.

The 2013 ministerial reform broke up the ministry into two entities. The departments in charge of regulation, monitoring, and supervision of the rail sector became the National Railway Administration (NRA), a bureau under the Ministry of Transport. The departments in charge of the railway service as well as the planning, design, and investment of railways became the China Railway Corporation (CRC), a wholly state-owned enterprise. The 18 regional railway administrations were likewise reorganized into subsidiary companies of the CRC. In addition, several large enterprises specializing in manufacturing of railway equipment (e.g., China Railway Rolling Stock Corporation and China Railway Construction Corporation), previously managed by the ministry, were placed under the supervision of the State-Owned Assets Supervision and Administration Commission (Lawrence et al., 2019, p. 8). Other organizations previously affiliated with the ministry, such as the railway police, have been gradually detached from the ministry and reassigned under the jurisdictions of other agencies.[6]

The CRC plays the role that the ministry had played in planning the construction of new high-speed rail projects, working with local governments. Each project involves establishing a joint venture of these two entities. The CRC and the investment vehicles of the provinces involved are the major shareholders. The shareholders usually provide 50% of the equity and rely on bank loans or corporate debt for the rest of the finance. The provinces often contribute their share of equity in the form of land (Lawrence et al., 2019, p. 9), which the joint ventures use as collateral in bank loans. The joint ventures typically function as entities to finance the infrastructure and manage contracts. They do not provide services. Once the rail is completed, the tracks and stations are transferred to the regional rail administrations, and the joint venture charges the train operators for the use of the infrastructure. The CRC determines the rate of charge. This model allows the CRC to maintain a coherent operational network (Lawrence et al., 2019, pp. 58–59). In a few cases, such as the Beijing–Shanghai high-speed railway, the joint ventures also perform services after the construction is completed. They collect ticket revenue and contract regional railway administrations for infrastructure maintenance and train services. This model allows the joint ventures to profit from the asset, but also creates some special zones within the national railway network operated by the CRC. Most railways adopt the first model, and in the second model, the CRC is also the main shareholder of

[6] The railway police, for example, are now under the jurisdiction of Ministry of Public Security.

the operating company. Overall, the CRC maintains its control over the operation of the national high-speed railway network.

Of course, the formation of the joint ventures follows the lengthy approval process described in Chapter 3. Local government takes the lead in calibrating and negotiating various details of the proposal to meet the regulators' requirements in this process. The CRC, which receives numerous proposals on a regular basis, plays a minimal role in helping local governments expedite approval. In fact, as I have mentioned, the CRC can be an obstacle, especially if it has a conflict with other ministries over project details, which requires localities to mediate between them to coordinate consensus. Once a project receives approvals, the local governments are also responsible for relocating households or facilities in the railway path. Property owners who are unhappy with the rates of compensation can significantly delay the process (known as the "nail-houses" in Chinese) or even cause social unrest (Deng, 2017; Hess, 2010). Local governments often combat this resistance by holding groundbreaking ceremonies before they finish requisitioning the land. If this pressure does not work, the ceremony may precede actual construction's start by months or years.[7]

High-speed railway projects bring tangible and intangible benefits to localities. Many lines have not yet achieved profitability, but those that do will make payments to local governments based on their shares in the joint venture. Lines and stations also benefit localities by reducing travel times, greenhouse emissions, road congestion, and road accidents, and by promoting local economic growth through improved access. The World Bank once calculated the economic returns to four Chinese high-speed rail projects that it had financed by taking these aspects into account, and the estimated returns range from 8% to 18% (Lawrence et al., 2019, p. 70). This return is significant, given the average return to equity among listed firms in the Chinese stock market was only 1.17% in 2018.[8] In addition to social and economic benefits, high-speed rails also raise localities' media profiles. The groundbreaking and opening ceremonies of new lines often generate significant media publicity

---

[7] The construction of the Jinhua–Ningbo railway, for example, started almost two years after the groundbreaking ceremony was held in 2017. The slow progress in land requisition was the main cause of delay. Interview with a railway expert in Beijing, January 16, 2020.

[8] The average return to asset in the same year is 5.68%. See Evergrande Research Institute. (2019, November 29). 中国上市公司质量报告 (*Quality research report of Chinese listed firms*), dfcfw.com, retrieved from http://pdf.dfcfw.com/pdf/H3_AP201912111371755979_1.pdf.

at the national level, which can attract increased investment in the localities and may boost the careers of local leaders.[9] As discussed in Chapter 2, the construction brings jobs and lucrative contracting opportunities to local residents. Many train stations are built not in the urban centers but in population-sparse suburbs (Zhang et al., 2020), which boosts land prices in these remote places and contributes to local extra-budgetary revenue.

The reliance on bank loans and corporate bonds in financing the construction of new tracks has created huge liabilities for both CRC and local governments. While the debt figures of the local governments remain opaque, the debt of CRC has been well publicized. According to the annual report of CRC in 2018, CRC has accrued a debt of 5.27 trillion RMB in total. The company paid 490 billion RMB on the debt, both principal and interests, in 2018 alone.[10] Thus the debt takes a heavy toll on the company's profitability. According to a more detailed report published in 2019, a majority of the company's 18 regional railway administrations are losing money, and the company as a whole only made two billion RMB of profits in 2018 despite having eight trillion RMB in assets (see Table 5.1). Local governments likely have accumulated a significant amount of debt as well, as they typically own 50% of the joint ventures created for the construction of new lines, and thus 50% of the joint venture's debt.[11] Many local governments also contribute their share of equity to the joint ventures by first taking loans using land as collateral. Thus they enter the joint ventures with an increased debt burden due to the railway project.

The amount of debt as revealed in the CRC's statistics suggests that for a long period of time, financial constraint has not been a primary concern for local governments.[12] A joint venture with central and local state-owned enterprises as the shareholders has privileged access to credit. Local branches of commercial banks consider joint venture firms created for such infrastructure projects to be high-quality clients, not only because of the sheer size of the loans but also because of a stable expectation regarding debtors' (i.e., the central and local governments) ability to pay back the money. The

[9] There is mixed evidence on whether increased media publicity actually increases officials' likelihood of obtaining a promotion. For recent discussion in the literature, see Gueorguiev and Schuler (2016) and Lu and Ma (2019).

[10] See Zhu, B. L. (2019, May 3). 负债5.27万亿创新高！中国铁路是经济火车头还是灰犀牛？ (*The debt of CRC reaches a new height of 5.27 trillion*), Sohu.com, retrieved from http://www.sohu.com/a/311558459_100008055.

[11] The numbers on local governments' debts remain opaque.

[12] The Chinese central government only began to deleverage and regulate excessive borrowing by local governments in 2018.

Table 5.1 The Financial Situation of Regional Railway Administrations (2018)[a]

Regional Railway Administrations	Net Profit (100 million RMB)	Asset (100 million RMB)	Debt Asset Ratio
Taiyuan	95.58	4036.90	39.81%
Wuhan	65.49	4029.09	33.82%
Zhengzhou	54.08	3728.45	29.46%
Shanghai	17.09	10061.25	36.95%
Xian	16.89	3339.71	36.88%
Nanchang	14.27	2970.85	14.96%
Jinan	−6.72	2633.76	32.38%
Hohhot	−20.05	2431.43	58.14%
Qinghai-Tibet Rail	−23.01	1605.76	27.68%
Guangzhou	−26.05	6262.79	38.08%
Nanning	−35.72	2899.87	45.79%
Urumqi	−43.69	1928.08	39.58%
Kunming	−49.49	2670.39	38.09%
Lanzhou	−57.48	4068.95	40.93%
Beijing	−61.39	5922.30	41.80%
Shenyang	−113.56	5890.00	48.35%
Harbin	−125.88	2832.60	70.72%
Chengdu	−126.75	9015.00	41.01%
CRC	20.45	80023.39	65.15%

[a] The table is adapted from a news report on the financial situation of CRC. See "The profitability of the regional railway administrations is disclosed for the first time." *Traveldaily.cn*, October 30, 2019, https://www.traveldaily.cn/article/132585.

Chinese central government also routinely uses monetary policy to encourage investments in infrastructure at times of economic slowdown. For example, the Chinese central government announced a four trillion yuan stimulus package following the 2008 global financial crisis, most of which went into building new infrastructure. According to economist Wu Jinglian, the package translated into three trillion yuan additional investments in the high-speed railway sector.[13]

[13] See Quan, X. J. (2018, August 8). 前车之鉴：2008年4万亿基建投资 (*Lessons from the past: the four trillion infrastructure investment in 2008*), jrj.com.cn, retrieved from https://finance.jrj.com.cn/2018/08/08083224922596.shtml.

Local governments therefore spare no efforts in soliciting permissions for rail infrastructure from the central government. Despite having no authority to approve the construction of new projects, local governments highlight proposals for new high-speed lines in local development plans and in government work reports during each year's local people's congresses to signal their intention and to coordinate preparatory work at local level. A quick search of the provincial 12th five-year plans (2011–2015) shows that every province except Tibet had proposed construction plans for high-speed railway lines.[14] Regional leaders also pay frequent visits to the CRC (as they did to the Ministry of Railways) and other central ministries in Beijing, meeting with central bureaucrats and seeking to make a strong case that their proposals should receive priority.[15] The Chinese media term such trips to Beijing "*pao bu qian jin* 跑部钱进" (literally meaning "run into ministries and then money comes in," and it is a homophone to the Chinese term for "running forward quickly"). In some extreme cases, local officials have even tacitly tolerated local mass mobilizations that demand a local high-speed railway station in order to gain some leverage in their bargaining with the upper-level governments (see Chapter 6 for more details).

Regional and temporal variations in getting high-speed rail projects from the central government represent observable outcomes in such bottom-up bargaining. Why do some localities get permissions for construction while others do not? Why do some localities, such as Yancheng, as noted in the introduction chapter, have to wait much longer than others? Localities do not lack motivation or financial leverage to build high-speed rails. The bigger challenges, as shown in Chapter 3, lie in the cumbersome procedures to bring on board various specialized agencies at the center. The critical task is not only to compel these institutions to acknowledge the feasibility of the project and throw in their support, but also to outdo potential competitors. Variations in localities' abilities (i.e., bargaining power) in achieving these goals are key drivers of disparities in rail infrastructure.

The high-speed railway program also provides an ideal setting to test the effect of localities' bargaining power. First, it is something completely new

---

[14] Based on my online search of 31 provinces' development plans.

[15] For an example, see Qu, S. N. (2016, March 3). 云南省委省政府在京与中国铁路总公司举行工作会谈 (*Yunnan party secretary and governor have meeting with the head of the China Railway Corporation in Beijing*), cpc.people.com.cn, retrieved from http://cpc.people.com.cn/n1/2016/0303/c117005-28169059.html.

for China. The existing (by the beginning of 2019) 29,000 km of high-speed rails across China's 30 provincial units were all built after 2004.[16] While pre-existing levels of the same type of infrastructure in the same regions might affect investments in projects such as highways or ports (also known as "path dependence"), the high-speed rails started with a clean slate. This fact makes localities' bargaining efforts a more prominent determinant of the allocation of policy benefits. Second, the institutions that regulate the construction and operation of the railways have not experienced fundamental changes in this relatively short period of time. This means that the outcomes of bargaining, which take place only several years apart from each other, are comparable. In contrast, the process of seeking to build an airport was very different in the 1980s. Airport construction used to be under the jurisdiction of the Central Military Commission, and now the authority mostly rests with the Civil Aviation Administration. So a longitudinal study of other types of projects would amount to comparing apples to oranges. Finally, the central government pledged that the high-speed rail network would eventually cover most municipalities with at least one million in population. So there is no province that cannot compete for railway service.[17]

Localities and their leaders have a considerable stake in the timing of the approval and construction of railway projects to serve their areas. Getting ahead in securing approval for one project likely forecloses the chances (at least for a long period) of a competing project close by. Even the difference of only one or two years in starting time is also meaningful, since most high-speed railways took just two to three years to complete.[18] The average tenures of provincial and municipal party secretaries are 3.76 years and 3.49 years, respectively (Landry et al., 2018, p. 1082). This means that falling behind in getting approval might not allow the incumbent regional leaders to claim credit when the lines are completed. These factors alleviate the concern that some localities do not wish to compete; as most of them do, outcomes largely reflect the localities' bargaining power.

---

[16] The only province that does not have high-speed rail is the Tibet autonomous region.

[17] This does not even exclude Taiwan, as China proposed a cross-strait railway bridge to extend the high-speed railway to the island. See Wang, Y. (2016, March 5). 十三五期间北京香港高铁将贯通 拟建设北京-台北高铁 (*The 13th five-year plan will have Beijing-Hong Kong high-speed rail completed, and proposes Beijing-Taipei high-speed rail*), Guancha.cn, retrieved from https://www.guancha.cn/Project/2016_03_05_353005.shtml.

[18] For example, the construction of the Shanghai–Hangzhou high-speed railway only took 20 months, and the 1318 km-long Beijing–Shanghai high-speed railway, the longest ever constructed, only took 38 months to complete.

5.3 Testable Hypothesis

This section briefly recapitulates the core argument advanced in Chapters 2 and 3: that bottom-up bargaining by local governments explains variations in the allocation of investments in rail infrastructure. This bargaining power lies in access to superiors and the ability to coordinate policy consensus among numerous specialized bureaucracies at higher levels.

Bargaining power is a rather time-invariant characteristic of bureaucratic units. It reflects the degree to which an agency possesses economic, political, or coercive resources that it can use to its advantage (Levi, 1988). Territorial governments and functional bureaucracies typically acquire institutionalized bargaining power through their positions within the regime. Political power and policy resources are allocated in an ascending manner according to party-state hierarchies. In China, provinces and cities have more power than counties and districts. Similarly, localities whose leaders hold concurrent appointments at a higher level have an advantage. Bureaucratic units capitalize on these privileges to gain tangible economic or policy benefits in the course of policy bargaining.

This argument of localized bargaining significantly differs from the conventional wisdom about patronage politics. The latter argument suggests that officials with close connections to the central ruler receive spoils such as government positions, bank loans, and transfers (Shih, 2004, 2008), and such connections are built around shared birthplaces, education, and workplace experience (Shih et al., 2012). While patronage politics mainly operates at the level of individual elites or constituents, the argument of localized bargaining focuses on agencies (e.g., territorial administrations) as a whole. This is not to deny that factional affiliations affect resource allocation. The argument instead calls for attention to a different factor that does not vary a lot based on which individuals hold the positions. In addition, while the patronage argument emphasizes the strategic calculation on the part of the ruler to allocate resources, the localized bargaining argument focuses on the bottom-up solicitation activities by the recipients.

5.4 Empirical Strategy

5.4.1 The Outcome Variable

My original data set on China's high-speed railway projects since 2004 is structured to allow event history analysis. For each month, each province is assigned a value of 0 until the event of interest (i.e., beginning of construction of a high-speed railway with at least 1 station inside the province) takes place, at which point the month is assigned a value of 1. I also code a separate variable on the completion of each railway by following the same rule. A limitation of the data is the fact that the first proposal takes place in closed-door meetings, which makes it impossible for me to measure exactly when a locality first proposed construction. By contrast, the commencement and end of construction are well-publicized by local and national media.

The Chinese high-speed railway network has tracks with three different speed limits: 200 km/hour, 250 km/hour, and 350 km/hour. While conventional rails run locomotive-powered trains, the high-speed rails run exclusively electric multiple unit (EMU) trains. The 350 km/hour lines are the main lines of national network, and the 250 km/hour and 200 km/hour are for regional connectors and intercity rails. After the 2010 Wenzhou train crash, the authority lowered the operating speed of high-speed trains. Now the EMU trains typically run at the speed of 300 km/hour on most of the line with a design speed of 350 km/hour, and at a speed of 200 km/hour on the 250 km/hour and 200 km/hour lines.[19] Table 5.2 presents a comparison of trains running under these two speed limits.

I limit the analysis to tracks with a 350 km/hour design speed limit.[20] This is primarily because some of the lines with lower speed limits were upgraded from existing lines. For example, the Dazhou–Chengdu railway, Jinhua–Wenzhou railway, and the Suining–Chongqing railway were all upgraded from existing lines and now run EMU trains at the speed limit of 200 km/hour. Lines with a design speed limit of 350 km/hour have all been newly constructed since 2004. The bargaining dynamics are very different between these two types. For example, when seeking to upgrade an existing line, there is no need to negotiate the path or requisition land for construction. Beyond that, there are also major differences in technical standards,[21] construction

---

[19] Ni, V. (2011, August 11). *After Wenzhou train wreck, China to implement universal slowdown on high speed trains*, china-briefing.com, retrieved from https://www.china-briefing.com/news/after-wenzhou-train-wreck-china-to-implement-universal-slowdown-on-high-speed-trains/.

[20] After the deadly high-speed railway crash accident in Wenzhou in July 2011, the Ministry of Railways reduced the speed limits for high-speed trains (now 300 km/h and 200 km/h for trains previously operated at 350 km/h and 250 km/h, respectively), despite the fact that the railways were designed and constructed at higher standards.

[21] The 350 km/h railway requires a 7,000-meter minimum horizontal radius, while railways at lower speed required much smaller minimum curve radii (2,000–5,500 meters). This means the construction of lines with a higher speed limit would affect a much larger area than those with lower speed limits. For a comprehensive comparison on the technical standards of different speed limits, see Lawrence et al. (2019) pp. 40–41.

Table 5.2 Comparison of Tracks Under Two Speed Limits[c]

	350–300 km/h	250–200 km/h
Fare-First Class (yuan/pkm)[a]	0.74	0.35
Fare-Second Class (yuan/pkm)	0.46	0.29
Passenger/Train (person)[b]	825	390
Revenue (yuan/pkm)	0.50	0.28
Operating Cost (yuan/pkm)	0.23	0.19
Net Profit (yuan/pkm)	0.27	0.09

a. yuan = Chinese RMB unit, pkm = passenger-kilometer

b. Assume 75% load factor.

c. The information in the table is adapted from Lawrence et al. (2019) p. 25 and p. 59.

methods,[22] and, most importantly, the amount of money required for the railways with different speed limits. Based on my data set, the 350 km/hour railways (18,249 kilometers in total) cost on average 126 million RMB per kilometer, while railways at lower speed limits (200–250 km/hour, 7,905 kilometers in total) cost 85 million RMB per kilometer. The efforts and time involved to solicit a new railway therefore are very different between these two tracks. Limiting the analysis to the newly built 350 km/hour lines thus allows more consistent comparison across cases.

The dataset ends in 2014 because the Chinese government began to allow private enterprises to take part in financing these projects through public–private partnerships (PPPs) after 2014. The central bureaucracies and the local governments were no longer the only players on the field. This changed the dynamics of approval, as private funding could dramatically increase a projects' chances of obtaining needed approvals. One of the first few PPP projects that the Chinese government approved, the Hangzhou–Shaoxing–Taizhou high-speed railway, has private enterprises contributing 51% of the equity.[23] Such projects were at first able to get very swift approvals, although difficulty increased over time. (The credit strain that the central government's effort to deleverage placed on the country's private enterprises in 2018 further

---

[22] The track of the 350 km/h lines is laid mostly on viaducts, while the track for 250 km/h lines goes on the ground.

[23] See Du, T. (2017, September 12). 首个民营高铁PPP项目--杭绍台铁路PPP项目落地 (The first PPP project—Hangzhou-Shaoxing-Wenzhou line is finalized), eeo.com.cn, from http://www.eeo.com.cn/2017/0912/312640.shtml.

complicated the pathway.) The relationships between the private enterprises and central and local governments and the roles firms played in obtaining approvals is not clear, but including this data would cloud my focus on intergovernmental bargaining. Some of the private firms, such as the Fosun International, a leading investor in the Hangzhou–Shaoxing–Taizhou high-speed rail project, are huge conglomerates with national influence spanning beyond their business domains. These firms might have their own channels of influencing policymaking at the center.

5.4.2 The Estimation Method

The dependent variable discussed above measures how long it takes for a locality to receive full permission for the construction of its first high-speed rail. It captures the period before an event occurs. Cox proportional hazards model is the most commonly used semi-parametric model to estimate the association between the length of time passed before an event and any covariates that might be related to the event. It has several advantages over other models, including being easy to implement and interpret, and being insensitive to the problem of censoring (i.e., observations that never experience the event of interest) in the sample (Allison, 2010). The model has the following form:

$$h(t \mid x_i\beta) = h_0\left(t\right)\exp\left(x_i\beta\right)$$

in which $h_0\left(t\right)$ is the baseline hazard and $x_i\beta$ is a vector of covariates that might be related to the event of interest and their coefficients. The equation estimates the hazard rate at time t for observation i.

5.4.3 Key Explanatory Variable

Following the discussion in Chapter 4, I measure provincial bargaining power by looking at whether the head of each province—the provincial party secretary—holds a dual appointment at the national level (e.g., a seat in the politburo, the vice chairman of the National People's Congress or National People's Political Consultative Conference, a vice premier, or a state councilor).

The CCP's central leadership determines the appointments of provincial party secretaries and their concurrent positions. Usually, politburo members are formally elected in the first plenum meeting of the central committee right after the national party congress that takes place every five years, and state-level positions are determined in the spring following the party congress. The selection of these positions involves deliberation, competition, and compromise among top-level party elites, in closed-door meetings prior to the party congress. No clear rules guiding the selection are public, although scholarship suggests performance, seniority, and relationship with the party's general secretary are important predictors of selection (e.g., Li & Zhou, 2005; Shih et al., 2012; Shirk, 2012; Zhang, 2014). In most cases, the selection of the national-level leadership positions is independent of the appointment of provincial leaders. Many leaders are appointed to serve concurrently as provincial party secretaries after they have gained national-level positions.[24] For some regions, the party secretaries are ex officio members of the politburo; leaders are also appointed to be the top administrators in these places to secure a seat in the politburo in the next party congress.[25]

The assignment of dual appointments is certainly not random. The rationale for such joint appointments is that the leaders who receive them work in jurisdictions where economic and social development and local governance requires coordination at the national level. Places that receive this treatment include the centrally administrated cities, coastal provinces that are the country's economic powerhouse (e.g., Guangdong), and ethnic minority regions (e.g., Xinjiang). While some scholars argue that these appointments are meant to strengthen central control (Huang, 1999; Sheng, 2019), others have contended the opposite (Bulman & Jaros, 2019). These positions, in addition to being one rank above regular provincial leaders, also give localities significant advantages in policy bargains. The empirical exercise of this chapter is interested in how localities utilize the political advantages vested in these positions and translate them into policy benefits. As Chapters 3 and 4 discussed, the dual appointments provide the localities an exclusive channel to voice their demands at a higher level, which might be crucial when the central authorities are considering projects in two neighboring jurisdictions.

---

[24] Bo Xilai, for example, was appointed to serve the party secretary of Chongqing, after his promotion into the politburo in the 17th party congress in 2007.

[25] For example, in May 2017, Cai Qi, a protégé of President Xi Jinping, was appointed party secretary of Beijing, which always has a seat in the politburo. Cai became a member of the politburo in the 19th party congress in fall 2017.

These appointments also give the localities additional advantages when they need to cut through bureaucratic gridlock at the central ministries to secure funding and permissions needed for construction.

I code cardinal provinces as 1 (i.e., their leaders also hold positions at the national level), and cleric provinces as 0. This is a time-dependent variable, as some provinces switched their status during the observational period.[26] The fine-grained nature of the monthly data allows me to capture the exact months when these personnel changes took place, reducing measurement errors commonly seen in data collected on a yearly basis.[27] Among the 4,092 province-months, provincial leaders held concurrent positions at a higher level in 753 (18.4%).

5.4.4 Accounting for Alternative Explanations

I include a battery of variables besides concurrent appointments that might also explain the variations in the outcome. These control variables are motivated by two theoretically relevant alternative explanations, as discussed in Chapters 1 and 2 ("loyalty purchasing" and "technocratic solutions"). The first control variable measures the connection between the provincial leader and the incumbent general party secretary. The patronage politics argument contends that top party leaders tend to favor their close associates with various types of government spoils (Shih, 2004, 2008). It is thus possible that the general party secretary might give priority to provinces governed by his factional members. Following the standard approach in the literature, I measure each provincial party secretary's connection with the general party secretary by looking at whether they have worked in the same bureaucratic agency within two administrative steps (Shih et al., 2012).[28] Among the 4,092 province-months, 504 (12.3%) have a provincial party secretary with a connection to the incumbent general party secretary at the time (i.e., Hu Jintao before November 2012, and Xi Jinping after November 2012).

---

[26] For example, the provincial party secretary of Hubei held a seat in the politburo from 2002 to 2007, whereas the party secretary of Chongqing has been holding a seat in politburo since 2007.

[27] For example, if a province started the construction in February under a party secretary without a concurrent position, and a new party secretary with a concurrent position assumed office in July of the same year, the yearly data might falsely attribute the event to the new leader.

[28] The original measure in Shih, Adolph, and Liu (2012) also includes whether the two officials were born in the same province or went to the same university. Recent discussions in the literature tend to focus more on the shared work experience, as this criterion minimizes potential measurement errors. See for example Ma (2016).

I also look at whether the provincial party secretary is the child of high-level officials at the minister level or above. These second-generation officials are called "princelings" in China, and they remain active and influential in both business and politics (Zhang, 2019). It is possible that these officials' social status gives them advantages in securing large infrastructure projects like railways from the central government. Among the 4,092 province-months, 232 (5.7%) have a provincial party secretary who is a princeling.

Additionally, I control for the age of the provincial party secretary. Chinese officials face various age limits for promotion and mandatory retirement, and provincial party secretaries must retire at 65. The age measure accounts for the possibility that officials' incentive to exert effort to develop the local economy—of which securing central investment in large infrastructure projects is an important part—might change as they age (Xi et al., 2015).

I also include a set of socioeconomic indicators at the provincial level to account for the "technocratic solution" explanation. They are gross domestic product (GDP), population, local revenue, length of existing railroad, and railway passenger volume. They are included under the premise that the central authorities, and especially the Ministry of Railways and its successor, the CRC, wanted to economize their investments and gave priority to those regions that need railways the most and those whose local conditions would promise reasonable returns for construction (Huang & Morgan, 2011).

Two logistical issues arise in coding these socioeconomic indicators with numerical values into the event history data. First, as the Chinese government does not report monthly economic statistics, I have to use yearly data for every month in a given year. This practice creates an artificial "jump" between December and January every year. Second and more importantly, the event history data only documents an observation until the event of interest takes place, which could potentially induce biases. For example, those observations that experienced the event late would have higher values for measures that are monotonically increasing (such as GDP) simply because they have stayed in the data set longer. This might lead to an incorrect conclusion that there is a negative association between these measurements and the likelihood of the event of interest. Amplifying this potential bias, most economic indicators in China grew on average at more than 10% year-to-year during the observational period. To deal with these issues, I transform the numerical values of each observation into rank percentiles, which are values ranging from 1/31 to 31/31, with the top-ranked province being 1/31 and bottom-ranked being 31/31. Such coding allows more consistent comparison across different provinces and over a long period of time. It also to some extent reflects the zero-sum nature of inter-jurisdictional competition for resources.

5.5 Results

5.5.1 Baseline Results

I first run the model with only the key covariate—whether the provincial party secretary holds concurrent positions at a higher level—and include three sets of control variables: individual characteristics of the provincial party secretary (connection with the top leader, princeling status, and age), socioeconomic indicators of the province (GDP, population, and local revenue), and existing rail conditions (lengths and passenger volume)—one at a time. The results are presented in model 1 through model 4 in Table 5.3.

The key covariate (whether the provincial leader holds a dual appointment) appears to be positively associated with the outcome throughout the four models, and such association is statistically significant beyond the 0.05-level across the models, except in model 2. The lack of significance in model 2 can be explained by the fact that locales where the leaders hold concurrent positions at a higher level are inherently different, socially and economically, from other provinces, and therefore excluding socioeconomic controls might have introduced biases in the estimation.

Most of the control variables do not appear to have a statistically significant association with the outcome. The notable exception is the railway passenger volume, which is negatively associated with the outcome. Because I use percentile rank measurement (i.e., places with larger passenger volume are assigned smaller rank values), the robust negative association suggests that places with a larger volume are more likely to secure a project and start the construction early on. This result is intuitive, as market and cost-benefit concerns should have played an important role when central bureaucracies evaluated the feasibility of a new railway project. In other words, the analysis lends some support to the "technocratic solution" explanation in addition to localized bargaining.

Table 5.3 Cox Proportional Hazards Models: Time to Begin Construction

	Model 1	Model 2	Model 3	Model 4
Dual Appointment	1.09 **	0.84	1.80 ***	2.07 ***
	(0.49)	(0.56)	(0.69)	(0.76)
Connection With Leader		0.30	−0.36	0.19
		(0.66)	(0.71)	(0.87)
Princeling		0.41	−0.27	−0.32
		(0.70)	(0.67)	(0.66)
Age		0.09	0.14*	0.15
		(0.07)	(0.08)	(0.09)
GDP (rank)			−3.93	0.55
			(3.92)	(4.89)
Population (rank)			−2.30	0.67
			(1.52)	(2.02)
Revenue (rank)			1.21	−3.47
			(3.41)	(4.54)
Existing Railway Length (rank)				1.24
				(1.20)
Railway Passenger Volume (rank)				−5.87 ***
				(2.13)
N	2293	2293	2293	2293
Wald	p = 0.03	p = 0.18	p = 0.00	p = 0.01

Standard errors in parentheses
*p<0.1; **p<0.05; ***p<0.01

The coefficient of the Cox proportional hazards model is interpreted as the logged hazard ratio, which corresponds to the ratio of the chances of the event between two levels of a variable, and such ratio does not depend on the specific t. In this way, the positive coefficient of the key covariate in the fully specified model 4 can be interpreted as follows: everything else equal, the chance of securing the first high-speed railway project and starting the construction for the provinces with a party secretary holding a dual appointment at a higher level is 7.9 times $(e^{2.07})$ the chance for those without. This substantial difference is also evidenced in the simulated survival curve in Figure 5.1. In the figure, the solid curve indicates the provinces with dual appointments, and the dashed curve indicates those without. The y-axis indicates the proportion of provinces that do not have at least one high-speed

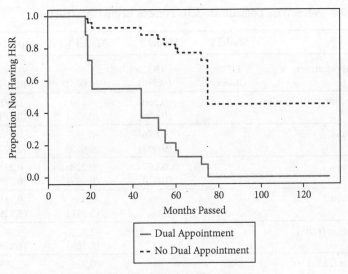

Figure 5.1 Survival Curves for Two Types of Provinces

rail. Both categories started at one, meaning that no province had high-speed railway at the beginning. As shown in the figure, the solid line declines at a much quicker pace than the dashed line, meaning provinces with dual appointments received approval for construction in a much quicker fashion.

To rule out the possibility that the results are sensitive to the assumptions of the Cox model, I also run the same specifications using the piece-wise logistic survival model. The results remain consistent with the estimates from the Cox proportional hazards model (see Table 5.4). The proxy for localities' bargaining power, the dual appointment, is positively associated with the outcome and statistically significant.

5.5.2 Explaining Variations in Completion Time

Having shown that greater bargaining power might help to secure a high-speed railway project and start the construction early on, we now look at whether such bargaining power would help localities get ahead in completing the construction. I replace the original outcome variable with the amount of time passed until the first high-speed railway was completed for each province, and I run the same model specifications as I did in the baseline models.

Table 5.4 Piece-Wise Logistic Models: Time to Begin Construction

	Model 1	Model 2	Model 3	Model 4
Dual Appointment	1.220**	0.937*	1.399**	1.246**
	(0.488)	(0.530)	(0.603)	(0.634)
Connection With Leader		0.360	−0.129	0.448
		(0.650)	(0.676)	(0.771)
Princeling		0.676	−0.087	−0.094
		(0.667)	(0.663)	(0.677)
Age		0.162**	0.228***	0.238***
		(0.078)	(0.089)	(0.089)
GDP (rank)			−0.989	0.719
			(3.397)	(3.929)
Population (rank)			−2.320*	−0.563
			(1.368)	(1.825)
Revenue (rank)			−0.739	−2.195
			(3.061)	(3.517)
Existing Railway Length (rank)				1.307
				(1.168)
Railway Passenger Volume (rank)				−3.384*
				(1.732)
Constant	−4.909***	−14.662***	−16.708***	−17.295***
	(0.259)	(4.740)	(5.301)	(5.508)
Observations	2,293	2,293	2,293	2,293
Log likelihood	−116.894	−114.150	−105.359	−103.326
Akaike Inf. Crit.	237.788	238.299	226.717	226.652

Note: *p<0.1; **p<0.05; ***p<0.01

As shown in Table 5.5, the coefficients of the key covariate are positive across four models but are not statistically significant at the 0.05-level.[29] Like the baseline results, in the fully specified model, none of the control variables is significantly associated with the outcome except the railway passenger volume measured in percentile rank.

This result suggests that additional bargaining power within the bureaucracy seems to only help when the locales need to compete with others to secure a project from the central government. It plays little role in expediting the constructions that have already begun. In other words, local leaders are more interested in getting railways approved than in having them built. With

---

[29] The results remain consistent when I run the piece-wise logistic regression with the same model specifications.

Table 5.5 Cox Proportional Hazards Models: Time to Completion

	Model 1	Model 2	Model 3	Model 4
Dual Appointment	0.94 (0.58)	0.94 (0.80)	1.72* (0.96)	1.52 (1.03)
Connection With Leader		0.23 (0.78)	−0.34 (0.96)	−0.21 (1.04)
Princeing		−0.57 (1.29)	−0.10 (1.60)	1.03 (1.82)
Age		0.03 (0.06)	0.02 (0.08)	−0.05 (0.09)
GDP (rank)			−7.28* (3.90)	−6.29 (4.65)
Population (rank)			−0.61 (1.88)	1.26 (2.16)
Revenue (rank)			3.35 (3.39)	2.65 (4.10)
Existing Railway Length (rank)				1.06 (1.35)
Railway Passenger Volume (rank)				−4.12** (2.03)
N	3300	3263	3263	3263
Wald	p = 0.11	p = 0.79	p = 0.05	p = 0.06

Standard errors in parentheses
*p<0.1; **p<0.05; ***p<0.01

an average tenure under four years (Jia et al., 2015; Landry et al., 2018; Li & Zhou, 2005), observing positive economic gains after the completion of a new railway inside of a party secretary's term is unlikely. The data show that most local leaders are already halfway through their tenure when the construction begins, and thus they will not be around to take credit when it is completed, let alone reap the gains of the long-term economic benefits the railway will generate.

5.5.3 Destination Provinces Only

One potential bias in the analysis so far is that some locales might benefit from the bargaining effort of the others, thereby acting as free riders—for example, if a railway connects A and B and happens to pass through C, and A and B but not C may have expended effort to make it happen. However, the data would also count C as having begun construction, even though it is the effort of A and B that made the project go forward. Stations at the two ends of a railway often receive the lion's share of profits from train tickets and have the most incentive to expend such effort. To avoid counting such free rides, I limit my analysis only to those provinces that are among one of the two ends of a railway project. By the end of 2014, 18 provinces have a high-speed railway of which they are one of the two ends, and 14 of them already have their first line completed. I run the same model specification for both the commencement and completion of construction using Cox proportional hazards model. The results are presented in Tables 5.6 and 5.7.

The coefficients for the dual appointment are positive and statistically significant across two tables, suggesting that having a provincial party secretary holding concurrent higher positions expedites both the start and the completion of the high-speed railway construction in the destination provinces. The coefficient of the variable in the full specification of Table 5.6 (3.13) is larger than the one from the same specification (2.07) in Table 5.3 (as is the z statistic), implying that the effect of dual appointments is more pronounced in the destination provinces than in pass-by provinces. What is noteworthy is that connection with the incumbent general party secretary and age also appear to be positively associated with the start of the construction, after eliminating the potential bias introduced by the pass-by provinces (Table 5.6). This partially lends support to the "loyalty purchasing" and career incentive arguments, as the central leader might favor the locales governed by his associates, and as those officials moving closer to the retirement age limit might exert more effort to get promoted. These two positive associations, however, are not significant in the completion model (Table 5.7), which is consistent with the aforementioned intuition that local leaders exert less effort—neither seeking help from their patrons nor on their own—to the events (completion of construction) where they would not be able to claim the credit.

5.5.4 Testing the Hypothesis at the Municipal Level

So far we have established a robust relationship between a province's institutionalized bargaining power and the central government's temporal

Table 5.6 Cox Proportional Hazards Models: Time to Begin Construction, Destination Provinces Only

	Model 1	Model 2	Model 3	Model 4
Dual Appointment	1.45 ***	1.25 **	2.48 ***	3.13 ***
	(0.51)	(0.60)	(0.82)	(1.03)
Connection With Leader		0.72	0.47	1.69*
		(0.68)	(0.74)	(0.96)
Princeling		0.59	0.14	0.20
		(0.73)	(0.69)	(0.72)
Age		0.07	0.19 **	0.23 **
		(0.07)	(0.09)	(0.10)
GDP (rank)			−5.56	−3.51
			(4.76)	(5.73)
Population (rank)			−1.77	1.67
			(1.82)	(2.59)
Revenue (rank)			1.88	−0.46
			(4.01)	(5.21)
Existing Railway Length (rank)				2.67*
				(1.36)
Railway Passenger Volume (rank)				−7.16 **
				(2.82)
N	2578	2578	2578	2578
Wald	p = 0.00	p = 0.05	p = 0.01	p = 0.02

Standard errors in parentheses
*p<0.1; **p<0.05; ***p<0.01

and regional priorities in granting permission for high-speed rail projects. This relationship points to the plausibility of the hypothesis that localities' bargaining efforts influence central government agencies' allocative decisions. How well does this logic extend to levels below the province? The bureaucratic politics at the sub-provincial level involves more interactions: municipal governments are bargaining with both the provincial government and, to a lesser extent, the central bureaucracy. For the purpose of simplicity, this study assumes that the competitions within a province approximate those at the national level among provinces and that a number of municipalities bargain for a greater share of resources from the provincial government. This assumption is consistent with the scholarly characterization of the Chinese polity as a multi-divisional

Table 5.7 Cox Proportional Hazards Models: Time to Completion, Destination Provinces Only

	Model 1	Model 2	Model 3	Model 4
Dual Appointment	1.21 **	1.48*	2.14 **	2.08 **
	(0.61)	(0.84)	(0.99)	(1.05)
Connection With Leader		0.88	0.97	1.12
		(0.83)	(1.16)	(1.24)
Princeling		−0.73	−1.35	−0.92
		(1.29)	(1.85)	(1.98)
Age		0.09	0.14	0.10
		(0.08)	(0.11)	(0.12)
GDP (rank)			−8.59	−9.15
			(5.66)	(6.71)
Population (rank)			1.69	3.54
			(2.51)	(3.10)
Revenue (rank)			3.52	4.38
			(4.85)	(5.93)
Existing Railway Length (rank)				1.53
				(1.60)
Railway Passenger Volume (rank)				−3.14
				(2.52)
N	3444	3341	3341	3341
Wald	p = 0.05	p = 0.28	p = 0.11	p = 0.14

Standard errors in parentheses
*p<0.1; **p<0.05; ***p<0.01

organization in which each province is rather self-contained and exercises its authority like a state within its territory (e.g., Landry, 2008; Maskin et al., 2000).

I code the bargaining power of each municipality in the same way as I did with the provinces. I look at whether the top leader (i.e., party secretary) of each municipality also has an appointment in the provincial decision-making bodies (e.g., standing committee of the provincial party committee, or deputy provincial governor). I run two sets of simplified models. The first, using a Cox proportional hazards model, looks at how long it takes for each municipality to receive permission to construct its first high-speed railway station. In addition to the dual appointment variable, in model 2 and

Table 5.8 Municipal Level: Time to Begin Construction (Cox Proportional Hazards Models)

	Model 1	Model 2	Model 3
Dual Appointment	1.20 *** (0.19)	1.22 *** (0.20)	1.14 *** (0.27)
Socioeconomic Controls	NO	YES	YES
Provincial Fixed Effect	NO	NO	YES
N	341	341	341
Wald	41 on 1 df, p = 0.00	59 on 5 df, p = 0.00	121 on 35 df, p = 0.00
R^2	0.09 (Max 0.99)	0.13 (Max 0.99)	0.42 (Max 0.99)

Note: *p<0.1; **p<0.05; ***p<0.01

3 I include controls of key social-economic indicators of each municipality (i.e., GDP, population, and fiscal revenue)[30] and provincial fixed effects, which account for unobserved heterogeneities at the provincial level. As shown in Table 5.8, the variable of dual appointment is positively and statistically significant across three specifications, suggesting these cities had priority even holding provincial-level factors at constant. The second exercise looks at the number of high-speed railway lines that each municipality is connected to. I use a simple OLS regression, and include the same set of control variables to estimate how the number of high-speed railways correlates with each city's bargaining power. The results, as presented in Table 5.9, show that the proxy for institutionalized bargaining power of the municipality is positively associated with being connected to more railways. While allocative decisions at the sub-provincial level involve more actors and are more complex, these results provide suggestive—although in no way conclusive—evidence that bargaining power helps localities gain an advantage in the race for high-speed railways.

---

[30] Similar to the estimation of the provincial models, I use the rank percentile transformation for the socioeconomic control variables. Because the dual appointment status and the relative ranks of municipalities remain stable in a short period of time, I use the rank of averaged social economic indicators during the observational period (2004–2014). The resulting estimation is a Cox proportional hazards model with time-invariant covariates.

Table 5.9 Municipal Level: Number of High-speed Railways (OLS Models)

	Model 1	Model 2	Model 3
Dual Appointment	1.304***	1.306***	1.032***
	(0.121)	(0.128)	(0.124)
Socioeconomic Controls	NO	YES	YES
Provincial Fixed Effect	NO	NO	YES
Observations	341	341	341
R^2	0.256	0.277	0.506
Adjusted R^2	0.253	0.266	0.449
Residual Std. Error	0.789 (df = 339)	0.783 (df = 335)	0.678 (df = 305)
F Statistic	116.385***	25.661***	8.931***
	(df = 1; 339)	(df = 5; 335)	(df = 35; 305)

Note: *p<0.1; **p<0.05; ***p<0.01

Additionally, I look at how many newly constructed high-speed railway stations are in each municipality. The intuition is that a station can bring long-term benefit to the locality, whereas construction of railway tracks only brings short-term benefit of investments in fixed assets. Therefore, the localities also have the incentive to bargain for more stations in their jurisdiction. Tables 5.10 and 5.11 present OLS and negative binomial estimation on the determinants of station numbers. Controlling for socioeconomic indicators (population, GDP, and fiscal revenue), number of counties in a city, as well as provincial fixed effects, cities with leaders sitting in the provincial decision-making bodies on average have 0.7 more stations than the ordinary cities (Model 4 in Table 5.10). Again, this result is consistent with the prediction of the argument.[31]

5.6 Concluding Remarks

This chapter examines how institutionally rendered bargaining power of territorial administrations shapes the political geography of China's high-speed

---

[31] I also conduct an additional analysis by including a dummy for provincial capitals, as their party secretaries always sit in the provincial party standing committee. The coefficient for dual appointment remains positive and statistically significant, even after the inclusion of the provincial capital dummy. This means that a seat in the provincial leadership gives non-capital cities significant policy advantages over those without such appointments.

Table 5.10 Municipal Level: Number of Stations (OLS Models)

	Model 1	Model 2	Model 3	Model 4
Dual Appointment	2.410***	0.926***	0.874**	0.711*
	(0.282)	(0.346)	(0.355)	(0.406)
Socioeconomic Controls	NO	YES	YES	YES
Number of County Units	NO	NO	YES	YES
Provincial Fixed Effect	NO	NO	NO	YES
Observations	337	285	285	285
R^2	0.179	0.327	0.328	0.460
Adjusted R^2	0.177	0.317	0.316	0.386
Residual Std. Error	1.840	1.721	1.723	1.632
	(df = 335)	(df = 280)	(df = 279)	(df = 250)
F Statistic	73.054***	33.968***	27.201***	6.257***
	(df = 1; 335)	(df = 4; 280)	(df = 5; 279)	(df = 34; 250)

Note: *p<0.1; **p<0.05; ***p<0.01

Table 5.11 Municipal Level: Number of Stations (Negative Binomial Models)

	Model 1	Model 2	Model 3	Model 4
Dual Appointment	1.278***	0.492*	0.452*	0.503*
	(0.223)	(0.258)	(0.265)	(0.280)
Socioeconomic Controls	NO	YES	YES	YES
Number of County Units	NO	NO	YES	YES
Provincial Fixed Effect	NO	NO	NO	YES
Observations	337	285	285	285
Log Likelihood	−496.876	−435.399	−434.843	−398.977
Akaike Inf. Crit.	997.752	880.797	881.687	867.953

Note: *p<0.1; **p<0.05; ***p<0.01

railway project. I find that cardinal localities are able to secure permissions for railway projects and commence construction earlier than their cleric counterparts. The effect of greater institutionalized bargaining power is less pronounced in pressing the completion of construction, suggesting that officials are less willing to exert efforts when they anticipate that they will not be able to claim the credit for such efforts.

The findings in this chapter depart notably from the existing literature in two aspects. First, most studies on the logic of distributive politics in nondemocracies focus on the political geography of reversible benefits, such as poverty relief programs (Magaloni, 2006) and bank loans (Shih, 2004). This chapter instead looks at the allocation of government investment that translates into lasting public goods. This distinction has important theoretical implications, as such investment should not be easily equated with "pork" that the incumbent would employ to please constituencies in electoral autocracies. Instead, this book proposes a bottom-up perspective that explains the distribution of such resources as a function of bargaining by territorial bureaucratic units.[32] Second, in contrast to the patronage politics thesis that emphasizes the role of informal, interpersonal connections between the ruler and the elites, the study in this chapter looks at the dynamics of power that are vested in officials' positions (Baturo & Elkink, 2014). It depicts an interesting juxtaposition of two seemingly contradictory aspects of authoritarian bureaucracy: the formalized bureaucratic ranks that stipulate power distribution among different constitutive units, and the lack of institutionalized norms and rules that govern resource competition among these actors within the bureaucracy.

This chapter mostly focuses on the "winners" in policy bargains. It assumes that those regional players without strong bargaining power can only acquiesce to the unfavorable terms presented to them. Yet, this might not be accurate. Officials in cleric localities could seek extra-institutional sources of leverage to strengthen their position. Chapter 6 explores one such source: mass mobilizations, which local officials strategically tolerate if protestors' demands are congruent with officials' intention to secure

---

[32] For bottom-up resource bargaining in other contexts, see for example, Treisman (1999).

more resources from above. The protestors in this case serve as a credible and costly signal to officials at the higher level that rejecting the demand of the localities might put social stability at further risk. "High-speed railway rallies" have been widespread across China in the past decade.[33] Thus, bargaining for high-speed rails takes place not only in closed-door meetings in Beijing, but also in the streets of small cities.

---

[33] For an account of several such events, see 高铁争夺战呈现出社运新特点 (*Competitions for high-speed railway reveal new features of social movement*), Zhigu Qushi, retrieved from https://mp.weixin.qq.com/s/M3UiAKCVMrOFaUd2ogXnmw.

6

The Power of the Masses

6.1 Introduction

On May 16, 2015, more than 20,000 residents in Linshui county, Sichuan province, took to the streets to protest a construction plan for high-speed railway released not long before.[1] The proposed line would connect Dazhou and Chongqing. It would stop in Guang'an, but not stop in Linshui. The two localities, which are adjacent, had been competing for a station for a long time, and Linshui residents were angered and disappointed by the plan. For days they had undertaken public mobilization, gathering over 10,000 signatures in a short time on a petition seeking a change to the direction of the track—directed at, according to the petition, "the relevant department of the state (国家有关部门)."[2]

While Chinese local officials generally spare no effort in repressing mass mobilization, local authorities in Linshui did very little. As protesters gathered signatures, they did not act. When the public demonstration began, local police did not try to quell the crowd until it had been going on for hours, when protesters began to burn cars in the streets. Even so, the protest had an impact: the Sichuan provincial government stated that the released plan was not final, and the location of the stations was subject to reconsideration.

Mass mobilizations about railway stations and other types of policy benefits like the one in Linshui have been increasingly common in China.[3] What do these protests tell us about the internal dynamics of policy bargains? What roles do local authorities play in these events? This chapter studies how the power of the masses shapes intra-elite bargaining on policy resources.

---

[1] For coverage of the protest, see, for example, Allen-Ebrahimian (2015).

[2] The petition letter was also uploaded online; see https://baike.baidu.com/pic/%E9%82%BB%E6 %B0%B4%E4%BF%9D%E8%B7%AF%E8%BF%90%E5%8A%A8/17583060/0/b21c8701a18b8 7d637d09ea2020828381e30fdf8?fr=lemma&ct=single#aid=0&pic=b21c8701a18b87d637d09ea20 20828381e30fdf8.

[3] For a summary of high-speed railway related protests between 2008 and 2015, see 高铁争夺战呈 现出社运新特点 (*Competitions for high-speed railway reveal new features of social movement*), Zhigu Qushi, retrieved from https://mp.weixin.qq.com/s/M3UiAKCVMrOFaUd2ogXnmw.

Localized Bargaining. Xiao Ma, Oxford University Press. © Oxford University Press 2022.
DOI: 10.1093/oso/9780197638910.003.0006

I argue that some jurisdictions in China have experienced "consent instability" in which local officials strategically tolerate bottom-up mobilizations
to strengthen their bargaining power. Specifically, "cleric" officials, who
oversee less influential segments of the regime and therefore lack other
bargaining power, often favor this strategy. They capitalize on local mass
mobilizations when the demand of the masses is congruent with elements of
their agenda that they are otherwise unable to pursue, especially those that
involve bargaining between the locality and higher levels of the government.
The protesters in the street function as a powerful bargaining chip for local
officials. They illustrate ex ante that rejecting the locality's demand brings a
risk of social instability, which brings the pressure of the masses to bear on
higher-level leaders.

Several institutional conditions of the Chinese party-state breed what
I call consent instability. The first is that the hierarchies of the party-state
create an uneven playing field for actors seeking policy resources from
above. Agents with higher ranks or those who capture traditionally important positions in the nomenklatura (cardinals) receive more resources
than others. Agents representing weak bureaucracies (clerics), in contrast,
have minimal bargaining power with their superiors. These weak players
therefore seek sources of bargaining power from outside the bureaucracy.
This chapter explores how such local officials tap the public pressure of
local citizenry to achieve their purposes. Second, cadre incentives are
not uniform across different levels of the party-state. Grassroots officials,
who have very little chance of getting promoted beyond their localities,
choose to prioritize the augmentation of local interests. Cadres at higher
levels, however, value their career prospects more than grassroots officials
do. This discrepancy of incentives explains why grassroots officials might
risk their own careers to tolerate citizen mobilizations that promote local
interests, and why officials at higher levels often concede when they face
such demands.

To provide greater details on the logic of consent instability, this chapter
uses a case study of eastern county C's response to a proposed government
merger. The dynamics in the county merger resemble those in high-speed
railway planning. Both involve intensive, closed-door bargaining between
localities and their superiors, and in both cases, grassroots authorities,
lacking bargaining power, had few options but to acquiesce to unfavorable
policy outcomes. I use the county merger case because I was able to gain access to a rich amount of first-hand information. Drawing on interviews with

local officials and residents, I show that county C officials tolerated protesters because their interests coincided with protesters' demands. The merger would significantly weaken their power and authority, and county officials successfully used local citizen mobilization to resist the higher-level officials' decision.

Local officials' tacit consent to mobilization makes the grassroots into a powerful weapon for weak bureaucrats, as it forces their superiors to consider the possibility that ignoring protesters' demands will imperil social stability. This strategy has also appeared in many localities' quests for infrastructure programs like high-speed railway stations. To offer a systematic assessment of the efficacy of using public pressure as leverage in intra-bureaucratic bargaining, I employ a survey experiment of 368 local officials. I use an endorsement experiment design in which the subjects (local cadres) evaluated a hypothetical budgetary earmark request from a leader at the grassroots. The subjects showed a significantly higher level of approval of the earmark when the request was backed by popular pressure that threatened the stability of the regime.

The consent instability model offers new insights into our understanding of how Chinese officials respond to sources of social instability. It shows that while, in keeping with the conventional understanding, many Chinese officials actively contain, stifle, and repress mass mobilizations, they might sometimes seek opportunities in popular contention.[4] Protesters send costly signals of local demand and help officials to extract concessions from above. Such a state–citizen relationship has been observed in various issue areas featuring intensive bargaining among multiple segments of the government, most of which are prominent in cases involving administrative redistricting or allocations of investment in large infrastructure projects (such as high-speed railways). It challenges the often-perceived elite-masses dichotomy in authoritarian politics,[5] pointing to the possibility that the masses can play a meaningful role in shaping interactions among the authoritarian elites.[6]

[4] For a thorough review of the state's role in popular contention, see Lorentzen (2017).

[5] For recent theoretical development on the elite and the masses aspects of authoritarian rule, see Svolik (2012).

[6] For earlier work on how state and society mutually empower one and another, see Migdal et al. (1994); for recent work on how social pressures shape elite interactions, see, for example, Slater (2010).

6.2 Defining "Consent Instability"

"Consent instability" refers to the strategic tolerance of mass mobilization by weaker bureaucratic actors, who use public pressure as bargaining leverage against their superiors. It involves two key actors. The first is local entities with relatively weak influence in the bureaucracy (or the "clerics"). Those are territorial administrations or functional bureaucracies that oversee less influential segments of the regime, such as local governments in more remote parts of the country or those lower in the hierarchy, or bureaus in charge of issues that are not key policy concerns of the party-state. These bureaucracies often get sidelined in the intra-bureaucratic competition for resources or preferential policies from above. They either have difficulties drawing attention from superiors or lack bargaining leverage in competing with more powerful peers. The second actor is a local citizenry with collective action potential. Through collective action, they demand policy changes, including improvements in local infrastructure, social welfare, and other locality-specific policies. These demands do not target local governments, but instead target higher-level officials who have the authority to make such decisions. Citizens express their demands through mobilizations that carry an implicit threat to social stability.

Consent instability involves the officials' strategic tolerance of—and in some cases, even collusion with (e.g., O'Brien et al., 2020)—citizens' expressions of demands toward upper-level officials. The public displays of constituents' discontent, particularly mass mobilizations, help strengthen officials' bargaining power in soliciting policy benefits. First, bottom-up mass mobilizations serve as *credible* evidence of public dissatisfaction.[7] They single out the demands of a particular locality from a myriad of noisy signals that leaders at higher levels receive, including those "cheap talks" by competing agents that claim the existence of similar demands from their constituents. When the demand of people in streets is congruent with what the officials want from above, public pressure becomes powerful leverage that officials can invoke to demand policy concessions that they are otherwise unable to pursue. Second, the disruptive effect of mass mobilizations illustrates ex ante the grave consequences (i.e., social instability) of rejecting a locality's demands, and brings the pressure of the masses to bear on the

---

[7] Jessica Weiss argues that authoritarian regimes' tolerance of anti-foreign protests serves a similar function in international negotiation by credibly signaling the regime's resolve. See Weiss (2013).

side of leaders above. Higher-level leaders face a choice between acceding to the demands of the localities. or rejecting them and being responsible for priming the local population to join a more fundamental challenge to social stability.

It is important to note that official consent does not necessarily mean local officials publicly organize or assist protesters against their superiors. Organizing protests against higher-level decisions is considered a serious disciplinary violation ("activities against party organization") in the CCP, and if found out, officials would face harsh sanctions. Observations suggest that local governments take the safer step of defecting from their usual practices in preventing and repressing mobilizations, and demonstrate a high degree of tolerance to protesters. Therefore, the role of local government in these events is more about consent than collaboration. In some rare cases, local officials also join mobilizations as individual participants.

Consent instability reflects an informal alliance between the local state and the citizens. It also departs from our traditional understanding of how local governments in China manage popular contention. It is nonetheless a strategic response by local officials facing various formal and informal institutional incentives and constraints. In the next section, I highlight two key institutional characteristics of the Chinese bureaucracy that give rise to consent instability.

6.3 The Institutional Setting

Two institutional features of the Chinese party-state create conditions for consent instability to emerge. The first is the unequal distribution of bargaining power among various bureaucratic units. Intra-bureaucratic bargaining for preferential policies often sidelines the weak segments of the bureaucracy. To strengthen their positions, they seek sources of bargaining power outside the bureaucracy (i.e., public pressure). At the same time, China's cadre management system imposes differential incentives. Grassroots officials who value departmental or community enrichment more than promotion use social instability as a tool to extract policy concessions from higher-level leaders.

6.3.1 Unequal Distribution of Bureaucratic Bargaining Power

Bargaining takes place in the day-to-day operation of the Chinese government (Lampton, 1992). Various bureaucratic units, who have diverse and often conflicting agendas, compete, negotiate, compromise, and collude among themselves to try to maximize their departmental interests (e.g., Mertha, 2009; Zhou, 2008). The unequal distributions of bargaining power among various bureaucratic units shape the outcomes of these interactions. Those with greater bargaining power are better positioned to secure preferential policy outcomes, which are often at the expense of those with relatively weak bargaining power.

The unequal distributions of bargaining power exist in two dimensions. First, units of different administrative ranks have unequal power in a straightforward hierarchical model. Higher-level officials can force those at the lower level to accept the terms they offer. For example, when officials at various levels of government disagree on the shares of specific taxes they collect, or the divisions of responsibilities in expenditure, the higher-level officials prevail because they have both explicit and effective power (e.g., Zhang, 2006; Zhou & Lian, 2011). Redistricting or administrative merger decisions have the same impact.

Bureaucracies of equal rank can also have unequal bargaining power. For example, provincial capitals usually have more influence over provincial policymaking than ordinary municipalities; municipal public security bureaus are considered more important—and therefore can garner more resources (e.g., Wang & Minzner, 2015)—than health or sports bureaus. Formal institutional arrangements recognize some of these differences: the heads of these more important locales or bureaus often have dual appointments at a higher level, as elaborated in Chapter 4. For example, the secretary of the provincial capitals always sits on the provincial party standing committee, and municipal public security bureau chiefs also carry concurrent titles such as deputy mayor.

Beyond such arrangements, nothing formal sets out the differences in bargaining power among officials of the same rank, but those who get lower priority recognize the informal norms and consensus that give them less bargaining power than their peers. Consequently, some of them take a risky path of seeking sources of power that strengthen their positions from outside the bureaucracy—such as the pressures of the citizenry.[8]

---

[8] This logic is also consistent with the sequence of bargaining generalized by Xueguang Zhou and Hong Lian, who argue that intergovernmental bargaining often starts with formal communication

6.3.2 The Differential Official Incentives

The strategic use of public pressure by weak officials to extract policy concessions from above hinges upon an important assumption: that officials at lower levels have less to lose than those at higher levels. To understand this point, we need to review the institution that governs officials' incentives—the cadre management system.

The cadre management system evaluates officials' performance in various aspects of governance, and links the evaluations to officials' career prospects (e.g., Edin, 2003; Whiting, 2004). Numerous empirical studies have found the system to be effective in supplying high-powered incentives for officials to pursue desired policy goals set by the regime, such as economic growth (Li & Zhou, 2005), revenue collection (Lü & Landry, 2014), and environmental regulation (e.g., He et al., 2020; Jia, 2012). The party has placed additional emphasis on social stability maintenance by sanctioning officials whose "negligence" in their work causes social instability.[9] The party also institutes what is called the "one-veto rule," which disqualifies an official for promotion if he fails in stability maintenance, no matter how well he performs in other aspects of local governance. Combined, these arrangements make social stability a top priority for local officials (e.g., Yan, 2016).

A single mass incident in an official's jurisdiction does not necessarily lead to sanction, however. If citizens mobilize in favor of policy change that authorities at higher levels determine, and direct their demands toward upper levels of government, leaders at higher levels will be directly responsible for failure in containing the situation, had they not reacted properly to appease the local population. Local officials who lack direct authority over the issues of contention can shed the responsibility for mobilizations if they communicate with their superiors about how to address the situation. Other improvisations that signal good work ethic can also ward off the accusation of negligence.[10]

among bureaucratic units, followed by altering the offer in an informal context. See Zhou and Lian (2011).

[9] See General Office of CCP and General Office of the State Council. (2016, February 27). 健全落实社会治安综合治理领导责任制规定 (Regulations on enhancing leadership responsibilities of comprehensive governance of public security), Item 20 in Chap. 5, xinhuanet.com, retrieved from http://news.xinhuanet.com/politics/2016-03/23/c_1118422119.htm.

[10] For example, Lee and Zhang (2013) note that the implementation of the one-veto rule leaves ample space for discretion at the grassroots. In many cases, grassroots officials are able to dodge sanctions through improvisations. Cai (2014b) also documents selective punishment of local officials. Local officials in a social stability maintenance unit I interviewed concurred with these

The officials' incentive structure also differs along the administrative ranks, as officials at different levels have different opportunities to advance. Most lower-ranked officials (including vice leaders and bureau chiefs) are not rotated but serve lifetime posts in one locale (Ang, 2016, p. 49). These officials, as Yuen Yuen Ang estimates, account for more than 99% of the Chinese bureaucracy (Ang, 2016, p. 106). Whereas promotion incentives are important to higher-level leaders (e.g., Li & Zhou, 2005), the incentives most relevant to lower-ranked officials "come in the form of compensation, not promotion" (Ang, 2016, p. 137). Grassroots officials receive a fixed salary and extra incentives based on the performance of the bureaucracy they oversee, with a greater reward for those whose departments obtain more income (Ang, 2016, p. 131). The autonomy grassroots officials enjoy in managing the local economy is an important source from which they generate surplus for the bureaucracies they lead (Oi, 1995).

The incentive structure empowers grassroots officials in a way that party leaders doubtless never intended. Higher-level officials, especially those in leadership positions, value promotion. Promotions at higher ranks are highly competitive and subject to political struggle (Shih et al., 2012). A stain on an official's résumé, including poor social stability management as evidenced by a mass protest on their watch, can block their hopes for advancement.[11] Officials at the grassroots level, in contrast, value compensation over promotion, and their compensation is closely tied to local and departmental interests. When higher-level orders confront local interests, officials at the lower level can use mobilization to extract concessions. The career ambitions of superiors make them vulnerable and cautious.

To summarize, two institutional characteristics of the party-state create space for "consent instability" to emerge. The unequal distributions of bargaining power place some bureaucracies in a weak position. The officials who oversee these agencies seek sources of bargaining power from outside the bureaucracy. Grassroots officials in these places often value the augmentation

observations. Interview with a deputy director of letter visit office of a coastal district, October 20, 2015. Interview with a deputy director of letter visit office of a coastal district, December 24, 2015.

[11] One of my interviewees, who works in a local social stability maintenance unit, commented on the political use of the "one-veto rule" as follows: "This is very complicated. If you are in good relation with 'the above' [superior], you are fine. If 'the above' is looking after you, this [the one-veto rule] becomes a good excuse to punish you. You know, this is something of Chinese characteristics." Interview with a staff member at the politics and law commission of the capital of a coastal province, October 22, 2015.

of local interests more than their own advancement. Therefore, they can risk using social instability as an extortionary tool to extract policy concessions from higher-level leaders.

The county C case study in Section 6.4 illustrates these dynamics. While the majority of the book focuses on the politics of high-speed railways, this chapter uses a county merger case to illustrate consent instability. The primary reason I selected this case is the availability of evidence. I was able to gain access to local leaders and residents involved in the incident, and gather rich first- and second-hand information on the background and development of the mobilization. I have not been able to gain similar access to information regarding mobilizations related to high-speed railways. The county merger case, fortunately, is comparable to cases in which local leaders used public pressure to pursue high-speed railway projects. In both cases, local governments with weak bargaining power (the clerics) have few institutionalized mechanisms of resisting unfavorable policy decisions imposed by their superiors.

6.4 A Case Study of "Consent Instability"

More than 1,000 residents of county C held a protest at the county government headquarters in 2013.[12] The impetus was that officials of a city, which I will call H, that administers the county had decided to turn county C into a district under its direct jurisdiction. Thus they were essentially proposing to merge the county with city H. County C, one of the most affluent in the city, was financially independent, which meant their strong tax base could provide amenities in the city and that county officials had autonomy that district officials lack. County C residents took their county's relatively independent status as a point of pride and argued that the merger would have a negative impact on various aspects of their lives, such as the quality of local public services. The gathering of over 1,000 people in front of the county government building opposing the merger plan was the culmination of expressions of dissatisfaction on various online and offline channels. While Chinese officials generally treat social stability as a priority, clear evidence suggests

---

[12] As I draw intensively from interviews with local officials, to protect the safety of these informants and also to comply with institutional requirements involving human subjects, I have removed all potential identifiers that could reveal the true identity of the informants. This includes specific names, positions, locations, and exact dates of the incidents.

that county C officials did little to prevent this protest and even sided with organizers. The city government hastily suspended the merger plan following the mass demonstration, stating that the plan was "still immature." The analyses of the preferences and behaviors of city officials, county officials, and the local population draw on 21 interviews with local officials and residents, as well as other primary sources regarding the incident that I acquired during the fieldwork.

6.4.1 Actors and Their Preferences

City H. Like many other cities in province K, the city H government presides over a relatively small urban center. This is the result of province K's long-term practice in managing its counties directly (省管县). Whereas counties exist administratively under cities, as elsewhere in China, they are economically accountable only to the province. The allocations of revenue, government investment, land quotas, and other resources take place directly between the provincial government and the counties. This management system means the city government can extract resources from districts within it, but not counties. City H, for example, controls the resources of only two districts. Because of this arrangement, many cities in province K lack resources to invest in infrastructure and urban construction and cannot develop their urban centers. The two largest cities in province K turned several of their counties into districts in the early 2000s, and have since then achieved rapid urbanization and growth. In turning county C into a district under its direct control, the government of city H sought to strengthen its capabilities. The provincial government endorsed the plan as a way to grow the provincial economy through a new wave of urbanization.

In the party hierarchy, city H government has more power than county C's government. The city enjoys higher political rank than the county despite the latter's relatively independent economic status.[13] The county officials would endure punishment if they openly opposed their superiors' decisions.

County C. As county C residents and county officials perceived, county C has benefited enormously from its relatively autonomous status. The deputy chief of the county's fiscal bureau told me that the county currently retains

---

[13] As in most cities in China, the city leaders hold the rank of bureau chief (*ting ji*), and the county leaders hold the rank of division chief (*chu ji*), which is two ranks below the city leader.

80% of its revenue and transfers the remaining 20% to the provincial government, whereas a merger would require it to turn over 50% or more of this revenue to the city government.[14] Further, the county would lose its annual land conversion quota to city H, along with its control of the land use right transfer fee. The county has relied on this large supplement of tax revenue for a number of its infrastructure projects.[15] A merger might give these funds to city H, which sought to develop an urban center.[16]

Beyond revenue allocation, county C would lose much of its control of various aspects of economic and social management, such as urban planning and the recruitment of public employees. A county official described the difference between the county and district structure in province K as follows:

> Our ranks won't change (if county C becomes a district). But as a district, we are only a "half government (半级政府)." We are functionaries of the city and only get to do whatever the city government wants us to do. Now [as a county] we are in full charge of ourselves.[17]

In interviews, I proposed that the change could have benefits, such as increased access to public services offered by the city, but county C officials dismissed these. Proud of the county's status as one of the "national top 100 counties (全国百强县)," the county's officials worry that joining city H—an average prefecture struggling with its own development—would impose liabilities on the county. An official at the county's development and reform bureau, for example, said that the county has never received help from the city, and he would not expect that to change if it became a district. He noted that the county sought help from the capital of province K or Shanghai when doctors needed a medical specialist in rare diseases, or the county's factories needed technical experts. "There has not been a single time we received help from city H," he noted. "They also don't have what we need."[18] There are also concerns that the county would face direct competition with the city's two districts in attracting outside investment, and that the merger would deprive

---

[14] Interview with a deputy director of the county fiscal bureau, November 13, 2015.

[15] The size of county C's land use-right transfer fee is about half the size of the formal revenue. Interviews with a deputy director of the county fiscal bureau and a section chief of the county land bureau, November 13, 2015.

[16] Interview with a section chief of the county land bureau, November 13, 2015.

[17] Interview with the director of the county policy research office, November 13, 2015.

[18] Interview with a deputy director of the county development and reform bureau, November 13, 2015.

the county of policy advantages it had before.[19] Throughout my interviews in county C, every official, including those within the county leadership,[20] was quite outspoken on the potential downsides of the merger. None, however, expressed support of the merger plan.

County C Citizens. Local citizens objected to the potential merger for similar reasons as county officials. Some expressed concern that the city government would not pay enough attention to their county, and they would lose services they currently enjoy. Some openly expressed reluctance to share their schools, hospitals, and other public facilities with city residents.[21] Local businessmen, who were already unhappy with the redundancy of the county's bureaucracy, worried that the merger would further increase their cost of doing business.[22] For example, a businessman who runs a private tutoring school told me that he would lose valuable time traveling 30 kilometers to the city to obtain permission for business activities.[23]

Many county residents voiced their concerns online once the plan became public. On the county's Baidu Tieba (the Chinese equivalent of Reddit) page, I identified 816 posts that discuss the merger, each of which had at least ten replies and many of which had many more.[24] Some posts suggested the city was trying to squeeze as much as it could from the county; others pointed to another county that had lost its independence under city H a decade ago and suggested its fate had been negative and that county C's would be as well. Akin to the nationalistic accounts that Chinese netizens often invoke, they appealed to local pride, portraying city H as an "invader" that sought to undermine the interests of the county. Some of these posts used derogatory terms to refer to city H. They called the merger a way of humiliating county residents, avowing they "would never be the conquered people (坚决不做亡县奴)."

---

[19] Interview with a deputy director of the county commerce bureau, November 13, 2015.

[20] Interview with a member of the county party standing committee, November 13, 2015. Interview with a secretary to the county executive, November 13, 2015.

[21] Interview with county resident A, June 24, 2015. Interview with county resident B, August 18, 2015. Interviews with county residents C and D, November 12, 2015. Interviews with county residents E and F, November 13, 2015.

[22] Interview with a deputy director of the county commerce bureau, November 13, 2015.

[23] Interview with local resident F, November 13, 2015.

[24] This number might underestimate the citizens' online participation, as the incident took place three years before I conducted the search, and many posts had been deleted. Because county C's name appears in these posts, to protect informants' identities, I do not include links to these posts.

6.4.2 Bureaucratic Bargaining Before the Demonstration

The bargaining between the county and the city took place long before the protest. According to county C officials, the city government conducted months of field investigation (调研) prior to the decision. The working group assigned to investigate the decision for the city summoned county officials (including bureau chiefs and township heads) and listened to their opinions regarding the merger plan.[25] These meetings took place behind closed doors, and at first, the public did not know about the merger plan. In these meetings, the city officials assured the county officials that the merger would not harm county C, but the county officials strongly opposed it from the very beginning. They had no trust in the city officials' assurances. In interviews with me, they cited the fate of district N, formerly county N, as a formerly autonomous and prosperous area where development had lagged behind after merging with city H.[26] The city government proceeded with the merger plan despite these objections.

I did not speak with city officials and therefore do not know why they ignored county officials' opinions, only to heed them later. Perhaps they underestimated the scale of opposition, believed only a fraction of county officials were seriously opposed and that they would eventually acquiesce to higher authority.

6.4.3 The Demonstration

Several weeks after meeting with county officials and disregarding their objections, the city officials informed these county officials that they would soon come down to the county and announce the merger publicly.[27] This never came to pass, but I believe that the statement of intention prompted county C officials to leak news of the merger plan, having concluded that the city was ignoring their objections. County residents began to post calls to action online to county C citizens to resist.

---

[25] Interview with a secretary to the county executive, November 13, 2015. Interview with a deputy director of county reform and development commission, November 13, 2015.

[26] Ibid.

[27] This section mainly relies on the coverage of the incident by a major commercial newspaper in China. Because the name of the county was mentioned in the news report, to protect the identity of the informants I do not include the title of the report, and later refer to it as "Report 1."

Attempts at offline resistance began with a request for a permit to demonstrate by a township branch of the county's business association. The request to the county's public security bureau alleged that "the merger would seriously undermine the interests of the county C people and the local business. After collective discussions among the members, [we] request permission to hold a demonstration with 150 anticipated participants in the square in front of the county government."[28] In line with the policy of all Chinese government agencies, the county's public security bureau declined the request, but the county's business association would continue to show leadership in the ensuing public response.

The demonstration went ahead *at the proposed date* without the permit, and far exceeded the number in the application. It attracted at least 1,000 protesters, most of them not members of the business association.[29] The business association distributed T-shirts and banners with printed slogans on the spot. The T-shirts declared "I love county C." Banners read "County C belongs to the people of County C!," "County C has over a thousand years of history, it cannot become a district overnight!," and "County C's half-million people will never be the conquered people (亡县奴)!"[30] Some participants held a piece of large white cloth and asked people passing by to sign it, indicating their support for the protest.[31] County residents live-broadcasted the event on social media, and one social media post includes a picture of the poster's small child wearing the "I love county C" shirt.[32]

Other signs of protest appeared in public in the form of stickers on cars. A foreign media outlet ran a photograph of such a sticker that stated, "County C people thank those who contributed to the development of our county, and will remember as criminals those who turn our county into a district."[33] A sticker on a taxi stated that the county police would fine anyone who did not have a sticker opposing the merger.[34] A local hotel's outdoor LED screen stopped displaying room rates in order to display a slogan opposing the merger.[35]

---

[28] The author acquired a copy of the letter online.

[29] Report 1 stated there were "several thousand." Online posters claimed there were over ten thousand participants, but this seems unlikely.

[30] I changed the number of people to protect the county's identity.

[31] Some overseas media outlets covered the demonstration with photos from the scene. To protect the identity of the informants, I refer to these reports, which I accessed on a foreign website, as "Report 2."

[32] Ibid.

[33] Report 2.

[34] Ibid.

[35] The photo was uploaded to a Baidu Tieba post.

6.4.4 County Officials' Response

The county government's refusal of a permit aligned with party policy, as did the county's other actions: deploying police forces to manage the crowd when the demonstrations took place but not taking any drastic measures that would further provoke public anger, and keeping their superiors in city H informed about the situation.

Yet, in addition to these standard responses, the officials demonstrated an unusual degree of tolerance. While they are cautious about suppressing protests once they have begun, local-level Chinese government officials often take measures to prevent them, but they did not in this case.[36] The permit request had notified the county of the intent to hold the demonstration, and the police could have preemptively contained the organizers. But they did not. The protesters showed up on the date listed in their application. Organizers were able to prepare T-shirts and banners ahead of time without police obstruction. The police also tolerated protesters' behavior such as entering the gate of the government compound and hanging banners with anti-merger slogans on the glass door of the government building in the course of the demonstration. A local resident who attended described the police as "gentle," concluding, "they were with us."[37]

Some officials participated in oppositional activities. Several officials from the county fiscal bureau and commerce bureau—the two bureaus the merger would most limit—were among the protesters in front of the county building.[38] Over 200 retired county cadres also wrote letters to the county leaders voicing their opposition regarding the merger.[39] On the same day, leaders of the local townships and industrial parks signed a petition letter threatening to resign altogether if the city government did not retract the decision.[40] In the letter, these local leaders said that their resistance (to preserve county independence) "will and must be supported by the half-million county residents."[41] They seemed to be fully aware that citizen mobilization would echo their action.

It seems obvious that the police and the local officials had the support of county leadership, or they would not have taken this risk. Perhaps nothing

---

[36] For example, Yan (2016).
[37] Interview with county resident B, August 18, 2015.
[38] Report 1.
[39] Ibid.
[40] Ibid.; the author also acquired a photocopy of the signed letter online.
[41] Ibid.

summarizes the intricate position of the county better than the words of a county C's party standing committee member, who told me that the county government supported the people, who were "the front stage," from "the backstage."[42] Ample evidence suggests that officials tolerated the mild instability that the demonstration created.

6.4.5 The Outcome of the County's Resistance

As the demonstration unfolded, the county officials quickly reported the situation to the city and waited for their directives. Hours after people gathered in the government square, the county's deputy party secretary walked out of the government building and spoke to the crowd. He told them that the city's and county's governments and party committees had "carefully considered" the merits of turning county C into a district and concluded it was premature. "Thanks, everyone, for supporting county C. Many thanks!"[43] The crowd cheered and quickly dissipated.

No formal sanctions punished county officials for working against their superiors. Here, the cadre evaluation system worked in their favor, because the impetus for the unrest was the city's interest in merging the county, and they had monitored, contained, and reported during the protest, as the swift joint response in making the announcement suggests. The protest had ended peacefully after the announcement, in contrast to a 2005 incident that led to the removal of several high-level county officials in Daye, where the Huangshi prefecture-level city sought to turn the county into a district. Protesters besieged the city government building and destroyed government property in that case, but county C officials avoided this outcome.[44]

The provincial authority treated the county officials who stood with the protesters as voluntary individual actors instead of part of a concerted scheme by the bureaus they represented. The provincial authority sent an informal warning in the form of an investigation team to have one-on-one meetings (约谈) with those township leaders who signed the petition against the merger, but did not enact further sanction.[45]

[42] Interview with a member of the county party standing committee, November 13, 2015.
[43] Report 1.
[44] See Wu, W. (2006, February 25). 湖北大冶两市委副书记被撤职 (Two deputy party secretaries of Daye removed from office), sina.com.cn, retrieved from http://news.sina.com.cn/c/2006-02-25/11558300186s.shtml.
[45] Interview with a member of the county party standing committee, November 13, 2015.

6.5 Consent Instability in the Broader Context

6.5.1 Consent Instability in Various Issue Areas

The details of the county C incident allow us to deduce the conditions under which consent instability takes place. It is triggered by upper-level decisions that put weak agencies in a disadvantageous position. Local citizens voice their dissatisfaction against such decisions, which empowers local officials at the bargaining table. Such conditions—which rely crucially on the preference congruence between local officials and citizenry—can appear in various issues areas and across different parts of the country.

In addition to county C in 2013, I am aware of several other cases where administrative redistricting led to consent instability. National media reported the Daye incident in Hubei in 2005[46] and the Longnan incident in Gangsu in 2008.[47] In both cases, thousands of residents protested the disempowerment or planned disempowerment of local government. Investigations conducted later reveal that local officials were involved in these events, much as they were in county C. In interviews, a professor at Zhejiang University told me that Huangyan county officials opposed its conversion into a district in 1994.[48] Most of the delegates of the local people's congress were entrepreneurs, and they opposed the merger for economic reasons. After the city government forced the conversion, they refused to perform their duties. In another case, retired cadres mobilized, unsuccessfully, against the redistricting of Shaoxing's two counties in 2013.[49]

The construction of high-speed railway stations is another issue area in which local officials have invoked local popular pressure to demand preferential consideration. In recent years, protesters have demanded local stations in the planned high-speed railway routes in at least a dozen small localities where local officials do not have the leverage to demand a station. Chinese media term such mobilizations "high-speed railway social movements (高铁

[46] See Wu, W. (2006, February 25). 湖北大冶两市委副书记被撤职 (*Two deputy party secretaries of Daye removed from office*), sina.com.cn, retrieved from http://news.sina.com.cn/c/2006-02-25/11558300186s.shtml.
[47] See 甘肃陇南11·17群体性事件初步控制 (The November 17th mass incident in Gangsu Longnan is under control), huanqiu.com, retrieved from https://china.huanqiu.com/article/9CaK rnJlcxc; also Interview with an official in the Development Research Center of the State Council, 19 July 2015.
[48] Interview with a professor of public administration at Zhejiang University, August 20, 2015.
[49] Ibid.

社运)."[50] As in county C's reversion of the merger, local officials have tolerated or even encouraged protesters, and many of these movements have had success.[51]

Like the cases in administrative redistricting, the congruence of preferences for high-speed railway between local authorities and citizens is an essential condition for consent instability to take place. The officials' preference for high-speed railways is straightforward. As elaborated in previous chapters, introducing high-speed railways brings short-term and long-term benefits to the local economy, which could contribute both to local officials' career advancement and more specific personal interests (e.g., contracting opportunities for connected local businesses). The local residents' preference for high-speed railways is more complex. Some might indeed benefit from improved transportation, but the number of people in need of frequent long-distance travel is not big compared to the population. The majority of local residents see the high-speed railway as an achievement of local development and a point of pride. In other words, the "benefits" might be imaginary.[52] As an increasing number of Chinese localities are connected to the national high-speed railway network, even local residents who seldom ride trains might see losing a high-speed railway station to a neighboring locale as a humiliation. Such localist sentiments based on the shared interests of an "imagined community" (Anderson, 2006) have the potential to mobilize more protesters, just as nationalism, its counterpart at the national level, does.

6.5.2 The Role of Intermediaries

Like in county C, local business owners have played an active role in many of these events elsewhere. For example, in 2015, a local business association in Jingzhou, Hubei, organized a rally and collected more than 10,000 signatures

---

[50] These locales are Shaoyang and Loudi in Hunan, Shiyan and Xiangyang in Hubei, Dengzhou and Xinye in Henan, Jingzhou and Jingmen in Hubei, and Linshui and Guangan in Sichuan. See 高铁争夺战呈现出社运新特点 (*Competitions for high-speed railway reveal new features of social movement*), Zhigu Qushi, retrieved from https://mp.weixin.qq.com/s/M3UiAKCVMrOFaUd2ogXnmw. Also see Allen-Ebrahimian, B. (2015, May 19). *These Chinese people want high-speed rail so badly they are fighting police to get it*, foreignpolicy.com, retrieved from https://foreignpolicy.com/2015/05/19/linshui-china-high-speed-rail-protest-police/.

[51] Take the Linshui incident as an example: Sichuan provincial government hastily announced that the route of the high-speed railway in question—Dayu Railroad—was not finalized and would be subject to further review following the protest.

[52] Interview with a scholar of contentious politics in Hong Kong, July 30, 2015.

from local citizens advocating the construction of a local station along the proposed Wuhan–Chengdu high-speed railway. When interviewed by a newspaper, the organizer emphasized that the business association "is a legal nonprofit organization founded under the permission of Jingzhou civil affairs bureau."[53] Local businesspeople (mine owners) also played a pivotal role in mobilizing the protesters in the Daye incident.[54]

The frequent presence of local business organizations might help explain why local governments were able to remain largely invisible in protests. Local businesses in China are highly dependent on the state, and businesspeople form close ties with local officials to survive and flourish (e.g., Dickson, 2008; Ong, 2012; Tsai, 2007). Thus these business associations likely serve as the crucial interlocutor between the state and the citizens in many cases. The state green-lit the mobilization from backstage, and the business associations mobilized the people in public. Because the local state did not publicly organize the protest by itself, they were able to (in most cases) avoid being identified and sanctioned by their superiors.

In contrast, local leaders in the Daye incident relied on members of local football fan associations and mine owners to mobilize the masses (Deng et al., forthcoming). While these organizations or individuals had rich social linkages and were able to mobilize a large number of local residents in a short period of time, they were also more difficult than business associations for local leaders to control behind the scenes.

6.5.3 The Risk of Consent Instability

A legitimate concern is how do local officials control the power of the masses once they unleash them, and what will happen if protesters get out of control. Yet, the use of mass mobilization as a bargaining tool depends on some risk of instability (Weiss, 2013, p. 3). If a protest appears perfectly controllable or staged, then its messages are likely dismissed as "cheap talks." Despite being genuine and spontaneous, consent instability is relatively easy for local governments to control. First of all, the appeals of the citizens are localist

---

[53] See Zhou, S. Y. (2015, April 20). 湖北两地 "竞争" 沿江高铁项目 荆州组织万人签名 (Two locales in Hubei "competed" for the high-speed railway along the Yangtze River, Jingzhou organized a rally with ten thousand people collecting signatures), xinhuanet.com, retrieved from http://www.xinhuanet.com/politics/2015-04/20/c_127707841.htm.

[54] See Mei, J. (2006, February 25). 大冶 "8·6" 事件始末 (*A detailed report on the August 6th incident in Daye*), soho.com, retrieved from http://news.sohu.com/20060225/n242011082.shtml.

(e.g., opposing redistricting, demanding a high-speed railway station) and do not pertain to individual grievances or official misconduct. Such localist appeals are unlikely to garner much popular support beyond the locality. Consequently, the potential protesters are limited to the people in the locale.

Second, as shown in the case of county C, the local government is aware of the mobilization ahead of time and thus can make preparation (e.g., dispatching police) to prevent the situation from getting out of control. In those few cases in which protesters began to attack government buildings or damage property (such as in Daye and Linshui), the local public security forces quickly stepped in and dispersed the crowds.[55] The ease with which they have done so reveals that lack of repressive capability is not the reason these mobilizations take place. Rather, repressive capability gives local officials the confidence to take a risk, expecting they can control the protests that they tacitly permit or support.

Finally, as shown in earlier discussions, there are intermediaries (such as local business associations) between local governments and protesters. These intermediaries give local governments some leverage in influencing the crowd. When mine owners (i.e., intermediaries) in Daye tried to organize the protest, some of the people they paid to join the protest had criminal records (these were also the people who attacked the building).[56] The mine owners lost control of these people and the protest ended in violence.

Whether the mobilization went out of control and became violent was a crucial criterion for whether officials involved would be punished by their superiors. As mentioned earlier, the state usually sanctions the party responsible for causing unrest. In these cases, the direct cause of contention, at least seen from outside, is the policy decisions by higher-level authorities. Superiors thus lack good reasons to punish county officials. But if the mobilization turns violent, then the superiors can accuse local officials of failure in containing the situation. In Daye, the protest was accused of "causing severe political consequences," and such accusation was not seen in other cases (including county C).[57] The scale and violence made the

---

[55] For example, the local public security force in Linshui stepped in after the local people's rally for a high-speed railway station went out of control. Wen, P. (2015, May 18). *Chinese pro-development protesters in bloody riot police confrontation in Linshui*, smh.com.au, retrieved from http://www.smh.com.au/world/chinese-prodevelopment-protesters-in-bloody-riot-police-confrontation-in-linshui-20150518-gh3zpv.html.

[56] See (2006, February 25). 湖北大冶官员公然组织上访策划打砸事件始末 (*A detailed report on how Hubei Daye officials plotted and organized petitioners in the Daye incident*), sina.com, retrieved from http://news.sina.com.cn/c/2006-02-25/04438298759s.shtml.

[57] See Mei, J. (2006, February 25). 大冶 "8·6" 事件始末 (*A Detailed Report on the August 6th Incident in Daye*), soho.com, retrieved from http://news.sohu.com/20060225/n242011082.shtml.

Daye incident a high-profile event and forced the Hubei provincial government to conduct a thorough investigation. When investigated, Daye officials were found to have colluded with organizers of the protest and were charged with plotting against the party organization. In many other cases, mild mobilizations did not trigger a thorough investigation from higher authorities.

6.6 Assessing the Power of the Masses

Consent instability in county C led to policy change. The case study, however, does not provide satisfying answers to every question. For example, why did the city authority ignore the county officials' opinion in the first place, yet concede when the protest took place? So far, we have conjectured that city leaders do not want to be responsible for causing greater instability. Is this just the result of the idiosyncratic situation in city H, or does it reflect a broader, more systematic pattern? Evidence on how things operate at the city level is scant. Officials at higher levels have been more difficult to approach than county-level officials such as those I interviewed.

To investigate whether this is a pattern that likely goes beyond the cases I know about, between December 2016 and May 2017 I conducted a survey experiment of 368 local officials. I recruited from the cadre training classes in the Master of Public Administration programs in two universities in Beijing.[58] The respondents constitute a subsample of the sample analyzed in Chapter 3.

6.6.1 The Respondents

By arrangement with the schools' staff, who helped with the distribution of the survey, only public officials participated. Table 6.1 describes the participants.

Of course, as I mentioned in Chapter 3, this is not a representative sample of Chinese local officials. It would be difficult to assemble such a sample

---

[58] To protect the identity of the respondents as well as the school officials who helped implement the survey, I do not disclose the names of the schools.

Table 6.1 Descriptive Statistics of the Subjects (N = 368)

Variable	Mean
Male (1 = male, 0 = female)	0.62
Age	41
College degree or above (1 = yes)	0.89
Party experience (years)	16.24
Length of service in government (years)	18.77
Rank at or above division chief (1 = yes)[1]	0.30
Rank at or above section chief (1 = yes)[2]	0.56
Rank at or above deputy section chief (1 = yes)[3]	0.83
Hold leadership position at work unit (单位) (1 = yes)	0.60

Notes: 1. Positions at the rank of division chief (处级) include county executive, municipal bureau chief, and section chief in provincial bureaus.

2. Positions at the rank of section chief (科级) include township executive, county bureau chief, and section chief in municipal bureaus.

3. Positions at the rank of deputy section chief (副科级) include deputy township executive, deputy county bureau chief, and deputy section chief in municipal bureaus.

because of the party's political control. Therefore, in line with past research, this study employs re-randomization within the sample to test causal hypotheses (Meng et al., 2017). Notwithstanding its limitations, the sample clearly has sufficient experience and knowledge of how local governments operate. More than 83% of participants have obtained the rank of deputy section chief or better, and over 60% report that they hold leadership positions at their work units, meaning they are cadres. The average work experience in the government is 18.77 years, much longer than the 10-year average in the benchmark survey study of Chinese local officials in the field (and also longer than the 16.72 years average of the full sample analyzed in Chapter 3). The subjects work in five provinces, including three coastal provinces and two inland provinces.

6.6.2 Survey Experiment Design

Officials are unlikely to admit to the dynamic of consent instability, even on an anonymous survey, which would signal regime weakness and suggest they themselves are a threat to the party-state. Thus, I employ an endorsement experiment design. The endorsement experiment design uses subtle cues to measure survey respondents' support of statements or policies that socially sensitive actors endorse, thus avoiding directly addressing sensitive political issues (Lyall et al., 2013).

Respondents were first divided into control, treatment, and placebo groups. This basic statement was used with each of the three groups:

> City A is under a tight budget this year. Mr. Wang, the party secretary of a district under the city, goes to the city's fiscal bureau, asking for a special earmark for a reconfiguration project [形象整修工程] of a main road in his district. [Control group: No additional sentence here. Treatment group: "Many of the local people have been strongly demanding the reconfiguration for a while due to the road's poor condition." Placebo group: "Mr. Wang claims that many of the local people have been strongly demanding the reconfiguration for a while due to the road's poor condition."]
>
> If you were in charge of the city's fiscal bureau, would you support the earmark?
>
> 1. Strongly oppose 2. Oppose 3. Neither support nor oppose 4. Support 5. Strongly Support

The objective of comparing the control group with the treatment group is to test whether public pressure has an impact. The objective of comparing the placebo group and the treatment group is to test whether a claim of public pressure has a different impact from actual public pressure. Since it is costless for Mr. Wang to fake the public pressure, his superiors may not believe him, and it may not be a useful bargaining tool. The comparison between the treatment and the placebo scenarios could also ameliorate the concern that the revelation of citizens' policy demands alone drives any observed treatment effect.

The wording of this hypothetical scenario does not reference merging districts or planning high-speed railway stations, even though the aforementioned cases involve these issues, because I expected to recruit city and county bureaucrats, who lack the power to influence such decisions. Such officials would have power over a special earmark on local projects, and using this scenario makes their responses more realistic and reliable.

Table 6.2 Baseline Result: Comparing the Control and Treatment Groups

	Estimate	Std. Error	t value	Pr(>|t|)
Intercept (control)	2.9403	0.19907	14.769	<0.001***
Treatment	0.7628	0.13271	5.748	<0.001***
Enumerator (class) fixed effect	Yes			

Table 6.3 Comparing the Control and Placebo Groups

	Estimate	Std. Error	t value	Pr(>|t|)
Intercept (control)	3.1948	0.2173	14.70	<0.001***
Placebo	0.3223	0.1461	2.206	0.0284*
Enumerator (class) fixed effect	Yes			

6.6.3 Results

I first compare the control and treatment groups. In addition to the key variable that identifies a respondent's group, I control for the enumerator fixed effect, as different staff members distributed the survey questionnaires in different classes. The results are presented in Table 6.2.

The level of support in the control group, as reflected in the coefficient for the intercept, is about 2.94, suggesting moderate opposition. This result likely reflects the central government's pressure on local government to cut back wasteful spending to "showcase" infrastructure projects. The language used in the survey—reconfiguration of a main road—suggests that the earmark could be used in such a project.

The coefficient for the treatment group is 0.76, and is statistically significant ($p < .001$). This means that the inclusion of a statement that local citizens also strongly demand such an earmark shifts the level of support to 3.7 (2.94 + 0.76), an almost 26% increase from that of the control group (2.94). This result lends strong support to the claim that officials consider public pressure in determining their actions.

I also compare the control with the placebo treatment, as shown in Table 6.3. The size of the coefficient for the placebo treatment is 0.32 and is significant at $p < .05$. I then run the analysis using the placebo group as the benchmark, and the difference between the placebo and treatment groups

Table 6.4 Comparing the Placebo and Treatment Groups

	Estimate	Std. Error	t value	Pr(>$|t|$)
Intercept (placebo)	3.4643	0.1885	18.382	<0.001***
Treatment	0.4338	0.1284	3.377	<0.001***
Enumerator (class) fixed effect	Yes			

is also large (0.43) and significant at $p < .001$, as shown in Table 6.4. Thus the support for the earmark was stronger in the placebo group than in the control group, but much weaker than in the treatment group. This is consistent with my hypothesis that *real* citizen demand has a stronger treatment effect than *claimed* citizen demand. Together, these results help illustrate why local officials need to risk social instability in order to have a strong bargaining tool.

6.7 Concluding Remarks

This chapter studies local officials' strategic use of instability in bureaucratic bargaining. I develop a theory of "consent instability" in which mass mobilizations—with appeals that are congruent with officials' agenda—could serve as powerful bargaining leverage for weak bureaucrats (the "clerics") to extract policy concessions from above. The chapter examines the institutional environment that gives rise to such a strategy, uses a detailed case study to show how officials' responses to a public protest deviate from the default mode of repression, and employs a survey experiment to assess the efficacy of public pressure in intra-bureaucratic bargaining.

The findings in this chapter not only further our understanding of bureaucratic bargaining, but also contribute to the literature on the multifaceted nature of stability maintenance in China. While conventional wisdom suggests that the Chinese state prioritizes stability and spares no effort in preventing social movements (e.g., Wang & Minzner, 2015; Yan, 2016), recent studies suggest a more nuanced picture (Lorentzen, 2017). Local states in China enjoy considerable autonomy, and differ in their strategies addressing sources of social instability (e.g., Cai, 2010; Yan & Zhou, 2017). Through interviews with local officials in Beijing and Shenzhen, Lee and Zhang (2013) find that grassroots officials and aggrieved citizens surprisingly "share a common interest in sustaining a certain level of instability," because "the existence of instability justifies demands for an augmented budget for the departments and personnel involved in preserving stability" (p. 1493). Similarly, O'Brien et al. (2020) find that local bureaucrats and business elites collude in mobilizing protests to protect their own interests. Weiss (2014) argues that the Chinese authority tolerates and capitalizes on nationalistic protests to generate bargaining power in international diplomatic negotiations. This chapter adds to this line of research by showing that local officials can benefit from the presence of protests in the intra-bureaucratic policy bargain and therefore have the incentive to tolerate citizen mobilization with congruent demand. These findings suggest that public displays of discontent are not always ominous for officials, and officials sometimes use (or even manipulate) such events to their advantage (e.g., Chen & Xu, 2016).

The findings in this chapter are also consistent with the notion that the Chinese state is far from monolithic. Instead, it is a segmented, multilayered system with actors of different interests competing for influence (Jaros, 2019; Mertha, 2009), and these actors occasionally seek allies within or outside the state against shared adversaries (e.g., Zhou, 2010). While a large body of literature suggests that the multilayered, decentralized system provides incentives for economic growth (e.g., Landry, 2008; Lü & Landry, 2014; Montinola et al., 1995), this chapter shows that such a system also breeds intergovernmental conflict and popular contention. The tension stems from the paradox of economic decentralization coupled with political centralization (e.g., Huang, 1996; Xu, 2011). Local states, which enjoy considerable policy autonomy in their jurisdictions, routinely confront attempts of top-down political control and develop various strategies of resistance to preserve their autonomy.

Finally, the model of consent instability also contributes to the comparative literature of authoritarianism by highlighting an elite–mass linkage in authoritarian politics. While students of dictatorships increasingly recognize that elites have greater influence than the masses in authoritarian political processes (Svolik, 2012), many scholars have importantly noticed that bottom-up citizen mobilizations, when they come at the right time and in the right forms, might empower authoritarian elites in unanticipated ways (e.g.,

O'donnell & Schmitter, 1986; Radnitz, 2010; Slater, 2010; Treisman, 1999). The argument developed in this chapter echoes this logic, and offers rich evidence on how Chinese local officials exploit public pressure to extract policy benefits from their more powerful counterparts within the regime. The question of how the masses might change the landscape of Chinese elite politics at various levels is a promising area for future research.

7

Conclusion

7.1 Review of Main Findings

This book begins with an attempt to understand the politics behind the largest infrastructure program in human history. The rapid expansion of China's high-speed rail network generates a host of interesting questions that have not received sufficient attention so far. What determines the allocation of rail investments in the first place? Why do some places get more central investments in rail infrastructure or have faster rollout in service than the rest? Why do some places need to wait while others get priority? What dynamics between the central and local authorities shape the allocations of investments? These empirical puzzles also echo some more general questions in the study of politics. What mechanisms bind the leaders to provide policy benefits to their constituents? What accounts for different levels and patterns of public works and services within a single country? What kind of institutional arrangements would serve the function of allocating resources among the regime insiders while at the same time also making such institutions self-enforcing and durable under authoritarianism?

The book explores how bottom-up policy bargains by territorial administrations (or localized bargaining) shape the allocation of policy benefits. Localities that are able to coordinate bureaucratic consensus among superiors and outcompete local rivals are more likely to secure preferential policy treatment. The bottom-up bargain model rests crucially on the preconditions that the authorities of decision-making and implementation are fragmented among numerous specialized bureaucracies. Such a structure not only limits the ability of the ruler to exert top-down control in the allocation of policy resources, but also renders bottom-up bargaining efforts by localities meaningful in determining policy outcomes. Localities, however, are not created equal. The outcomes of policy solicitations vary according to localities' bargaining power, which is derived from various sources. Combining interviews, case studies, policy documents, data analysis, and surveys of local officials, this book shows that some localities acquire

Localized Bargaining. Xiao Ma, Oxford University Press. © Oxford University Press 2022.
DOI: 10.1093/oso/9780197638910.003.0007

enhanced bargaining power in soliciting investment in rail infrastructure through their privileged positions within the party-state's hierarchy, and some others strengthen their bargaining positions by riding on the power of local constituents.

Unlike the prevailing theories in distributive politics, which often assume that the leaders at the top make strategic choices in allocating policy benefits among constituents, this book advances a "demand-side" story that emphasizes the important role played by the actors located on the receiving end of policies. Rulers do not govern alone. They rely on technocrats, experts, and local officials to formulate policies, enforce rules, and implement decisions. Yet these actors within the regime are not just impersonal tools of the ruler. They proactively use their positions and power to enlarge their personal or departmental interests. Not only are the state actors "autonomous" (e.g., Geddes, 1990; Nordlinger, 1981), so are the agencies within the state. Territorial administrations, for example, use their indispensable position in implementing policies to try to sway higher authorities' decisions to their favor. The eventual patterns of distribution, therefore, also to some extent reflect the intention and efforts of these "recipients." This story also corroborates the long-held assumption that authoritarian states are far from monolithic. The perennial tensions and bargaining taking place among various regime insiders set the tone for the variegated and often self-contradictory policy outcomes we observe under authoritarianism.

The book's focus on the internal dynamics of bureaucracies also contributes to our understanding of the patterns of power-sharing in authoritarian regimes. In recent years, scholars in comparative politics begin to pay attention to the roles of various institutions (such as party, legislature, constitution, election) in facilitating credible power-sharing agreements between the authoritarian ruler and the elites (e.g., Boix & Svolik, 2013; Lu & Ma, 2019; Magaloni, 2008; Svolik, 2012). There is insufficient attention to the question of how these institutions per se also affect the allocative patterns of wealth and benefits among the regime's elites. This book contributes to this line of studies by arguing that an elaborative bureaucracy with fragmented decision-making authorities plays the twin functions of tying the autocrat's hands while creating spaces that allow bottom-up competition for policy spoils among regime insiders (in this book's case, the territorial administrations). The resulting policy outcomes are more inclusive of various interests within the regime, thereby contributing to the longevity of authoritarian rule.

In the process of thinking about and writing the book, numerous relevant ideas have crossed my mind. While I want to be focused on the main argument of the book, I also do not want to see these thoughts get buried. Here I list, in a rather unorganized fashion, a few thoughts on issues related to the subject of the book. I hope they will provoke ideas for future studies by scholars who are interested in Chinese politics and comparative institutions in general.

7.2 Interests Articulation, Decentralization, and Regime Resilience

In 2003, Andrew Nathan argued that China has instituted a range of institutions that would serve to perpetuate CCP's rule (Nathan, 2003). Coined as "authoritarian resilience," this argument counters the prevailing expectation at the time that China, along with the world's remaining authoritarian regimes, would inevitably move toward democratization (Fukuyama, 1992). One of the crucial institutions in Nathan's argument is the "input institution," which allows citizens to voice opinions, issue complaints, and make demands. The idea is that these institutions would not only bolster the legitimacy of the party-state by making citizens feel that they have some influence over the policy process, but also diffuse potential collective aggression against the regime by directing citizens' grievances against specific, local-level agencies.

Nathan's argument predated the production of an influential line of studies that focuses on a set of relevant institutions but from a different theoretical perspective. The starting point of this line of research is the classical "dictator's dilemma," that efforts to consolidate authoritarian rule, such as censorship or repression of dissidents, paradoxically leave small problems in governance unnoticed until they fester and become major crises that could shake the foundations of authoritarian regimes (Wintrobe, 1998). The autocrats therefore need mechanisms that help solve the regime's information problem while still keeping their grip on power. Scholars of Chinese politics have identified a range of institutional arrangements that would serve such purposes, such as a constrained legislative system (e.g., Manion, 2016; Truex, 2016, 2017), consultative or deliberative outlets online or offline (e.g., Distelhorst, 2017; Distelhorst & Fu, 2019; Distelhorst & Hou, 2017; Gueorguiev, 2014; He & Warren, 2011; Meng et al., 2014), and even loosened enforcement of law or relaxed repression of citizens' expressions or actions (e.g., Gallagher, 2017; Heurlin, 2016; Lorentzen, 2013, 2014). The intuition is that these measures or institutions facilitate citizens' expression of grievances and opinions, enabling the central government (or higher levels of authorities) to heed information on local problems and take preemptive measures to address them.

One limitation in this influential and growing line of literature is that the institutions that have been studied so far deal mostly with rather individualized expressions by ordinary citizens. Few studies, however, have asked the question of what kind of arrangements allow the articulation of interests and facilitate information exchanges among the regime's elites and organized interests. As mentioned in the introduction chapter, what counts critically in the survival of authoritarian regimes is the relationship among the authoritarian ruling elites. The existence of rampant information problems among the elites, however, threatens the stability of authoritarian rule (Lu & Ma, 2019; Shih, 2010; Svolik, 2012; Wintrobe, 1998). In democracies, political elites signal their intentions through participation in contested elections, appearances on media, or open debates on policy issues. Yet similar institutions are often nowhere in existence under autocracies. Some autocrats even purposefully engineer secrecy to increase their leverage as the "first mover" in power struggles against rivals (Svolik, 2012, chapter 3). Not knowing others' intentions or behaviors leads to a toxic environment that breeds suspicion, fear, and miscalculation among the elites, which often culminate in elite splits or even regime changes. Some autocracies establish institutions that regularize elite interactions (e.g., politburo meetings, party congresses) to reduce information paucity. Yet such information exchanges are limited to an exclusive group of top-level elites (Lu & Ma, 2019). We know little about how the bulk of authoritarian elites, and the institutions they represent, communicate and settle conflicts over the allocation of critical resources among themselves.

The bottom-up policy bargains documented in this book provide a regularized, controllable mechanism for a much broader group of elites and organized interests within the regime to articulate their demands. The participants of this "input institution" are not ordinary citizens but instead powerful regime insiders and the agencies they represent. The behaviors of solicitation send information of what localities (or functional bureaucracies) want to their superiors. The outcomes and, to a lesser extent, the process of bargaining is also more transparent, likely observable by most of the participants (i.e., other regional administrations) of the system. The articulation of these players' interests not only reduces possibilities of miscalculation among the elites, but also enables the state to formulate policies that are more inclusive of various interests within the regime.

In her seminal book *The Political Logic of Economic Reform in China*, Shirk (1993) notes a conspicuous lack of institutional mechanisms for territorial administrations to participate in economic policymaking (pp. 107–116). The State Council, the chief institution responsible for making and implementing economic and social policies, constitutes only functional ministries. The only venue where provinces could meaningfully participate in deliberation on economic issues is the Central Economic Work Conference (中央经济工作会议), which is typically held once a year. In these meetings, provinces with disproportionate economic or population size have equal representation. Such an institutional framework leads to "disenfranchisement of provinces (Shirk, 1993, p. 112)" in policymaking, despite the provinces' prominent role in growing the economy. The argument and findings in this study suggest that provinces (and other layers of local government) work actively to influence central economic policymaking through more frequent, informal policy bargaining. Their differential bargaining power and strategies translate into different policy outcomes. Future studies that try to summarize the recipe for China's economic success and political stability should not overlook this important aspect of interest articulation by territorial administrations.

This story also echoes recent developments in the state-building literature, which argues that an elaborative and extensive bureaucratic system can substitute the function of a representative legislature in reducing information asymmetry between the ruler and the constituents. The transmission of information within a large bureaucratic system inevitably provokes competition among agents who seek to convince their superiors. While most of such competition seems to focus on social and economic policies, whether regime elites use the same mechanisms to resolve political or ideological differences remains unclear. If not, then what kind of institutional arrangements, if there are any, serve as the mechanisms to settle these disputes merits further investigation.

The bottom-up interest articulation by regional governments might not be afforded in every authoritarian country. Like permitting citizens to express their views or grievances, it entails that the state grants a certain degree of freedom to the subjects. Why does the ruler allow powerful players

in the regime to take proactive actions (even just on social or economic policies) while not worrying that they would use such autonomy against him?
An important variable that often gets overlooked is the scale of the country.
Cross-country analyses often treat units (countries) in the sample of analyses
as qualitatively equivalent, yet the variations in the scales of countries can
create different dynamics in domestic politics. Yasuda (2015) is among the
first to focus on the scale of China, arguing that the issues associated with the
scale of a large country (such as challenges in multilevel coordination, and
problem identification) are to blame for China's regulatory failures in food
safety.

In the case of this book's subject, the scale of China, territory-wise and
population-wise, leads to decentralization and the creation of numerous territorial administrations at different levels. Information asymmetry caused by
the scale of the country necessitates the empowerment of local authorities
that are closer to the people, as well as information channeling from grassroots agents to the decision-makers at higher levels. The large number of
territorial administrations (which is also a consequence of the scale) allows
the central government to give localities some degree of autonomy in pursuing their interests, including localized bargaining that seeks to prioritize
territorial interests, and not to worry that such autonomy would threaten
the authority of the central government. The difficulties of coordinating collective actions against the center increase with the number of subnational
units. If a large country only has a handful of subnational units, or has one
unit that enjoys disproportionally large influence (such as Russia under the
Soviet Union), then localities' actions in pursuing policy influence might
overshadow the authority of central leaders. China had a brief history of
having six greater administrative areas under the central government (and
the provinces were placed further below) after 1949, all headed by powerful
revolutionaries. The system was abolished in the early 1950s as Mao feared
that the cultivation of these few local power bases would challenge his authority (Lin, 2017).[1] The center–province structure that replaced the greater
administrative areas significantly reduced the threats that any individual regional government can impose on the central authority, and also made the
emergence of provincial interests in the reform era more tolerable to the
center (Liu et al., 2018; Shirk, 1993).

---

[1] The CCP briefly restored the party organs at the greater administration area level between 1960
and 1966 in an attempt to coordinate regional development. The administrative structure of greater
administration areas was never restored.

When taking the effect of scale into consideration, we also need to think about the external validity of prevailing theories on how decentralization or de facto federalism has promoted economic growth in China (e.g., Jin et al., 2005; Landry, 2008; Maskin et al., 2000; Montinola et al., 1995; Xu, 2011). Instituting a system of decentralization is one thing, and making the institution self-enforcing is another. As discussed in several places in the book, the bottom-up, localized bargaining takes place as a result of contradictory aspects of centralization and decentralization in the Chinese system, namely that localities that are largely on their own have something to gain from their superiors. Why could decentralization in China withstand waves of central leaders' impulses to centralize power? The case of China might suggest that decentralization is more likely to emerge, sustain, and succeed in a country with a large territory and population, and a sizable number of subnational units that share roughly equal abilities in influencing their superiors. Future studies that apply the framework of decentralization in explaining policy outcomes should also be cautious of the scope conditions that make decentralization persist in the first place.

7.3. Power Sharing of Different Types

One key argument advanced in this book is that fragmentation of authorities in the bureaucracies curbs the dictatorial tendency of central leaders and creates spaces for localities to proactively solicit greater shares of interest in social and economic policies. The mechanisms of this argument have been elaborated in earlier chapters, and I will not repeat them here. One implication of this argument is that it would be easier for the ruler to exert top-down controls in issue areas with a centralized decision-making authority. The example I used is personnel appointment. Unlike building high-speed rails, appointing and promoting officials does not need the assistance of technocrats and experts from various specialized agencies; the power of personnel, therefore, is centralized in the hands of the organization department, through which top party leaders control the careers of party and government officials.[2] Under this condition, one then might question the validity of

---

[2] This does not imply that the organization department is without expertise. The central organization department keeps and manages an extensive list of several thousands of officials at the center and provincial levels.

power sharing through bureaucratic fragmentation. If the ruler controls personnel appointment, he could replace leaders of any uncooperative agencies with only his appointees. Eventually, all agencies would be staffed by rulers' close associates and fall in line. Then what prevents the ruler from making policy decisions at his will?

The intuition of bureaucratic control through personnel appointment seems straightforward. This prediction, however, needs to address challenges from the bureaucratic and political perspectives. Bureaucratically, as we have discussed in Chapter 2, the degree to which the political appointees of bureaucratic agencies can achieve their goals relies on the cooperation of career bureaucrats and experts within the agencies. Because of the gaps in experience and expertise in specialized fields, the political appointees are likely to be influenced by bureaucrats, sometimes even without noticing it themselves. Such a problem would only be exacerbated if the ruler parachutes in an outsider with no prior experience to head the agency. In addition, as shown in Chapter 3, bureaucratic checks emerge not just from an uncooperative bureaucracy but also from costs of coordinating agreement among multiple bureaucracies. Some tensions between bureaucracies exist by design, irrespective of whether the heads of these agencies pledge their loyalty to the same leader. The fact that there are multiple agencies overseeing the same policy area makes the rise of bureaucratic conflicts inevitable (as exemplified by the high-speed railway project). Apolitical disagreements over technical parameters of policy proposals, combined with a push to defend and enlarge one's own departmental interests, create gridlocks that could drown any ambitious policy initiatives in prolonged delays. The slow progress in the development of Xiong'an New Area, which was personally initiated by President Xi Jinping in early 2017, provides a vivid example. Despite being the signature project of arguably the most powerful CCP leader since Mao, the construction of the new area has been significantly delayed. According to media reports, the inaction was caused by a prolonged and still ongoing process of coming up with a construction design, which took input from a large number of central ministries as well as local authorities in Hebei.[3]

Extending the logic of between-bureaucracy tensions into the political realm, it is also true that leaders who belong to the same faction are not necessarily friends. The bounds of a clientelistic network are formed between

---

[3] See Zhang, W. H. (2019, February 24). 两年过去了，雄安新区为何几乎没动一砖一瓦？ (*Why has the Xiong'an New Area not moved a brick after two years?*), thepaper.cn, retrieved from https://www.thepaper.cn/newsDetail_forward_3032347.

individual officials (clients) and their patrons, not between officials. In a recent study, Chen and Hong (2021) found that career pressures prompted Chinese local leaders to wage negative media campaigns against officials in the same faction. They directed local state media under their control to report negative news on their co-faction peers to outrival them for promotion. Officials who received such negative coverage indeed saw their chances of promotion decline. It is entirely possible that similar incentives to outperform factional peers would lead to chicanery or sabotage between leaders of different functional bureaucracies that would cause the policies in question to flounder. The mixture of ever-present tensions among bureaucratic units, and occasional clandestine rivalries between leaders that head these organizations, ensures that even a ruler who can staff the entire bureaucracy with his people still could *not* expect the bureaucracy to turn his orders into policy outcomes like a well-oiled machine.

In addition, I also want to challenge the assumption that centralized personnel control allows the ruler to appoint whoever he wants to serve in important leadership positions. The Leninist party system has some important self-constraining features that are often glossed over under the label of authoritarianism. Shirk (1993), for example, points out that the party's general secretary in fact needs to be attentive to the demands of central committee members, who hold the statutory power in electing the former. In terms of personnel appointments, the CCP's paramount leader enjoys a much smaller degree of latitude compared to his democratic counterparts (the US president, for example). Unlike elected politicians in democracies—who can appoint whomever she or he prefers, even a political novice, to cabinet membership—the elaborative rules of promotion in Leninist parties prohibit the party's paramount leader from doing the equivalent. Some of the most constraining rules include that a position can only be filled by an official who already holds the same rank or one level below that rank. In the latter case, the appointment is considered a promotion. Rank-skipping promotion rarely takes place in the post-Mao CCP. This means that when a general party secretary intends to fill a leadership vacancy at a ministry or a province, he cannot appoint a trusted personal secretary, a friend from childhood, a classmate in college, or even his own daughter. Instead, he would have to choose from a pool of officials who already hold the rank of minister or governor or those of their deputies. When a new general party secretary comes to power, the people who are in positions that are ranked high enough to be considered for promotion to ministerial or provincial leadership positions have been appointed to their current positions by the previous general party secretary. It takes a significant amount of time to promote one's own associates, step by step, from lower levels. Officials usually need to serve in one position for a period of time before they can be promoted to the next level.[4] Again, no one can skip any rank in between to reach a higher level. This entails that the pool of candidates that a new general party secretary could consider for his ministers or governors includes a large number of protégés left by the previous general party secretary. The ability of the incumbent to act on his will would be inevitably limited by this army of high-ranking officials who are closer to the ruler's immediate predecessor (Ma, 2016). Such "intergenerational power sharing" is made possible because of strict rules in promotion. The costs of overriding such a system are potentially prohibitive, as the system steadily creates expectations of upward career mobility that commits the loyalty of millions of rank-and-file officials to the party (Geddes, 1999; Liu, 2020; Svolik, 2012).

This analysis suggests that the biggest enemy of an ambitious leader who attempts to centralize power is not his rivals in the party, but perhaps the very party that he commands. Those who have successfully concentrated power have, maybe against their own intentions, weakened the party to some extent. For example, Mao's centralization of power during the Cultural Revolution came at the price of shuttering the party's organizations and rules (including those on promotion) and replacing experienced revolutionaries and technocrats at various levels with farmers and factory workers without prior political experience (e.g., Bai & Zhou, 2019). Future studies that explore the longevity of Leninist systems should take into consideration these inherent features of the party-state that constrain the power of its leaders.

In the Spring of 2018, the CCP Central Committee passed the decision to "deepen the reform of the party and state institutions." The decision proposed the reorganization and realignment of central party and state institutions to achieve "modernization in state governance" while tightening the party's control over all spheres of government.[5] The main measures included the creation of several commissions aimed at providing overall guidance and coordination in broad issue areas at the party center, such as the creation

[4] As noted in Chapter 5, an average tenure for a provincial or municipal leader lasts for three to four years.

[5] See (2018, March 21). 中共中央印发《深化党和国家机构改革方案》 (*The CCP central committee releases the decision to deepen the reform of the party and state institutions*), Xinhuanet.com, retrieved from http://www.xinhuanet.com/2018-03/21/c_1122570517.htm.

of the Central Commission for Overall Law-Based Governance (中央全面依法治国委员会) and the Central Comprehensively Deepening Reforms Commission (中央全面深化改革委员会), along with the merger of state or party institutions with overlapping authorities and the creation of the new ones. These included the incorporation of the State Administration of Civil Service into the party's Central Organization Department, and the incorporation of the General Administration of Press and Publication and the China Film Administration into the Central Publicity Department. The Ministry of Supervision and the National Bureau of Corruption Prevention were merged into the newly formed National Supervisory Commission, which is overseen by the Central Commission for Discipline Inspection.

These measures have put an end to the trend of separating the state organs from the party that began in the 1980s. The removal of bureaucratic divisions between the party and state organs of similar functions, and the centralization of previously fragmented authorities in certain areas, allow President Xi Jinping, who is also the General Party Secretary, to exert greater control over key state organizations. Yet these measures are unlikely to change what has been argued in this book. Most of the departmental mergers take place in the political, personnel, and ideological realms. In addition to the mergers with the Central Organization Department, the Central Publicity Department, and the National Supervisory Commission mentioned earlier, the Chinese Academy of Governance was also merged into the Central Party School. As discussed in Chapter 2, these areas do not require the same level of technical expertise as those pertaining to the building of high-speed rails or the like. The party also does not rely on these institutions to generate economic growth. The bureaucrats in these departments therefore could be replaced with lower cost, and consequently are more likely to become targets of reorganization. The majority of specialized bureaucracies in the State Council were not affected by the changes.[6] Nor did the decision completely resolve the issue that there are often multiple ministerial authorities overseeing one issue area. The decision, in fact, created several new ministry-level institutions under the State Council, including the Ministry of Veterans Affairs, the Ministry of Emergency Management, and the China International Development Cooperation Agency. The total number of

---

[6] One major exception is the merger of the Ministry of Land and Resources, the State Oceanic Administration and the State Bureau of Surveying and Mapping, and the creation of the new Ministry of Natural Resources.

ministry-level institutions under the State Council after the reorganization (49)[7] still dwarfs the number of executive departments in the US cabinet (15) or that of Japan (12), suggesting a high level of institutional differentiation in the Chinese central government. The Ministry of Land, Infrastructure, Transport and Tourism in Japan oversees the issues that are governed by seven different ministries or ministerial-level organizations in China, including the National Development and Reform Commission, the Ministry of Transport, the Ministry of Natural Resources, the Ministry of Housing and Urban–Rural Development, the Ministry of Water Resources, the Ministry of Culture and Tourism, and the China Railway Corporation.

While the long-term effects of the 2018 ministerial reorganization in the political, ideological, personnel realms are yet to be observed, it is rather clear that the institutional differentiation and decentralization of authorities in the making of many social and economic policies will still be a defining feature of the Chinese bureaucracy in the foreseeable future. How these enduring features shape new challenges or initiatives by Chinese leaders, such as the Belt and Road Initiative, merits careful examinations by scholars in the future.[8]

7.4 From Elite Localism to Popular Localism

The analysis in this book paints a picture of rising localism in China. Although Chinese local leaders are primarily accountable to their superiors who appoint them, some of them instead become passionate defenders of local interests and try to obtain more resources from their superiors to strengthen the political and economic influence of their jurisdictions. The rise of localism on the part of local leaders (the "elite localism") is not surprising by itself. Some of the party-state's institutions, such as the performance evaluation of leading cadres and yardstick competition between regions, are designed to align the interests of officials with those of their constituents (Zhou, 2007). The fact that local leaders' own political fortunes

---

[7] This figure includes the number of ministries and that of other organizations (such as the State-owned Assets Supervision and Administration Commission) under the direct supervision of the State Council. It does not include state-owned enterprise like the China Railway Corporation.

[8] Some scholars have pointed out that bureaucratic fragmentation has led to decentralized implementation of the Belt and Road Initiative (BRI), through which local governments and business groups try to devise programs under the title of BRI that would in fact serve their own purposes (e.g., Hale et al., 2020; Ye, 2019).

(i.e., career advancement) depend largely on how well their regions per-form induces officials to proactively defend and fight for the interests of their jurisdictions. The emergence of elite localism, therefore, is by design largely a product of the CCP's cadre management institutions.

The mentality of prioritizing local interests at any cost, however, is not al-ways a blessing, particularly at times of crisis. For example, it is reported that some local governments competed to withhold consignments of medical supplies shipped through their jurisdictions during the outbreak of the co-ronavirus in early 2020. One of the most high-profile incidents was a leaked document showing that the Qingdao government ordered confiscation of 100,000 masks shipped from South Korea that authorities in Shenyang had ordered, after Shenyang withheld 100,000 masks that Qingdao had ordered from Japan.[9] These actions allegedly stopped after they drew heavy criticism online and invited investigation from higher levels.

Parallel to the rise of institutionally engineered localism on the part of local leaders is the surge of localist identity among ordinary citizens. One manifes-tation of the existence of such identities is the growth of numerous online forums and bulletin boards dedicated exclusively to discussions of local de-velopment issues. One typical site is the Baidu Tieba—China's equivalent of Reddit, where each Chinese city and province has its own discussion board. The site also has other dedicated discussion boards on themes such as urban development, skyscrapers, subways, high-speed rails, or local economic sta-tistics. Millions of users on these boards engage daily in lively discussions and debates on local development issues and on comparisons across locali-ties. I frequently visit these outlets as a part of doing my research, and also got to know and meet offline with some of their users. Their passions and interest in local development appear to be genuine. Typically young males, these people are not shy about expressing their pride in their localities, mostly their hometowns, and are very knowledgeable about details of their localities' de-velopment programs. They are also particularly vocal in defending against potential (often imagined) encroachment of local interests by other places or higher levels of government. Falling behind in development is considered a major humiliation, and these netizens often spend hours online arguing with others like themselves about why their localities are superior. They have held

[9] See Huang, K. (2020, February 7). *Chinese cities fight for mask shipments in scramble to stop co-ronavirus*, scmp.com, retrieved from https://www.scmp.com/news/china/society/article/3049508/chinese-cities-fight-mask-shipments-scramble-stop-coronavirus.

offline activities from time to time through shared WeChat or QQ groups. This kind of "popular localism" is a crucial part of this book's argument. As has been discussed in Chapter 6, these spontaneous sentiments of defending local interests are important drivers behind "consent instability." Without an opinion base that supports the agendas of local governments, local officials have little to mobilize to put additional pressure on their superiors. Despite being a loosely connected community that mostly exists online, these people also prove that they have the abilities to organize themselves, as revealed in the case studies of "consent instability."

Two important questions to ask are what gives rise to popular regionalism, and what consequences does it have on Chinese politics? I lay out some hypotheses for future studies to explore. On the origins of popular localism, one possibility is that it is the product of the growing individual demand for political participation in a rather confined environment. Rising income and education levels, as well as a quickly expanding middle class, create strong demand for political participation in China, like elsewhere in the world (Inglehart & Welzel, 2005). People want to get involved in politics and have a say in policies that will affect their livelihood. Such demands are evidenced in the rising activism by urban residents to organize and manage their own neighborhood associations (e.g., Read, 2003; Yip & Jiang, 2011; Zuo, 2016). Yet, beyond the basic neighborhood level, there are few institutional channels through which urban residents can legally participate in local governance. The regime has kept a tight control over political participation, silencing expressions of dissent on political and ideological matters. When local social and economic policies become the only few areas in domestic politics where there is some latitude of freedom in online discussions, these topics naturally attract a large number of netizens eager to vent their opinions. Some of these discussions can be very contentious (just like most political discussions), such as economic rivalries among nearby localities, which further attract more participants to the discussions. Most discussions and demands by lo-calist activists call for advancements of local interests, which are also more or less congruent with what local state actors prefer. These discussions and their communities are therefore dealt with a greater degree of tolerance by the regime and the local state.

Another relevant factor in the rise of local identities might be the growing prominence of nationalism in contemporary China. The CCP has launched a systematic campaign to propagate nationalism to bolster the regime's legitimacy in the aftermath of the 1989 pro-democracy movement (Liu & Ma,

2018). The defining cleavages of the world, in the official narratives, have shifted from capitalism versus socialism (and classes) to the Chinese nation versus hostile foreign powers (e.g., He, 2007; Zhao, 1998). There are many similarities in the messages of nationalistic propaganda and those of localist appeals, such as the creation of a division between "the us" and "the others," and an emphasis on how the individual's fate and status depend critically on those of the country (or a region). The constant indoctrination of patriotism and nationalistic narratives might unintentionally hand localists the playbook and ingredients to rise and thrive. As noted in Chapter 6, the protestors in county C's anti-merger movement and those in demanding high-speed railway protests adopted the language of anti-foreign protests, portraying forces that sought to weaken the localities' standing as "enemies" or "traitors." In a recent survey study, Hines et al. (2020) also find that when primed with nationalistic messages of the regime, Chinese respondents demonstrate a higher level of support for localist policies such as reduced social benefits to migrant workers. If we consider nationalism as the result of "imagined communities (Anderson, 2006)," then localism ought to be more appealing, as the well-being of local communities would more directly affect one's life.

A final question is what does the rise of popular localism mean for China's future. The optimistic prediction is that popular localism would broaden citizen participation, increase accountability on the part of local officials, and improve overall quality of local governance, which, hopefully, would one day induce a transition to a more democratic governing structure at the national level. The pessimistic prediction is that localism would fuel the increasing divisions (e.g., the urban versus the rural, the poor versus the rich, etc.) within the society, and local officials, under the pressure of localist constituencies, would pursue short-sighted policies and do greater damage to the country as a whole.

I want to end this book with a brief historical note. The early 1900s saw the rise of numerous railway activist groups across China's southern provinces advocating the construction of railways and protection of local railway rights from outside (mostly foreign) encroachment (Rankin, 2002). The early railway activists were local intellectuals, gentry, and merchants who recognized the value of railways in modernizing China. The mobilizations gradually gained a nationalistic and populist undertone and attracted a growing number of ordinary people as competition over railway ownership between localities and foreign powers or the Qing central government intensified (e.g., Zheng, 2018). These "railway protection movements (保路运动)"

culminated in a massive protest joined by tens of thousands across Sichuan province in the early fall of 1911 against Qing government's decision to nationalize locally built railways. Although the protest ended in bloodshed and repression, it nevertheless triggered a broader revolution against the Qing government across the country, which eventually brought an end to the monarchial rule that had lasted for two millennia in China. If history is any indication of the future, we should be optimistic. In some sense, localist demand for railways precipitated the coming of China's modern era. It is possible that they will continue to make a difference.

Bibliography

Acemoglu, D., & Robinson, J. A. (2000). Why did the West extend the franchise? Democracy, inequality, and growth in historical perspective. *The Quarterly Journal of Economics, 115*(4), 1167–1199.

Ahart, A. M., & Sackett, P. R. (2004). A new method of examining relationships between individual difference measures and sensitive behavior criteria: Evaluating the unmatched count technique. *Organizational Research Methods, 7*(1), 101–114.

Ahmed, A. T., & Stasavage, D. (2020). Origins of early democracy. *American Political Science Review, 114*(2), 502–518.

Albertus, M., & Menaldo, V. (2012). Dictators as founding fathers? The role of constitutions under autocracy. *Economics & Politics, 24*(3), 279–306.

Allen-Ebrahimian, B. (2015, May 19). These Chinese people want high-speed rail so badly they are fighting police to get it. *Foreign Policy.* https://foreignpolicy.com/2015/05/19/linshui-china-high-speed-rail-protest-police/

Allison, P. D. (2010). *Survival analysis using SAS: A practical guide.* SAS Institute.

Almond, G. A. (1958). A comparative study of interest groups and the political process. *American Political Science Review, 52*(1), 270–282.

Anderson, B. (2006). *Imagined communities: Reflections on the origin and spread of nationalism.* Verso Books.

Ang, Y. Y. (2012). Counting cadres: A comparative view of the size of China's public employment. *The China Quarterly, 211*, 676–696.

Ang, Y. Y. (2016). *How China escaped the poverty trap.* Cornell University Press.

Arendt, H. (1963). *Eichmann in Jerusalem: A report on the banality of evil.* Penguin.

Auerbach, A. M. (2019). *Demanding development: The politics of public goods provision in India's urban slums.* Cambridge University Press.

Bai, Y., & Jia, R. (2019). When history matters little: Political hierarchy and regional development in China, AD 1000–2000. *Ifo DICE Report, 16*(4), 50–54.

Bai, Y., & Zhou, T. (2019). "Mao's last revolution": A dictator's loyalty–competence tradeoff. *Public Choice, 180*(3–4), 469–500.

Bardhan, P. (2002). Decentralization of governance and development. *Journal of Economic Perspectives, 16*(4), 185–205.

Bardhan, P., & Mookherjee, D. (2006). Decentralisation and accountability in infrastructure delivery in developing countries. *The Economic Journal, 116*(508), 101–127.

Baron, D. P., & Ferejohn, J. A. (1989). Bargaining in legislatures. *American Political Science Review, 83*(04), 1181–1206.

Baturo, A., & Elkink, J. A. (2014). Office or officeholder? Regime deinstitutionalization and sources of individual political influence. *The Journal of Politics, 76*(03), 859–872.

Bell, D. A. (2015). *The China model: Political meritocracy and the limits of democracy.* Princeton University Press.

Belsky, R. D. (2005). *Localities at the center: Native place, space, and power in late imperial Beijing.* Harvard University Asia Center.

Berry, C. R., & Fowler, A. (2016). Cardinals or clerics? Congressional committees and the distribution of pork. *American Journal of Political Science, 60*(3), 692–708.

Blaydes, L. (2010). *Elections and distributive politics in Mubarak's Egypt.* Cambridge University Press.

Boix, C., & Svolik, M. W. (2013). The foundations of limited authoritarian government: Institutions, commitment, and power-sharing in dictatorships. *The Journal of Politics, 75*(02), 300–316.

Brownlee, J. (2007). Hereditary succession in modern autocracies. *World Politics, 59*(4), 595–628.

Bueno de Mesquita, B., Smith, A., Siverson, R. M., & Morrow, J. D. (2005). *The logic of political survival* (Vol. 1). MIT Press.

Bulman, D. J. (2016). *Incentivized development in China: Leaders, governance, and growth in China's counties.* Cambridge University Press.

Bulman, D. J., & Jaros, K. A. (2019). Leninism and local interests: How cities in China benefit from concurrent leadership appointments. *Studies in Comparative International Development, 54*(2), 233–273.

Burns, J. P. (1987). China's nomenklatura system. *Problems of Communism, 36*(5), 36–51.

Cadot, O., Röller, L.-H., & Stephan, A. (2006). Contribution to productivity or pork barrel? The two faces of infrastructure investment. *Journal of Public Economics, 90*(6), 1133–1153.

Cai, M. (2012). *Land-locked development: The local political economy of institutional change in China.* Dissertation. The University of Wisconsin—Madison.

Cai, Y. (2008). Local governments and the suppression of popular resistance in China. *The China Quarterly, 193*, 24–42.

Cai, Y. (2010). *Collective resistance in China: Why popular protests succeed or fail.* Stanford University Press.

Cai, Y. (2014a). Managing group interests in China. *Political Science Quarterly, 129*(1), 107–132.

Cai, Y. (2014b). *State and agents in China: Disciplining government officials.* Stanford University Press.

Cammisa, A. M. (1995). *Governments as interest groups: Intergovernmental lobbying and the federal system.* Greenwood Publishing Group.

Campante, F. R., & Do, Q.-A. (2014). Isolated capital cities, accountability, and corruption: Evidence from US states. *American Economic Review, 104*(8), 2456–2481.

Campos, J. E., & Root, H. L. (2001). *The key to the Asian miracle: Making shared growth credible.* Brookings Institution Press.

Castells, A., & Solé-Ollé, A. (2005). The regional allocation of infrastructure investment: The role of equity, efficiency and political factors. *European Economic Review, 49*(5), 1165–1205.

Chen, J., Pan, J., & Xu, Y. (2016). Sources of authoritarian responsiveness: A field experiment in China. *American Journal of Political Science, 60*(2), 383–400.

Chen, J., & Xu, Y. (2017). Why do authoritarian regimes allow citizens to voice opinions publicly? *The Journal of Politics, 79*(3), 792–803.

Chen, L. (2018). *Manipulating globalization: The influence of bureaucrats on business in China.* Stanford University Press.

Chen, T., & Hong, J. Y. (2021). Rivals within: Political factions, loyalty, and elite competition under authoritarianism. *Political Science Research and Methods, 9*(3), 599–614.

Cheng, T.-J., Haggard, S., & Kang, D. (1998). Institutions and growth in Korea and Taiwan: The bureaucracy. *The Journal of Development Studies, 34*(6), 87–111.

Chung, J. H., & Lam, T. (2004). China's "city system" in flux: Explaining post-Mao administrative changes. *The China Quarterly, 180*, 945–964.

Coase, R. H. (1937). The nature of the firm. *Economica, 4*(16), 386–405.

De Long, J. B., & Shleifer, A. (1993). Princes and merchants: European city growth before the industrial revolution. *The Journal of Law and Economics, 36*(2), 671–702.

Debs, A. (2007). *The wheel of fortune: Agency problems in dictatorships.* Working paper. Department of Political Science, Yale University.

Deng, Y. (2017). "Autonomous redevelopment": Moving the masses to remove nail households. *Modern China, 43*(5), 494–522.

Deng, Y., Yang, Z., & Ma, X. (forthcoming). Riding on the power of the masses? How different modes of mass mobilization shape local elite bargaining in China. *Journal of Chinese Governance*, 1–24. https://doi.org/10.1080/23812346.2021.1945284.

Dickson, B. (2008). *Wealth into power: The communist party's embrace of China's private sector.* Cambridge University Press.

Dickson, B. (2016). *The dictator's dilemma: The Chinese Communist Party's strategy for survival.* Oxford University Press.

Distelhorst, G. (2017). The power of empty promises: Quasi-democratic institutions and activism in China. *Comparative Political Studies, 50*(4), 464–498.

Distelhorst, G., & Fu, D. (2019). Performing authoritarian citizenship: Public transcripts in China. *Perspectives on Politics, 17*(1), 106–121.

Distelhorst, G., & Hou, Y. (2017). Constituency service under nondemocratic rule: Evidence from China. *The Journal of Politics, 79*(3), 1024–1040.

Djordjevic, J. (1958). Interest groups and the political system of Yugoslavia. In H. W. Ehrmann (Ed.), *Interest groups on four continents* (pp. 197–228). University of Pittsburgh Press.

Downs, A. (1967). *Inside bureaucracy.* Little, Brown.

Edin, M. (2003). State capacity and local agent control in China: CCP cadre management from a township perspective. *The China Quarterly, 173*, 35–52.

Eisenstadt, S. N., & Roniger, L. (1980). Patron–Client relations as a model of structuring social exchange. *Comparative Studies in Society and History, 22*(01), 42–77.

Evans, P. B. (1995). *Embedded autonomy: States and industrial transformation.* Cambridge University Press.

Evans, P. B., & Rauch, J. E. (1999). Bureaucracy and growth: A cross-national analysis of the effects of "Weberian" state structures on economic growth. *American Sociological Review, 64*(5), 748–765.

Falleti, T. G. (2005). A sequential theory of decentralization: Latin American cases in comparative perspective. *American Political Science Review, 99*(3), 327–346.

Fukuyama, F. (1992). *The end of history and the last man.* Free Press.

Fukuyama, F. (2011). *The origins of political order: From prehuman times to the French revolution.* Farrar, Straus and Giroux.

Gallagher, M. E. (2017). *Authoritarian legality in China: Law, workers, and the state.* Cambridge University Press.

Gandhi, J. (2008). *Political institutions under dictatorship.* Cambridge University Press.

Geddes, B. (1990). Building "state" autonomy in Brazil, 1930–1964. *Comparative Politics, 22*(2), 217–235.

Geddes, B. (1999). What do we know about democratization after twenty years? *Annual Review of Political Science*, 2(1), 115–144.

Geddes, B. (2004). *Authoritarian breakdown*. Manuscript. Department of Political Science, UCLA.

Geddes, B., Wright, J. G., Wright, J., & Frantz, E. (2018). *How dictatorships work: Power, personalization, and collapse*. Cambridge University Press.

Gehlbach, S., & Keefer, P. (2011). Investment without democracy: Ruling-party institutionalization and credible commitment in autocracies. *Journal of Comparative Economics*, 39(2), 123–139.

Gereffi, G. (1990). Paths of industrialization: An overview. In G. Gereffi & D. Wyman (Eds.), *Manufacturing miracles: Paths of industrialization in Latin America and East Asia* (pp. 3–31). Princeton University Press.

Gerschenkron, A. (1962). *Economic backwwardness in historical perspective: A book of essays*. Belknap Press of Harvard University Press.

Glaeser, E. L., La Porta, R., Lopez-de-Silanes, F., & Shleifer, A. (2004). Do institutions cause growth? *Journal of Economic Growth*, 9(3), 271–303.

Golden, M. A., & Picci, L. (2008). Pork-barrel politics in postwar Italy, 1953-94. *American Journal of Political Science*, 52(2), 268–289.

Goldstein, R., & You, H. Y. (2017). Cities as lobbyists. *American Journal of Political Science*, 61(4), 864–876.

González de Lara, Y., Greif, A., & Jha, S. (2008). The administrative foundations of self-enforcing constitutions. *American Economic Review*, 98(2), 105–109.

Gueorguiev, D. D. (2014). *Retrofitting communism: Consultative autocracy in China*. PhD Thesis. UC San Diego.

Gueorguiev, D. D., & Schuler, P. J. (2016). Keeping your head down: Public profiles and promotion under autocracy. *Journal of East Asian Studies*, 16(1), 87–116.

Guy, R. K. (2017). *Qing governors and their provinces: The evolution of territorial administration in China, 1644-1796*. University of Washington Press.

Haber, S. (2007). Authoritarian government. In B. Weingast & D. Wittman (Eds.), *The Oxford handbook of political economy* (pp. 693–707). Oxford University Press.

Habyarimana, J., Humphreys, M., Posner, D. N., & Weinstein, J. M. (2007). Why does ethnic diversity undermine public goods provision? *American Political Science Review*, 101(04), 709–725.

Haggard, S. (1990). *Pathways from the periphery: The politics of growth in the newly industrializing countries*. Cornell University Press.

Hale, T., Liu, C., & Urpelainen, J. (2020). *Belt and road decision-making in China and recipient countries: How and to what extent does sustainability matter?* Report. ISEP, BSG, and ClimateWorks Foundation. https://sais-isep.org/wp-content/uploads/2020/04/ISEP-BSG-BRI-Report-.pdf.

Hall, P. A., & Thelen, K. (2009). Institutional change in varieties of capitalism. *Socio-Economic Review*, 7(1), 7–34.

Hansen, J. M. (1991). *Gaining access: Congress and the farm lobby, 1919-1981*. University of Chicago Press.

He, B., & Warren, M. E. (2011). Authoritarian deliberation: The deliberative turn in Chinese political development. *Perspectives on Politics*, 9(02), 269–289.

He, G., Wang, S., & Zhang, B. (2020). Watering down environmental regulation in China. *The Quarterly Journal of Economics*, 135(4), 2135–2185.

He, Y. (2007). History, Chinese nationalism and the emerging Sino–Japanese conflict. *Journal of Contemporary China, 16*(50), 1–24.

Heilmann, S. (2018). *Red swan: How unorthodox policy-making facilitated China's rise.* Chinese University Press.

Heilmann, S., & Melton, O. (2013). The reinvention of development planning in China, 1993–2012. *Modern China, 39*(6), 580–628.

Hess, S. (2010). Nail-houses, land rights, and frames of injustice on China's protest landscape. *Asian Survey, 50*(5), 908–926.

Heurlin, C. (2016). *Responsive authoritarianism in China.* Cambridge University Press.

Hicken, A. (2011). Clientelism. *Annual Review of Political Science, 14,* 289–310.

Hines, R. L., Wallace, J. L., & Weiss, J. C. (2020). *Rallying and dividing: Nationalism and China's urban-rural gap.* Working paper. Department of Government, Cornell University.

Hodler, R., & Raschky, P. A. (2014). Regional favoritism. *The Quarterly Journal of Economics, 129*(2), 995–1033.

Hollyer, J. R., Rosendorff, B. P., & Vreeland, J. R. (2011). Democracy and transparency. *The Journal of Politics, 73*(4), 1191–1205.

Hollyer, J. R., Rosendorff, B. P., & Vreeland, J. R. (2018). *Transparency, democracy, and autocracy: Economic transparency and political (in)stability.* Cambridge University Press.

Hou, Y. (2019). *The private sector in public office: Selective property rights in China.* Cambridge University Press.

Huang, J. (2000). *Factionalism in Chinese communist politics.* Cambridge University Press.

Huang, J., & Morgan, C. (2011). Case studies examining high speed rail station location decisions from an international perspective. *2011 Joint Rail Conference,* 517–526.

Huang, Ji. (2010). *The hidden communication: Study on the Beijing office in contemporary China.* Doctoral Dissertation. Central China Normal University.

Huang, Y. (1996). Central–local relations in China during the reform era: The economic and institutional dimensions. *World Development, 24*(4), 655–672.

Huang, Y. (1999). *Inflation and investment controls in China: The political economy of central-local relations during the reform era.* Cambridge University Press.

Huang, Y. (2008). *Capitalism with Chinese characteristics: Entrepreneurship and the state.* Cambridge University Press.

Huntington, S. P. (1968). *Political order in changing societies.* Yale University Press.

Hurst, W. (2006). The city as the focus: the analysis of contemporary Chinese urban politics. *China Information, 20*(3), 457–479.

Inglehart, R., & Welzel, C. (2005). *Modernization, cultural change, and democracy: The human development sequence.* Cambridge University Press.

Jaros, K. A. (2019). *China's urban champions: The politics of spatial development.* Princeton University Press.

Jensen, M. C., & Meckling, W. H. (1976). Theory of the firm: Managerial behavior, agency costs and ownership structure. *Journal of Financial Economics, 3*(4), 305–360.

Ji, C., & Ma, X. (2021). *Revolutionaries for railways.* American Political Science Annual Meeting, Seattle.

Jia, R. (2012). Pollution for promotion. *Unpublished Paper.*

Jia, R., Kudamatsu, M., & Seim, D. (2015). Political selection in China: The complementary roles of connections and performance. *Journal of the European Economic Association, 13*(4), 631–668.

Jiang, J., & Zhang, M. (2020). Friends with benefits: Patronage networks and distributive politics in China. *Journal of Public Economics, 184*, 104143.

Jin, H., Qian, Y., & Weingast, B. R. (2005). Regional decentralization and fiscal incentives: Federalism, Chinese style. *Journal of Public Economics, 89*(9), 1719–1742.

Johnson, C. (1982). *MITI and the Japanese miracle: The growth of industrial policy: 1925–1975.* Stanford University Press.

Kale, S. S. (2014). *Electrifying India: Regional political economies of development.* Stanford University Press.

Kan, N. (1998). *Daijin [Ministers].* Iwanami Shinsho.

Kato, Y. (2011, February 23). *The highspeed railway legacy of Liu Zhijun. Financial Times* (Chinese). http://www.ftchinese.com/story/001037078?full=y&archive.

Kennedy, S. (2009). *The business of lobbying in China.* Harvard University Press.

Kitschelt, H., & Wilkinson, S. I. (2007). *Patrons, clients and policies: Patterns of democratic accountability and political competition.* Cambridge University Press.

Knight, J., & Miller, G. J. (2007). *Democracy, bureaucracy and credible commitment.* Working paper. Washington University in St. Louis.

Kohli, A. (2004). *State-directed development: Political power and industrialization in the global periphery.* Cambridge University Press.

Kokkonen, A., & Sundell, A. (2014). Delivering stability—primogeniture and autocratic survival in European monarchies 1000–1800. *American Political Science Review, 108*(02), 438–453.

Kolkowicz, R. (1970). Interest groups in Soviet politics: The case of the military. *Comparative Politics, 2*(3), 445–472.

Köll, E. (2019). *Railroads and the transformation of China.* Harvard University Press.

Kornai, J. (1980). *Economics of shortage.* North-Holland Pub. Co.

Kornai, J. (1992). *The socialist system: The political economy of communism.* Oxford University Press.

Kramon, E., & Posner, D. N. (2013). Who benefits from distributive politics? How the outcome one studies affects the answer one gets. *Perspectives on Politics, 11*(02), 461–474.

Kuhn, P. A. (1992). *Soulstealers: The Chinese sorcery scare of 1768.* Harvard University Press.

Kung, J. K., & Chen, S. (2011). The tragedy of the nomenklatura: Career incentives and political radicalism during China's Great Leap famine. *American Political Science Review, 105*(01), 27–45.

Kuran, T. (1991). Now out of never: The element of surprise in the East European revolution of 1989. *World Politics, 44*(01), 7–48.

Lam, T. (2009). The county system and county governance. In J. H. Chung & T. Lam (Eds.), *China's local administration: Traditions and changes in the sub-national hierarchy* (pp. 163–187). Routledge.

Lam, T. (2010). Central–provincial relations amid greater centralization in China. *China Information, 24*(3), 339–363.

Lampton, D. M. (1992). A plum for a peach: Bargaining, interest, and bureaucratic politics in China. In K. G. Lieberthal & D. M. Lampton (Eds.), *Bureaucracy, politics, and decision making in post-Mao China* (pp. 33–58). University of California Press.

Lampton, D. M. (2015). Xi Jinping and the National Security Commission: Policy coordination and political power. *Journal of Contemporary China, 24*(95), 759–777.

Landry, P. F. (2008). Decentralized authoritarianism in China. *New York: Cambridge University Press, 6*, 31.

Landry, P. F., Lü, X., & Duan, H. (2018). Does performance matter? Evaluating political selection along the Chinese administrative ladder. *Comparative Political Studies, 51*(8), 1074–1105.

Lasswell, H. D. (1936). *Politics: Who gets what, when, how.* McGraw-Hill.

Lawrence, M., Bullock, R., & Liu, Z. (2019). *China's high-speed rail development.* The World Bank.

Lee, C. K., & Zhang, Y. (2013). The power of instability: Unraveling the microfoundations of bargained authoritarianism in China. *American Journal of Sociology, 118*(6), 1475–1508.

Lei, Z., & Zhou, J. (2019). Private returns to public investment: Political career incentives and infrastructure investment in china. NYU Department of Politics working paper.

Levi, M. (1988). *Of rule and revenue.* University of California Press.

Lewis, P. H. (2002). *Latin fascist elites: The Mussolini, Franco, and Salazar regimes.* ABC-CLIO.

Li, H., & Zhou, L.-A. (2005). Political turnover and economic performance: The incentive role of personnel control in China. *Journal of Public Economics, 89*(9), 1743–1762.

Lieberthal, K. G. (1992). Introduction: The 'fragmented authoritarianism' model and its limitations. In K. G. Lieberthal & D. M. Lampton (Eds.), *Bureaucracy, politics, and decision making in post-Mao China* (pp. 1–30). University of California Press.

Lieberthal, K. G. (2004). *Governing China: From revolution through reform.* W.W. Norton.

Lieberthal, K. G., & Oksenberg, M. (1988). *Policy making in China: Leaders, structures, and processes.* Princeton University Press.

Lin, Y. (2017). *Chongkao Gao Gang, Rao Shushi "Fandang" Shijian [Reexamining the "anti-party" incident of Gao Gang and Rao Shushi].* Chinese University Press.

Lipset, S. M. (1959). Some social requisites of democracy: Economic development and political legitimacy. *American Political Science Review, 53*(1), 69–105.

Liu, C., & Ma, X. (2018). Popular threats and nationalistic propaganda: Political logic of China's patriotic campaign. *Security Studies, 27*(4), 633–664.

Liu, H. (2020). *Authoritarian co-optation with upward mobility: Merit-based elite recruitment in China.* Working paper.

Liu, M., Shih, V. C., & Zhang, D. (2018). The fall of the old guards: Explaining decentralization in China. *Studies in Comparative International Development, 53*(4), 379–403.

Liu, M., Wang, J., Tao, R., & Murphy, R. (2009). The political economy of earmarked transfers in a state-designated poor county in western China: Central policies and local responses. *The China Quarterly, 200,* 973–994.

Lorentzen, P. (2013). Regularizing rioting: Permitting public protest in an authoritarian regime. *Quarterly Journal of Political Science, 8*(2), 127–158.

Lorentzen, P. (2014). China's strategic censorship. *American Journal of Political Science, 58*(2), 402–414.

Lorentzen, P. (2017). Designing contentious politics in post-1989 China. *Modern China, 43*(5), 459–493.

Lu, F., & Ma, X. (2019). Is any publicity good publicity? Media coverage, party institutions, and authoritarian power-sharing. *Political Communication, 36*(1), 64–82.

Lu, W. W., & Tsai, K. S. (2019). Inter-governmental vertical competition in China's urbanization process. *Journal of Contemporary China, 28*(115), 99–117.

Lü, X. (2015). Intergovernmental transfers and local education provision—evaluating China's 8-7 national plan for poverty reduction. *China Economic Review, 33,* 200–211.

Lü, X., & Landry, P. F. (2014). Show me the money: Interjurisdiction political competition and fiscal extraction in China. *American Political Science Review, 108*(03), 706–722.

Lyall, J., Blair, G., & Imai, K. (2013). Explaining support for combatants during wartime: A survey experiment in Afghanistan. *American Political Science Review, 107*(04), 679–705.

M.A. (2011, February 3). On the wrong track? *The Economist*. http://www.economist.com/blogs/gulliver/2011/02/high-speed_rail_china.

Ma, D. (2011, March 30). *China's long, bumpy road to high-speed rail. The Atlantic*. https://www.theatlantic.com/international/archive/2011/03/chinas-long-bumpy-road-to-high-speed-rail/73192/

Ma, H. (2009). *Research on Beijing office of local government*. Doctoral Dissertation. Peking University.

Ma, X. (2016). Term limits and authoritarian power sharing: Theory and evidence from China. *Journal of East Asian Studies, 16*(1), 61–85.

Ma, X. (2017, April). *The politics of paying the visits: Interprovincial trips by Chinese local leaders*. Midwest Political Science Association Annual Meeting, Chicago.

Ma, X. (2019). Consent to contend: The power of the masses in China's local elite bargain. *China Review, 19*(1), 1–29.

Mabuchi, M. (2009). *Gyosei Gaku (Public Administration)*. Yuhikaku.

MacFarquhar, R., & Schoenhals, M. (2009). *Mao's last revolution*. Harvard University Press.

Magaloni, B. (2006). *Voting for autocracy: Hegemonic party survival and its demise in Mexico*. Cambridge University Press.

Magaloni, B. (2008). Credible power-sharing and the longevity of authoritarian rule. *Comparative Political Studies, 41*(4–5), 715–741.

Magaloni, B., Diaz-Cayeros, A., & Estévez, F. (2007). Clientelism and portfolio diversification: A model of electoral investment with applications to Mexico. In H. Kitschelt & S. Wilkinson (Eds.), *Patrons, Clients, and Policies: Patterns of Democratic Accountability and Political Competition* (pp. 182–205). Cambridge University Press.

Malesky, E. J. (2008). Straight ahead on red: How foreign direct investment empowers subnational leaders. *The Journal of Politics, 70*(1), 97–119.

Malesky, E., & Schuler, P. (2010). Nodding or needling: Analyzing delegate responsiveness in an authoritarian parliament. *American Political Science Review, 104*(3), 482–502.

Manion, M. (1985). The cadre management system, post-Mao: The appointment, promotion, transfer and removal of party and state leaders. *The China Quarterly, 102*, 203–233.

Manion, M. (2016). *Information for autocrats: Representation in Chinese local congresses*. Cambridge University Press.

March, J. G., & Olson, J. P. (1983). Organizing political life: What administrative reorganization tells us about government. *American Political Science Review, 77*(2), 281–296.

Maskin, E., Qian, Y., & Xu, C. (2000). Incentives, information, and organizational form. *The Review of Economic Studies, 67*(2), 359–378.

McCubbins, M. D., & Schwartz, T. (1984). Congressional oversight overlooked: Police patrols versus fire alarms. *American Journal of Political Science, 28*(1), 165–179.

McGregor, R. (2010). *The party: The secret world of China's communist rulers*. Penguin UK.

Menaldo, V. (2012). The Middle East and North Africa's resilient monarchs. *The Journal of Politics, 74*(3), 707–722.

Meng, A. (2020). *Constraining dictatorship: From personalized rule to institutionalized regimes*. Cambridge University Press.

Meng, T., Pan, J., & Yang, P. (2017). Conditional receptivity to citizen participation: Evidence from a survey experiment in China. *Comparative Political Studies*, 50(4), 399–433.

Mertha, A. C. (2006). Policy enforcement markets: How bureaucratic redundancy contributes to effective intellectual property implementation in China. *Comparative Politics*, 38(2), 295–316.

Mertha, A. C. (2009). "Fragmented authoritarianism 2.0": Political pluralization in the Chinese policy process. *The China Quarterly*, 200, 995–1012.

Migdal, J. S. (2001). *State in society: Studying how states and societies transform and constitute one another*. Cambridge University Press.

Migdal, J. S., Kohli, A., & Shue, V. (1994). *State power and social forces: Domination and transformation in the Third World*. Cambridge University Press.

Miller, G. J. (2000). Above politics: Credible commitment and efficiency in the design of public agencies. *Journal of Public Administration Research and Theory*, 10(2), 289–328.

Miller, G. J., & Whitford, A. B. (2016). *Above politics: Bureaucratic discretion and credible commitment*. Cambridge University Press.

Min, B. (2015). *Power and the vote: Elections and electricity in the developing world*. Cambridge University Press.

Montinola, G., Qian, Y., & Weingast, B. R. (1995). Federalism, Chinese style: The political basis for economic success in China. *World Politics*, 48(01), 50–81.

Moustafa, T. (2007). *The struggle for constitutional power: Law, politics, and economic development in Egypt*. Cambridge University Press.

Myerson, R. B. (2008). The autocrat's credibility problem and foundations of the constitutional state. *American Political Science Review*, 102(01), 125–139.

Nathan, A. J. (2003). Authoritarian resilience. *Journal of Democracy*, 14(1), 6–17.

Naughton, B. (1996). *Growing out of the plan: Chinese economic reform, 1978–1993*. Cambridge university press.

Naughton, B. (2005). The new common economic program: China's eleventh five year plan and what it means. *China Leadership Monitor*, 16, 1–10.

Naughton, B. (2007). *The Chinese economy: Transitions and growth*. MIT press.

Nichter, S. (2008). Vote buying or turnout buying? Machine politics and the secret ballot. *American Political Science Review*, 102(1), 19–31.

Niskanen, W. A. (1971). *Bureaucracy and representative government*. Transaction Publishers.

Niskanen, W. A. (1973). *Bureaucracy-servant or master?: Lessons from America*. Institute of Economic Affairs.

Nordlinger, E. A. (1981). *On the autonomy of the democratic state*. Harvard University Press.

North, D. C. (1990). *Institutions, institutional change and economic performance*. Cambridge University Press.

North, D. C., & Weingast, B. R. (1989). Constitutions and commitment: The evolution of institutions governing public choice in seventeenth-century England. *The Journal of Economic History*, 49(04), 803–832.

O'Brien, K. J., & Li, L. (1999). Selective policy implementation in rural China. *Comparative Politics*, 31(2), 167–186.

O'Brien, K. J., Li, L., & Liu, M. (2020). Bureaucrat-assisted contention in China. *Mobilization: An International Quarterly*, 25(SI), 661–674.

O'donnell, G., & Schmitter, P. C. (1986). *Transitions from authoritarian rule: Tentative conclusions about uncertain democracies.* JHU Press.

Oi, J. C. (1989). *State and peasant in contemporary China: The political economy of village government.* University of California Press.

Oi, J. C. (1995). The role of the local state in China's transitional economy. *The China Quarterly, 144*, 1132–1149.

Ong, L. H. (2012). Between developmental and clientelist states: Local state–business relationships in China. *Comparative Politics, 44*(2), 191–209.

Ostrom, E. (1990). *Governing the commons: The evolution of institutions for collective action.* Cambridge University Press.

Pan, J., & Chen, K. (2018). Concealing corruption: How Chinese officials distort upward reporting of online grievances. *American Political Science Review, 112*(3), 602–620.

Payson, J. A. (2020a). Cities in the statehouse: How local governments use lobbyists to secure state funding. *The Journal of Politics, 82*(2), 403–417.

Payson, J. A. (2020b). The partisan logic of city mobilization: Evidence from state lobbying disclosures. *American Political Science Review, 114*(3), 677–690.

Pei, M. (2016). *China's crony capitalism.* Harvard University Press.

Pfeffer, J. (1981). *Power in organizations.* Pitman Publications.

Qian, M. (1982). *Traditional government in imperial China: A critical analysis.* Chinese University Press.

Radnitz, S. (2010). *Weapons of the wealthy: Predatory regimes and elite-led protests in central Asia.* Cornell University Press.

Rankin, M. B. (2002). Nationalistic contestation and mobilization politics: Practice and rhetoric of railway-rights recovery at the end of the Qing. *Modern China, 28*(3), 315–361.

Read, B. L. (2003). Democratizing the neighbourhood? New private housing and homeowner self-organization in urban China. *The China Journal, 49*, 31–59.

Rigger, S. (1999). *Politics in Taiwan: Voting for democracy.* Routledge.

Robertson, G. B. (2010). *The politics of protest in hybrid regimes: Managing dissent in post-communist Russia.* Cambridge University Press.

Robinson, J. A., & Verdier, T. (2013). The political economy of clientelism. *The Scandinavian Journal of Economics, 115*(2), 260–291.

Romer, T., & Rosenthal, H. (1978). Political resource allocation, controlled agendas, and the status quo. *Public Choice, 33*(4), 27–43.

Rosenberg, H. (1968). *Bureaucracy, aristocracy, and autocracy: The Prussian experience, 1669–1815.* Harvard University Press.

Ross, S. A. (1973). The economic theory of agency: The principal's problem. *The American Economic Review, 63*(2), 134–139.

Saito, J. (2006). *Pork barrel politics in contemporary Japan.* Dissertation. Yale University.

Scott, J. C. (1969). Corruption, machine politics, and political change. *American Political Science Review, 63*(04), 1142–1158.

Sen, A. K. (1999). *Development as freedom.* Anchor.

Shambaugh, D. (2008). Training China's political elite: The party school system. *The China Quarterly, 196*, 827–844.

Sheng, Y. (2010). *Economic openness and territorial politics in China.* Cambridge University Press.

Sheng, Y. (2019). The regional consequences of authoritarian power-sharing: Politburo representation and fiscal redistribution in China. *Japanese Journal of Political Science, 20*(3), 162–189.

Shi, M., & Svensson, J. (2006). Political budget cycles: Do they differ across countries and why? *Journal of Public Economics, 90*(8), 1367–1389.

Shih, V. C. (2004). Factions matter: Personal networks and the distribution of bank loans in China. *Journal of Contemporary China, 13*(38), 3–19.

Shih, V. C. (2008). Factions and finance in China. *Cambridge University Press.*

Shih, V. C. (2010). *The autocratic difference: Information paucity.* Mimeo: Northwestern University.

Shih, V. C., Adolph, C., & Liu, M. (2012). Getting ahead in the communist party: Explaining the advancement of central committee members in China. *American Political Science Review, 106*(01), 166–187.

Shih, V. C., & Zhang, Q. (2007). Who receives subsidies? A look at the county level in two time periods. In V. Shue & C. Wong (Eds.), *Paying for progress in China: Public finance, human welfare and changing patterns of inequality* (pp. 157–177). Routledge.

Shirk, S. L. (1993). *The political logic of economic reform in China.* University of California Press.

Shirk, S. L. (2012, November 5). Age of China's new leaders may have been key to their selection. *China File.* https://www.chinafile.com/reporting-opinion/viewpoint/age-chi nas-new-leaders-may-have-been-key-their-selection.

Singh, P. (2015). *How solidarity works for welfare: Subnationalism and social development in India.* Cambridge University Press.

Skilling, H. G. (1966). Interest groups and communist politics. *World Politics, 18*(3), 435–451.

Slater, D. (2010). *Ordering power: Contentious politics and authoritarian leviathans in Southeast Asia.* Cambridge University Press.

Smith, B. B. (2007). *Hard times in the lands of plenty: Oil politics in Iran and Indonesia.* Cornell University Press.

Solinger, D. J. (1986). China's new economic policies and the local industrial political process: The case of Wuhan. *Comparative Politics, 18*(4), 379–399.

Solinger, D. J. (1996). Despite decentralization: Disadvantages, dependence and ongoing central power in the inland-the case of Wuhan. *The China Quarterly, 145,* 1–34.

Solinger, D. J. (2001). Why we cannot count the "unemployed." *The China Quarterly, 167,* 671–688.

Solinger, D. J. (2006). Interviewing Chinese people: From high-level officials to the unemployed. In M. Heimer & S. Thøgersen (Eds.), *Doing fieldwork in China* (pp. 153–167). Lexington Books.

Spegele, B. (2011, April 15). China puts brakes on high-speed trains. *Wall Street Journal.* http://www.wsj.com/articles/SB10001424052748703983104576262330447308782.

Stewart, P. D. (1969). Soviet interest groups and the policy process: The repeal of production education. *World Politics, 22*(1), 29–50.

Stokes, S. C., Dunning, T., Nazareno, M., & Brusco, V. (2013). *Brokers, voters, and clientelism: The puzzle of distributive politics.* Cambridge University Press.

Svolik, M. W. (2012). *The politics of authoritarian rule.* Cambridge University Press.

Tarrow, S. G. (1994). *Power in movement: Social movements, collective action, and politics.* Cambridge University Press.

Treisman, D. (1999). *After the deluge: Regional crises and political consolidation in Russia*. University of Michigan Press.

Tremewan, C. (1994). *The political economy of social control in Singapore*. Palgrave Macmillan.

Truex, R. (2016). *Making autocracy work: Representation and responsiveness in modern China*. Cambridge University Press.

Truex, R. (2017). Consultative authoritarianism and its limits. *Comparative Political Studies, 50*(3), 329–361.

Truex, R. (2020). Authoritarian gridlock? Understanding delay in the Chinese legislative system. *Comparative Political Studies, 53*(9), 1455–1492.

Truman, D. B. (1951). *The governmental process: Political interests and public opinion*. Alfred A. Knopf.

Tsai, K. S. (2007). *Capitalism without democracy: The private sector in contemporary China*. Cornell University Press.

Tsai, L. L. (2007). *Accountability without democracy: Solidary groups and public goods provision in rural China*. Cambridge University Press.

Tsai, L. L. (2017). Bringing in China: Insights for building comparative political theory. *Comparative Political Studies, 50*(3), 295–328.

Tsebelis, G. (1995). Decision making in political systems: Veto players in presidentialism, parliamentarism, multicameralism and multipartyism. *British Journal of Political Science, 25*(3), 289–325.

Tullock, G. (1965). *The politics of bureaucracy*. Public Affairs Press.

Wallace, J. L. (2016). Juking the stats? Authoritarian information problems in China. *British Journal of Political Science, 46*(01), 11–29.

Wang, Y. (2014). *Tying the autocrat's hands*. Cambridge University Press.

Wang, Y., & Minzner, C. (2015). The rise of the Chinese security state. *The China Quarterly, 222*, 339–359.

Weber, M. (1978). *Economy and society: An outline of interpretive sociology*. University of California Press.

Weber, M. (2013). *From Max Weber: Essays in sociology*. Routledge.

Wechsler, H. J. (1979). T'ai-tsung (reign 626–49) the consolidator. In D. C. E. Twitchett (Ed.), *The Cambridge history of China* (Vol. 3, pp. 188–241). Cambridge University Press.

Weiss, J. C. (2013). Authoritarian signaling, mass audiences, and nationalist protest in China. *International Organization, 67*(1), 1–35.

Weiss, J. C. (2014). *Powerful patriots: Nationalist protest in China's foreign relations*. Oxford University Press.

Whiting, S. H. (2001). *Power and wealth in rural China: The political economy of institutional change*. Cambridge University Press.

Whiting, S. H. (2004). The cadre evaluation system at the grass roots: The paradox of party rule. In B. Naughton & D. Yang (Eds.), *Holding China together: Diversity and national integration in the post-Deng era* (pp. 101–119). Cambridge University Press.

Whiting, S. H. (2011). Values in land: Fiscal pressures, land disputes and justice claims in rural and peri-urban China. *Urban Studies, 48*(3), 569–587.

Wibbels, E. (2005). *Federalism and the market: Intergovernmental conflict and economic reform in the developing world*. Cambridge University Press.

Williamson, O. E. (1983). Credible commitments: Using hostages to support exchange. *The American Economic Review, 73*(4), 519–540.

Wintrobe, R. (1998). *The political economy of dictatorship*. Cambridge University Press.

Wittfogel, K. (1957). *Oriental despotism: A comparative study of total power.* Yale University Press.

Wong, C. P. W. (1997). *Financing local government in the People's Republic of China.* Oxford University Press.

Wong, C. P. W. (2000). Central–local relations revisited: The 1994 tax-sharing reform and public expenditure management in China. *China Perspectives, 31,* 52–63.

Wong, C. P. W., & Bird, R. M. (2008). China's fiscal system: A work in progress. In L. Brandt & T. G. Rawski (Eds.), *China's great economic transformation* (pp. 429–466). Cambridge University Press.

Woo-Cumings, M. (1999). *The developmental state.* Cornell University Press.

Wright, J. R. (1996). *Interest groups and congress: Lobbying, contributions, and influence.* Allyn & Bacon.

Xi, T., Yao, Y., & Zhang, M. (2015). Competence versus incentive: Evidence from city officials in China. *Working Paper Series, China Center for Economic Research.*

Xu, C. (2011). The fundamental institutions of China's reforms and development. *Journal of Economic Literature, 49*(4), 1076–1151.

Yan, X. (2016). Patrolling harmony: Pre-emptive authoritarianism and the preservation of stability in W County. *Journal of Contemporary China, 25*(99), 406–421.

Yan, X., & Zhou, K. (2017). Fighting the prairie fire: Why do local party-states in China respond to contentious challengers differently? *China: An International Journal, 15*(4), 43–68.

Yang, D. L. (2002). *Beyond Beijing: Liberalization and the regions in China.* Routledge.

Yasuda, J. K. (2015). Why food safety fails in China: The politics of scale. *The China Quarterly, 223,* 745–769.

Ye, M. (2019). Fragmentation and mobilization: Domestic politics of the belt and road in China. *Journal of Contemporary China, 28*(119), 696–711.

Yeo, Y. (2009). Remaking the Chinese state and the nature of economic governance? The early appraisal of the 2008 'super-ministry' reform. *Journal of Contemporary China, 18*(62), 729–743.

Yip, N., & Jiang, Y. (2011). Homeowners united: The attempt to create lateral networks of homeowners' associations in urban China. *Journal of Contemporary China, 20*(72), 735–750.

Yu, X. (2012). *Deng Xiaoping yu Bao Yugang (Deng Xiaoping and Yue-Kong Pao).* Huawen Chubanshe (Chinese Publisher).

Zeng, Q. (2020). Managed campaign and bureaucratic institutions in China: Evidence from the targeted poverty alleviation program. *Journal of Contemporary China, 29*(123), 400–415.

Zhang, C. (2017). Reexamining the Electoral Connection in Authoritarian China: The Local People's Congress and Its Private Entrepreneur Deputies. *The China Review, 17*(1), 1–27.

Zhang, M., Xu, J., & Chung, C. K. L. (2020). Politics of scale, bargaining power and its spatial impacts: Planning for intercity railways in the Pearl River Delta, China. *The China Quarterly,* 1–25.

Zhang, Q., & Liu, M. (2019). *Revolutionary legacy, power structure, and grassroots capitalism under the red flag in China.* Cambridge University Press.

Zhang, Q., Liu, M., & Shih, V. (2013). Guerrilla capitalism: Revolutionary legacy, political cleavage, and the preservation of the private economy in Zhejiang. *Journal of East Asian Studies, 13*(3), 379–407.

Zhang, T. H. (2019). The rise of the princelings in China: Career advantages and collective elite reproduction. *Journal of East Asian Studies, 19*(2), 169–196.

Zhang, Y. (2006). *Caizheng fenquan yu shengyixia zhengfujian guanxi de yanbian—Dui 20 shiji 80 niandai A sheng caizheng tizhi gaigezhong zhengfujian guanxibianqian de geanyanjiu* (Fiscal decentralization and the evolution of sub-provincial intergovernmental relations: A case study). *Shehuixue Yanjiu* (Sociological Studies), *3*, 39–63.

Zhang, Y. (2014). Testing social ties against merits: The political career of provincial party chiefs in China, 1990–2007. *Journal of Chinese Political Science, 19*(3), 249–265.

Zhao, S. (1998). A state-led nationalism: The patriotic education campaign in post-Tiananmen China. *Communist and Post-Communist Studies, 31*(3), 287–302.

Zheng, X. (2018). *The politics of rights and the 1911 revolution in China.* Stanford University Press.

Zhou, L.-A. (2007). Governing China's local officials: An analysis of promotion tournament model. *Economic Research Journal, 7*, 36–50.

Zhou, L.-A. (2016). The administrative subcontract: Significance, relevance and implications for intergovernmental relations in China. *Chinese Journal of Sociology, 2*(1), 34–74.

Zhou, X. (2008). *Jiceng Zhengfujian de 'gongmouxianxiang'—Yige zhengfu xingwei de zhiduluoji* (Collusion between local governments: An institutional logic of governmental behavior). *Shehuixue Yanjiu* (Sociological Studies), *6*, 1–21.

Zhou, X. (2010). The institutional logic of collusion among local governments in China. *Modern China, 36*(1), 47–78.

Zhou, X., & Lian, H. (2011). *Zhengfujian shangxiaji bumenjian tanpan de yige fenximoxing—Yi huanjing zhengce shishi weili* (Bureaucratic bargaining in the Chinese government: The case of environmental policy implementation). *Zhongguo Shehuikexue* (Social Sciences in China), *5*, 80–96.

Zuo, C. V. (2016). Attitudes and actions of homeowner activist leaders in contemporary China. *China Review, 16*(1), 151–167.

Index